Indian Self-Propelled Railway Vehicles in HO Scale

by Glyn Thomas, BSc(Hons), MBA, MBCS, CITP

Edited by Julian Rainbow and David Churchill

Design and typesetting by .... Glyn Thomas
Published by....................................IngramSpark
Printed by ....IngramSpark

ISBN 979-8-218-48453-8

Cover Photo: ICF EMU no. 445 near Wadala Road, 23/11/1981. See "ICF EMU, 1962 (Broad Gauge)" on page 105 [Tim Edmonds]

Back Cover Photo: Kalka-Simla Railway railcars nos. 1 and 4 at Barog, 20/10/1994. See "Kalka-Simla Railcars, 1911-1933 (2' 6" Gauge)" on page 41 [John Tolson, Transport Treasury, JMT13238]

About the Author

Glyn Thomas was born in London, England to South African parents.

Glyn's family has long connections with British colonial railways - his great-grandfather, Henry Norman Thomas, worked for Babcock and Wilcox building the Manx Electric Railway on the Isle of Man. Henry eventually moved to South Africa to setup the Durban tramway system, and he became General Manager of Transport for Durban Corporation.

Growing up too late to see the end of mainline steam on railways at home in Britain, Glyn travelled extensively in the 1980s and 1990s visiting railways around the world that continued to use steam, either in accompanied groups or independently. He first visited India in 1982 with a Warwickshire Railway Society trip, and made subsequent independent visits in 1989 and 2010.

Glyn is a keen modeller with interests in railways around the world. In the 1990s he built an Indian-themed HO-scale layout, but needed to abandon it due to a job move to the USA (it has recently been revived). More recently, he has modelled US railroads. Photos of his layouts have appeared in Model Railroader, and he has had articles published in Continental Modeller, Model Railroad Craftsman, and NMRA magazine. He is a National Model Railroad Association's Master Model Railroader.

Indian Steam Locomotives Book

Glyn's first book, Indian Steam Locomotives in HO Scale (ISBN 978-1-901613-04-9), was published by the British Overseas Railways Historical Trust in 2021 and is still available through them (website: borht.org.uk).

Indian Rolling Stock Book

Indian Rolling Stock in HO Scale (ISBN 979-8-218-03652-2), was published in 2022 and is available from bookshops, or on eBay.

British Overseas Railways Historical Trust

The author is indebted to the British Overseas Railways Historical Trust and it's Chairman, Julian Rainbow, MPhil., BSc., (Hons), MCInstCES, ARICS, ProfGCE, for assistance in the preparation of this book. The book includes photographs from the BBCIR Electrification album in the Trust's collection, and Julian has edited the text.

The British Overseas Railways Historical Trust was formed in 1984 to bring this past aspect of Britain's greatness to the public attention as an example to present day engineers, industrialists and businessmen. The aims of the trust are:

- To promote the study of the history of railways in the Commonwealth (excluding the UK).

- To promote the study of the British contribution to railways in other parts of the world.

- To locate and preserve any existing archive material and to make it available to researchers and historians.

- To establish a museum to tell the story of Britain's remarkable contribution in giving railways to the world, which will contain a representative collection of export locomotives and rolling stock.

- To create a library of relevant publications.

- To work with other groups with similar aims.

The Trust has been set up as a registered charity to protect its collections.

All aspects of British overseas railways are covered, e.g. business history, engineering history, biography, equipment manufacturers and exporters, consultants, finance, politics. We also encourage modelling (primarily HO Scale).

Table of Contents

Introduction

Western Railway EMUs at Bombay Central carshed, contrasting the older BBCIR sets with more modern ICF sets, approx. 1970. See "BBCIR EMU, 1928 (Broad Gauge)" on page 97 [IRFCA]

This book is intended as a companion to "Indian Steam Locomotives in HO Scale" and "Indian Rolling Stock in HO Scale", providing information on the self-propelled equipment that was commonly seen on Indian Railways. Like the companion volumes, this book focuses on Indian Railways during the 20th Century. See the steam locomotive book for a brief history of the railways during this period.

For the purposes of this book, I have defined self-propelled railway vehicles as those used for carrying passengers, including various forms of railcar and multiple unit, using different forms of power (steam, petrol, diesel, and electric). I have not covered self-propelled vehicles used by the railways' engineering or maintenance of way departments, such as inspection trolleys, cranes, and track maintenance machines, although there is some cross-over, especially with the earliest machines.

In the past, Indian self-propelled vehicles have received patchy attention from enthusiasts. There has been significant interest in some of the narrow gauge examples, especially those provided to the Kalka-Simla line. Broad- and metre gauge equipment, including the Electric Multiple Units (EMUs) provided for the suburban networks have received very little attention. This is clearly a major omission, because the building of electrified suburban railways led to massive expansion of the cities, and created the dominant urban Indian culture. Fortunately, modern domestic and Indian diaspora enthusiasts have started to take an interest in the multiple-unit scene, and there are some good resources available for anyone interested in 21st Century developments.

During the colonial era larger self-propelled vehicles were almost exclusively built overseas (mainly in Britain) and imported to India for final assembly and commissioning. In the 1930's, Indian railway workshops started to build smaller railcars built around standard road truck chassis and engines - Walford Engineering of Calcutta even tried to make a commercial business of this. The use of imported equipment for mainstream operations continued through the 1950s, especially with the supply of EMUs for the expansion of the Bombay suburban network. Indian-built EMUs starting to appear in the late 1950's, firstly from Jessops of Calcutta (Kolkata) and later (in the early 1960s) from the Integral Coach Factory (ICF) in Perambur, a suburb of Madras (Chennai). ICF ultimately became the dominant manufacturer of EMUs and later DMUs for the late 20th Century. Moving into the 21st Century, it is possible that Bharat Earth Movers Limited (BEML) will eventually overtake ICF.

The following sections describe developments in steam, petrol, diesel, and electric self-propelled vehicles during the 20th Century.

Steam

Steam railcars were invented during the 1840's but weren't widely used in the early years. In 1902, the London and South Western Railway (LSWR) in Britain introduced a steam railcar for service around Portsmouth. This influenced other railways and shortly afterwards, several Indian railways ordered broad gauge examples. While some of these had reasonably long lives, the initial orders weren't repeated.

A more successful variant on the steam railcar concept was a range of steam railcars and multiple-units developed by Sentinel Waggon Works of Shrewsbury, England (known simply as "Sentinel") and sold from the late 1920's to the 1950's. Both narrow gauge and broad gauge examples were used in India. Sentinel railcars supplied to nearby Ceylon (Sri Lanka) had long lives and one example was still being used for enthusiast excursions in the early 2000s.

Clayton Wagon Works developed a competitor to the Sentinel steam railcar in the late 1920's, using a compact conventional piston driven engine originally designed for road engines. Only one example was sent to India for the EBSR in 1928. While no photographs of the Indian railcar have been found, it was probably similar to New Zealand Railway's RM class of 1926, used on the Klarow branch, and South Africa RM11 of 1929, used on the Milnerton and Cape Flats lines. That incarnation of the Clayton company went out of business in 1929.

The Maharajah Schindia of Gwalior was always interested in novel technologies, and had a personal steam railcar built for his 2'-gauge Gwalior Light Railway. 3 more cars derived from this design were used in general traffic on that line.

The following table lists known Indian steam railcars.

Broad Gauge Sentinel Railcar Built for the BNR [Historical Railway Images]

Gauge	Railway	Builder	Type	Numbers	Year
2' 0"	Gwalior	KS	1 x Maharajah's railcar, 1904; 3 x railcar, 100 (1908),101 (1910),103 (1914).†	-, 100-103	1904-1914
5' 6"	NWR	VF	1 x railcar†	1	1905
5' 6"	GIPR	KS	1 x railmotor†	1	1905
5' 6"	SIR		Madras Railway, 3 x railmotor†****	1-3	1905-6
5' 6"	MSMR	K	3 x CB class railcars†	1-3	1906
5' 6"	EIR	NW, 1350-4	5 x M class railcars†*		1907
2' 6"	BNR	Sentinel	3 x SPC class (Satpura Lines)†	1-3	1925-6
5' 6"	BNR	Sentinel	2 x railcars†	4-5	1926
5' 6"	NWR	Sentinel	9 x SC class articulated railcars, includes the 3 from GIPR†	2-10	1926-7
2' 6"	BLR	Sentinel	2 x E class†	27-28	1927
5' 6"	GIPR	Sentinel	3 x railcars†**	2-4	1927
5' 6"	EIR	Sentinel	3 x railcars†	5310-2	1928
Metre	BBCIR	Sentinel	3 x twin-articulated railcars†*****	573-575	1928
Metre	NSR	Sentinel	2 x SSC Class railcars†	1-2	1928
Metre	EBSR	Clayton	1 x railcar, class M†		1928
2' 6"	NWR	Sentinel	3 x ZZTL class (Kangra Valley)† ‡	2-4	1932

† Reported in Hughes, Steam Locomotives of India, Volumes 1-4

* Rebuilt as 0-4-0T shunters in 1927 (includes Phoenix)

** To NWR in 1933

**** 10' 6" wide, see Railway Times, 1905

***** Out of use at Ajmer by 1944

‡ 11 upper class plus 15 lower class, later 36 lower class

Petrol and Diesel

KSR RMC10 Railcar at Barog. See "Kalka-Simla Railcars, 1911-1933 (2'6" Gauge)" on page 41 [Historical Railway Images]

Karl Benz patented an early gasoline-powered internal combustion engine in 1885 and ushered in the automobile age. Early cars were small, under-powered, and unreliable. It wasn't until about 1910 with mass produced cars being introduced around the world, that internal combustion engines could be considered for rail transportation - it was around this time that Indian railways started to experiment with railcars.

A successful early application of petrol motors to rail use was Motor Rail's tramcar design for Karachi tramways from 1909 onwards. While tramcars are out of scope for this book, adaptations of the design for rail use were supplied to Bhavnagar State Railway and the South Indian Railway in 1914-15. On the SIR, they were initially used on a 3-mile section from Mandapam to the Ceylon steamer pier, crossing the Pamban Viaduct. Later they may have been used elsewhere and a slightly larger version of the design was bought in 1925.

The Kalka-Simla Railway (or Kalka-Shimla Railway), with large numbers of first class passengers needing to visit the government during summer months[1], was an enthusiastic experimenter with a range of railcars for expedited first-class service. These were generally fuelled by petrol, but several were converted to diesel during World War 2.

Rudoft Diesel's design for a Rational Heat Motor was first successfully run in 1896. However, it took until the 1930s for diesel engines to become the predominant internal-combustion engines for rail use.

India has never been a major user of Diesel Multiple-Units (DMUs). Examples were introduced on the broad and metregauge during the 1940's and 1950's, but the orders weren't repeated. ICF introduced their own metre gauge design in the 1960's and small numbers were produced, including variants, up to today. In the 1990's, BEML provided small 4-wheel broad and metre gauge railcars for use on lines with low passenger numbers.

ICF has also introduced updated DMUs for the broad gauge starting in the 1990's and these have been produced in larger numbers.

The following table lists petrol and diesel powered self-propelled units know to have run in India.

Motor Rail "Simplex" Railcar for the South Indian Railway at the builder's plant in Lewes, England. The car could carry 70 passengers [The Engineer, 16/04/1915]

---

1 Between 1864 and 1947, Simla was the summer capital of British India; government officials moved there during summer months to avoid the oppressive heat of the plains.

Gauge	Railway	Builder, Works No	Type	Numbers	Year
2' 0"	Matheran Light Railway	DrC	1 x 8-seat railcar petrol-mechanical‡	1	1909
2' 6"	Cutch State Railway	McEwan, Pratt	1 x railcar (shooting car) 2-A-2PM.		1910
2' 6"	NWR	LP	1 x railcar, 17 HP (Kalka-Simla).	1	1911
2' 0"	Gwalior	DrC, 442 (via KS)	2w-2PMR "B" Body, 20 HP 1 ton 12 cwt, 6 seats‡		1912
2' 6"	NWR	LP	2 x railcar, 30 HP (Kalka-Simla).	2-3	1913
2' 0"	Gwalior	DrC, 526 (via KS)	2w-2PMR "B" Body, 20 HP 1 ton 17 cwt, long chassis with KS body‡		1914
2' 6"	Nasik Tramway	DrC/MP, 606-7	2 x Bg "Tramcar" 0-4-0+4PMR, 40 HP, W&P engine, 4 cyls 115x150mm, 3 speed, 20" wheels, 5 ton 13 cwt, 34 seats [Drewry book has photo].‡	1-2? φ	1915
Metre	SIR	MR	3 x SIM Class railcar	1-3*	1915
Metre	Bhavanagar SR	MR	1 x railcar, capacity 50 passengers, tare 5.85 tons, gross 8.85 tons, survived beyond 1951 as class EZZT†	2030, later 241	1915
2' 6"	Nasik Tramway	DrC 791-2	2 x railcars 2w-2PMR 40 HP Bg engine, 4 ton 7 cwt 40 seat‡	3-4? φ	1916
2' 0"	DHR	MR	1 x railcar 40 HP, 9 passengers†		1920
2' 0"	Kulasekarapatnam Light Railway	MR, 1953, 2073, 2136-7	4 x railcars, 40 HP; possibly also some local railmotors converted from road trucks.†		1920/1/3
2' 6"	NWR	DrC 903-4	2 x railcar, 45 HP, 2-4-2 (Kalka-Simla) 6 ton 3 cwt, Bg engine, 4 cyls 16 seat.‡	5-6	1921
Metre	SIR	DrC	2 x Nilgiri 0-4-0PM railcars‡		1923
2' 6"	Gaekwar's Baroda State Railways	DrC, 1418	1 x 2w-2PMR inspection car, 20 HP, Bg engine, 4 cyls 1T12C.‡		1925
Metre	SIR	MR	1 x SIM class railcar	3	1925
5' 6"	NWR	DrC, 1491	2w-2PMR B Body 20 HP 2T13C Bg engine, 4 cyls, 9 seats.‡		1926
5' 6"	Probably NWR	DrC 1634	w-2PMR B Body 20 HP 1T19C Bg engine, 4 cyls 9 seats.‡		1927
2' 6"	NWR (Kalka-Simla)	DrC, 1628	1 x railcar, 40 HP, 0-4-0PMR 4 ton 9 cwt, 9 seat.‡,	7	1927
2' 6"	NWR (Kalka-Simla)	DrC 1625-7	4 x railcar, 85 HP, 0-4-0+4PMR 8 ton 2 cwt, Bg engine, 6 cyls, 12 seat + 10cwt luggage.‡	8-11	1927
2' 0"	Matheran Light Railway		14-seat railcar petrol-mechanical (Dodge engine)†	2	1927
2' 0"	Matheran Light Railway	Brookville	4wPM, Type D with Ford engine		1928
5' 6"	NWR	DrC 1657-8	2w-2PMR chassis 30/35 HP 2T10C Bg engine, 4 cyls 12 seats.‡		1928
5' 6"	NSR	EE/Bg, 2000	2w-2PMR 25 HP Mdws engine, 4EL‡		1930
5' 6"	NWR	EE, 2004	2w-2PMR 25 HP Mdws engine, 4 cyls.‡		1930
Metre	NSR	EE/Bg, 2001	1 x 17 HP railcar 2W-2PMR, Mdws 4EH‡		1930
2' 6"	NWR	Wkm	1 x railcar, 58 HP (Kalka-Simla).¤	12	1931
Metre	Jamnagar and Dwarka Railway		Local railcar using a Ford 20 HP engine, plus trailer, 30 passenger capacity†		1932
2' 6"	Gaekwar's Baroda State Railways	AW	4 x railcar, 80 HP diesel-electric, survived to the 1940s.§	103-106	1932
2' 0"	Matheran Light Railway	Koppel/ Grashame	2 x 12-seat railcar petrol-mechanical (with Dodge engine).**	898-899	1932-4
2' 6"	NWR	AW	1 x railcar, 90 HP diesel§	14	1933

Gauge	Railway	Builder, Works No	Type	Numbers	Year
2' 6"	GIPR	AW	1 x railcar (Pulgaon-Arvi), 122 HP, two bogie, 6-cylinder engine, 58 lower class seats.§		1934
5' 6"	MSMR	AW	6 x YZZT Railcars (Diesel Electric, 160 HP).§	1-6	1934
2' 0"	Gwalior	Wkm	1 x railcar .¤	798	1934
Metre	Junagadh State Railway	BRCW/Dorman	2 x railcars (diesel… 70 HP), 54 seat.	1-2	1934
2' 6"	Martin & Co. (Shahdara-Saharanpur Light Railway)	Wkm	1 x 4wPM railcar (rebuilt 4wDM, 1959) .¤	RC1	1935
Metre	Jodhipur-Bikaner Railway	DrC, 2073-4 EE, 940-1	2 x railcars 24 HP 2w-2PMR Ford engine, 4 cyls (one for the Maharajah (to Middle East in 1942), one for inspections).†‡		1936
Metre	Udaipur-Chitorgarh Railway		2 x railcar.		1937
Metre	ARTC	Wkm	2 x railcars, 40-seat, works nos. 2379-80, order no. 10457, Ford V8 engines.¤	1-2	1937-1938
Metre	Jodhipur-Bikaner Railway	BkSR	1 x bogie railcar, with 2 x Ford V8 truck engines, capacity 2 upper class and 63 lower class passengers †; possibly out of service by 1943***	1	1938
5' 6"	NWR	Ganz	11 x diesel mechanical railcars.	90-100	1938
2' 6"	Martin & Co (Baraset-Basirhat Light Railway)		4 x 55 HP diesel-mechanical railcar		1938-40
Metre	Jamnagar and Dwarka Railway		Local railcar using Ford V8 30 HP engine†		1930s
Metre	Jamnagar and Dwarka Railway		Local railcar using Rolls Royce 60 HP engine†		1930s
Metre	Morvi Railway		3 x local railcars using road truck parts.†		1930s
5' 6"	NSR	DrC	4 x DB class Railcars (164 HP diesel)	1-4	1939
Metre	Morvi Railway		1 x diesel railcar for the Maharajah's use		1941
2' 0"	Gwalior	Wkm	1 x railcar for use by the Maharajah's entourage .¤		1947
5' 6"	NSR	EE/Bg, 1878	2w-2PMR 'Pay Car' 30 HP 3T11C F(V8)		1949
Metre	NSR	EE/Bg 1879	2w-2PMR 'Pay Car' 30 HP 3T9C Ford V8 engine		1949
2' 0"	Martin & Co. (Howrah-Amta Light Railway)		1 x local 4wDM railcar, 90 HP †	RC1	1951, rebuilt 1958
Metre	Indian Railways (Southern Railway)		12 x Japanese DMUs (see Isao Tsujimura paper - says 1953)		1952
Metre	Indian Railways	Fiat	12 x railcars, YRD1 class.		1955
5' 6"	Indian Railways (Northern Railway and Southern Railway)	Commonwealth Engineering.	24 x DMU		1958
2' 6"	Martin & Co. (Shahdara-Saharanpur Light Railway)	Walford****	2 x local 4wDM railcars	RC2-3	1959-61
Metre?	Southern Railway and others	ICF	6 x 2-car diesel multiple unit, with Ashok Leyland engines.		1964-1971

Gauge	Railway	Builder, Works No	Type	Numbers	Year
2' 6"	Various		4wDM + 4-wheel trailer sets using Ashok Leyland engines, approximately 44 cars (11 sets?).	7000-7043	1968-1980s
2' 0"	Gwalior		8 x 4wD, class NRD1, "power cars"	1001-8	1986-7
Metre	Indian Railways		Bogie railcars with Ashok Leyland engines.		c. 1990
Metre	Indian Railways		4wDM railcars with Ashok Leyland engines.		c. 1990
Metre	Indian Railways		4 x 4wDM railcars with Ashok Leyland engines, converted from NG.		c. 1990
5' 6"	Indian Railways	ICF	177 x DEMU cars built between 1993 and 2000		1993 onwards
5' 6"	Indian Railways		20 x 4wDM railcars, Ashok Leyland engines, class WRB and WRB1		1997-
5' 6"	Indian Railways	ICF	2 x DHMU power cars		2000
2' 6"	Various		4wDM + 4-wheel trailer sets using Asklok Leyland engines, approximately 12 cars (4 sets?).	10601-10612?	1999-2004?

† See Hughes, Indian Locomotives

‡ Reported in The Railway Products of Baguley-Drewry Ltd and its Predecessors, Allen Civil and Roy Etherington

§ Reported in Armstrong Whitworth A Pioneer of World Diesel Traction, Brian Webb

¤ Reported in The Wickham Works List, Keith Gunner and Mike Kennard

* No. 3 to Aden in 1916

** See Jeff Scherb in Narrow Gauge and Shortline Gazette, May-June 2005, railcar numbers may date from Indian Railway renumbering

*** Railway Board Reports via David Churchill

**** See Indian Railway Gazette, 3/38 and Railway Gazette, 7/38

φ Numbers implied from Leek and Manifold Railway photos by Robert Gretton (via David Churchill)

KSR Railbuses nos. 1 and 4 at Barog, 25/1/1992. See "Kalka-Simla Railcars, 1911-1933 (2' 6" Gauge)" on page 41 [Laurie Marshall, DRHS Collection]

Electric

ICF EMU no. 445 near Wadala Road, 23/11/1981 [Tim Edmonds]

It is with electric traction that the self-propelled railway vehicle made the most impact on Indian Railways. In the 1920s, the Great Indian Peninsula Railway (GIPR) started a major electrification program. On its mainline, electrification would make it easier to operate over the steep ghat sections between the coastal plain and the Deccan Plateau. Bombay (Mumbai), the city at the centre of its operations was growing rapidly and putting strain on the steam-operated commuter network. The GIPR decided to build a new harbour branch for suburban trains, and electrify the suburban lines using EMUs built by Cammell Laird and using 1,500V DC traction. The Victoria Terminus to Kurla service was inaugurated on 3rd February, 1925.

The GIPR's success in electrifying its suburban network was soon replicated on the Bombay, Baroda, and Central India Railway (BBCIR), which operated commuter lines northwards from Bombay. It used similar equipment from Cammell Laird, and started electric operations on 5th January, 1928.

The South India Railway (SIR) centred its operations at Madras (Chennai). It also introduced electrified suburban services in 1930, but this time on the metre gauge, with 1,500V DC power.

Before World War 2, Calcutta's hinterland was too widely dispersed to make electrification economically viable. However, the city grew rapidly during the war and with the influx of refugees from East Pakistan following Partition. Its electrification program started in the early 1950s. Suburban lines from Howrah to the north-west were inaugurated in 1957, using a 3,000V DC system.

Even as lines around Howrah were being electrified, there was growing concern about the strain that electrified railways were putting on domestic electricity grids. French engineers were consulted, and a decision was made to adopt the more efficient 25kV AC system for future railway electrification. Work on the 3,000V DC around Calcutta was transitioned to 25kV AC, and the existing 3,000V DC lines were converted.

In the 1960's, with the equipment provided to the Madras suburban system nearing the end of its useful life, the decision was made to convert that line to 25kV AC and equip it with new EMUs from ICF. This work was eventually completed in 1967. (This line was eventually converted to broad gauge in the early 2000's.)

In Mumbai (former Bombay), the maturity of the network precluded rapid transition to 25kV AC. Conversion eventually took place between 2003 and 2016. During the conversion period, many EMUs were fitted for dual-voltage working.

The following table lists electric self-propelled vehicle known to have run in India during the 20th Century. Hughes reports 16 classes of 1,500V DC EMUs, WCU1 to WCU16, and 4 classes of 25kV AC EMUs, WAU1 to WAU4 in 1990. It hasn't been possible to map most of these classes to types.

Gauge	Railway	Builder	Type	Class (if known)	Year
5' 6"	GIPR	Cammell-Laird	53 4-car sets, 1,500V DC (7 in service by 1926, 13 by 1927, 33 by 1928, 38 in 1929, 53 in 1931). The earliest cars had wooden bodies with later ones built of steel. 2 spare motor cars kept in reserve		1925-1931
Metre	SIR	Wingrove & Rogers, Liverpool	1 x railcar §		1926
5' 6"	BBCIR	Cammell-Laird	40 4-car sets, 1,500V DC (16 in service in 1928, 37 in 1929, and 40 in 1930**)	WCU2	1928-30
Metre	SIR	EE	24 3-car sets, 1,500V DC (17 in service by 1932, 24 in 1934**)		1930-1934
5' 6"	CR	MetroVic, BTH, Metropolitan Cammell and BRCW	24 4-car sets, 1,500V DC - 32 to WR		1951
5' 6"	WR	MetroVic, BTH, Metropolitan Cammell and BRCW	32 4-car sets, 1,500V DC		1951
Metre	SR	Breda	6 4-car sets, 1,500V DC (later converted to 25kV AC)		1956
5' 6"	CR	Breda	24 4-car sets, 1,500V DC		1956
5' 6"	CR/WR	(Hitachi - WCU6, Nippon - WCU7, Toshiba)	74 Japanese 4-car sets, same as EE design, 1,500V DC; withdrawn c. 1974 because they were vacuum braked	WCU6, WCU7	1956-8*
5' 6"	CR/WR	Jessops	16 3-car sets ordered in 1959, 1,500V DC; orders continued into the 1970's - total number unknown. Initially used imported British and Japanese electrical gear; later versions used domestic electrical gear from HEI.		1959-1970's
5' 6"	ER	MetroVic	36 motor coaches and 68 trailers, 3,000V DC†	WAU1	1958
5' 6"	ER	SIG	16 3-car units 3,000V DC, later converted to dual voltage - 3,000V DC/ 25kV AC, EPB; Converted to 1,500V DC for use on WR in 1968, withdrawn 2012**	WAU2	1958-9 (converted c. 1964)
5' 6"	ER	MAN	16 3-car 3,000V DC units plus a spare motor coach, with electrics from AEG; dual voltage (25kV AC from the outset?) **		1958-9
5' 6"	ER	Jessops	16 3-car 3,000V DC units, with electrics from AEI**		1959-60
5' 6"	ER	ICF	1 unit, with power by HEI†	(prototype)	1962
5' 6"	ER	ICF	4 units, with power by Hitachi, Japan and AEI, United Kingdom, 25kV AC†	(prototypes)	1963-4
Metre	SR	ICF	102 cars, (possibly 17 sets) with traction equipment by Nichimen, Japan, 25kV AC; additional trailers were supplied in later years		1965-6
5' 6"	ER		31 4-car units 25kV AC, 19 with Saxby and Farmer EPB and 12 with Knorr EPB‡	WAU3	1966
5' 6"	ER, SER	ICF	70 4-car units 25kV AC; with BEML electrical equipment; Westinghouse/Saxby and Farmer/Knorr EPB between 1967-9 2848 25kV AC EMU cars were produced between 1962 and 2000	WAU4	1967 onwards
5' 6"	CR/WR	ICF	861 1,500V DC cars between 1969 and 2000		1969 onwards

Gauge	Railway	Builder	Type	Class (if known)	Year
5' 6"	CR/WR	ICF	20(?), with chopper control with BARC; EMU MEMU Technology on IR says 5 units		1981 (prototype) 1993
Metre	SR	ICF	25 motor cars, with Thyristor control, traction equipment from GEC		1989-93
5' 6"	SR, WR, others?	ICF	Main-line EMU, 25kV AC - 488 cars produced between 1993 and 2000	MEMU	1993 onwards

§ Per Simon Darvill via David Churchill, Wingrove and Rogers acquired British Electric Vehicles (BEV) of Churchtown, Lancashire in 1926. BEV built battery-electric vehicles, mainly for industrial use. This was listed as a passenger vehicle and may have been similar to a railcar built for the British Admiralty in 1924.

* Reported as 1955 by Japan Association of Rolling Stock Industries (JARI)

** Reported on indiarailinfo.com

† Reported in Railway Gazette

‡ Reported in "EMU MEMU Technology In IR", Indian Railways Institute of Electrical Engineering, Nashik Road, (IRIEEN) 2014

** Statistics from Administrative Reports for Indian Railways from David Churchill

Pakistan and Bangladesh

Following Partition, both East and West Pakistan lost their ready access to Indian coal at economic prices. Their response was to increase their reliance on oil instead. In the short-term, steam locomotives were converted to burn oil. In the longer term this accelerated the movement towards diesel traction on the railways, and in West Pakistan, limited electrification of the main line truck routes.

Both regions (eventually separate countries following the 1971 war) were enthusiastic about diesel railcar operation. West Pakistan had long-term experience with railcar operation, using the Ganz railcars supplied to the North Western Railway in 1938. By Partition, when these units were allocated to West Pakistan, the teething problems had been resolved, and the units continued in regular service until about 1962.

West Pakistan also experimented with a locally produced railcar, using Japanese equipment. While the results of the experiment aren't widely recorded, no more railcars of this type were produced.

In 1959-60, West Pakistan turned to Linke Hofmann Busch for a class of broad gauge bogie railcars and trailers. A much larger order for railcars with above-floor engines plus trailers was placed with Hitachi in 1967. The Hitachi units were particularly successful and remained in service into the 1990s. At least one other class of similar design was provided by an unknown builder.

The East Pakistan/ Bangladesh railway network was smaller and predominately metre gauge. Railcars were introduced there in the 1960s, using 3-car units that externally resembled the West Pakistam LHB units.

Gauge	Railway	Type	Numbers	Year
5' 6"	PWR	24 x Linke-Hofmann-Busch railcars and trailers.		1959-60
5' 6"	PWR	1 x railcar, domestic build with Japanese parts.		1964
5' 6"	PWR	34 railcars and 92 trailers from Hitachi.		1968
5' 6"	PWR	36 railcars and trailers from Germany*.		1968
Metre	PER	4 railcars and 8 trailers (railcar + 2 trailer sets).		Service introduced in 1964

* Railway Gazette, March 1968 - further details have not been discovered

East Pakistan Railcar and trailers [Railway Gazette]

The Electrification of Indian Suburban Railways

Bombay/ Mumbai

The Bombay, Baroda and Central India Railway (BBCIR) was the first railway to operate suburban services in India, north from Bombay Back Bay (Churchgate) to Virar, in 1867. This line was susequently extended south to Colaba by 1873. Mainline trains initially terminated at Grant Road, and were extended to Colaba once the extension was built.

BBCIR's competitor in Bombay, the Great Indian Peninsula Railway (GIPR), operated suburban line to the north-east of the city. GIPR was the first Indian railway to use electric traction. Between 1925 and 1930, its mainlines to Igatpuri and Poona were electrified in order to use electric traction on the challenging ghat sections between the coastal plain and the Deccan plateau. In the Bombay area, electrification was required to increase capacity on the heavily used suburban network. The 'Harbour Branch', built in 1910 between Kurla and Reay Road, was electrified and extended south to Victoria Terminus, including the elevated Wadibunder section between Dockyard Road and Sandhurst Road. Construction of the elevated section of the Harbour line at Wadibunder was considered to be a major engineering achievement at the time.

The first electric suburban service on the Harbour Branch between Bombay Victoria Terminus (VT) and Kurla was inaugurated by the Governor of Bombay, Sir Leslie Wilson, on February 3rd, 1925. Suburban services initially extended to Kalyan, 45 miles from Bombay. Kurla, at the junction of the mainline and the Harbour Branch, became the location of the car shed for the electrified suburban lines. 1,500V DC was selected based on experiences at Newport-Shildon on the North-Eastern Railway in Britain, and Melbourne on Victorian Railways in Australia. Initially, hydro-electric power was provided by Tata group, with sub-stations at Dharavi (near Matunga), Kalyan, and Thana (Thane).

Suburban services on the GIPR mainline started in 1927. When the line was extended, the railway built it's own steam-turbine power plant at Kalyan. Following electrification of the Bhor Ghat section, mainline EMU services extended as far as Poona for Race Specials.

The first section of the BBCIR network to be electrified was Colaba-Borivali. The entire section was quadrupled in preparation for electrification and started electric operations on 5th January, 1928. Initially, steam services continued to serve the northern stations from Borivali to Virar. BBCIR electrification used 1,500V DC and was very similar to the connected GIPR electrified network.

During the late 1920s, BBCIR built the new Bombay Central station for its mainline trains, and long-distance services were diverted to it starting in 1930. The line between Churchgate and Colaba was abandoned in 1933 in order to provide space for development in downtown Bombay. Suburban services subsequently terminated at the rebuilt Churchgate station. In 1936, electrification was extended all the way to Virar, eliminating the need for steam services.

The final 20th Century development of the GIPR suburban network was the electrification of Kurla to Mankhurd as an extension of the Harbour Branch after World War 2.

During the 21st Century, expansion of the network has resumed, with construction of new lines including the Trans-Harbour line (Navi Mumbai to Thana), the Vasi Road to Roha line, and the Nerul to Uran line. In addition to these lines, Mumbai is investing in an extensive metro network.

Between 2003 and 2016, Indian Railways undertook the monumental task of converting the Mumbai suburban network from 1,500V DC to 25kV AC. During the period, many EMUs were converted to dual-power, so they could operate under either system. At around the same time, many of the Mumbai lines transitioned to 12-car trains, and starting in 2015 the mainline received 15-car trains.

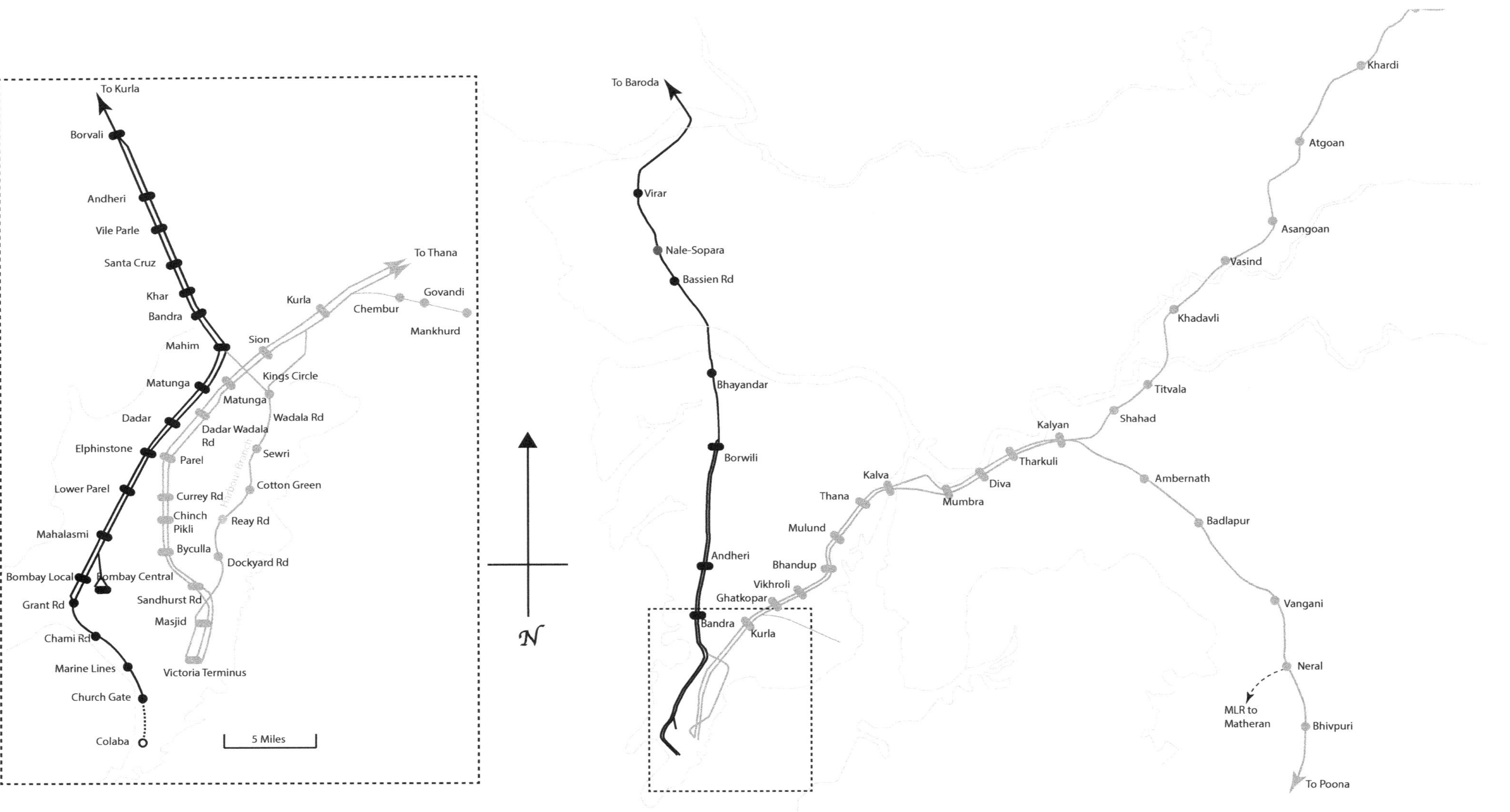

Bombay Suburban Network in 1956 (per the Overcrowding Committee Report), Showing GIPR and BBCIR Lines

Madras/ Chennai

In 1930, the South Indian Railway (SIR) initiated metre gauge electric services out of Madras using 1,500V DC power supplied via overhead wires. The suburban section, operated by EMUs, extended 18.5 miles from Madras Beach to Tambaram. The metre gauge mainline station at Egmore was 2.75 miles from Beach, and steam-hauled mainline and outer suburban trains ran alongside the electrified line from Egmore to Tambaram.

In the 1960's, it was decided to expand the Madras suburban electric network and convert the entire system to 25kV AC traction. The line was extended from Tambaram to Viluppurum in 1965 and conversion to 25kV AC was completed in 1967.

The north-westward Madras Central–Gummidipundy (formerly Gummudipundi) broad gauge section introduced electrified suburban services on April 14th, 1979[1].

In the early 21st Century, a major project converted the metre gauge suburban lines to broad gauge. The conversion was completed in 2004.

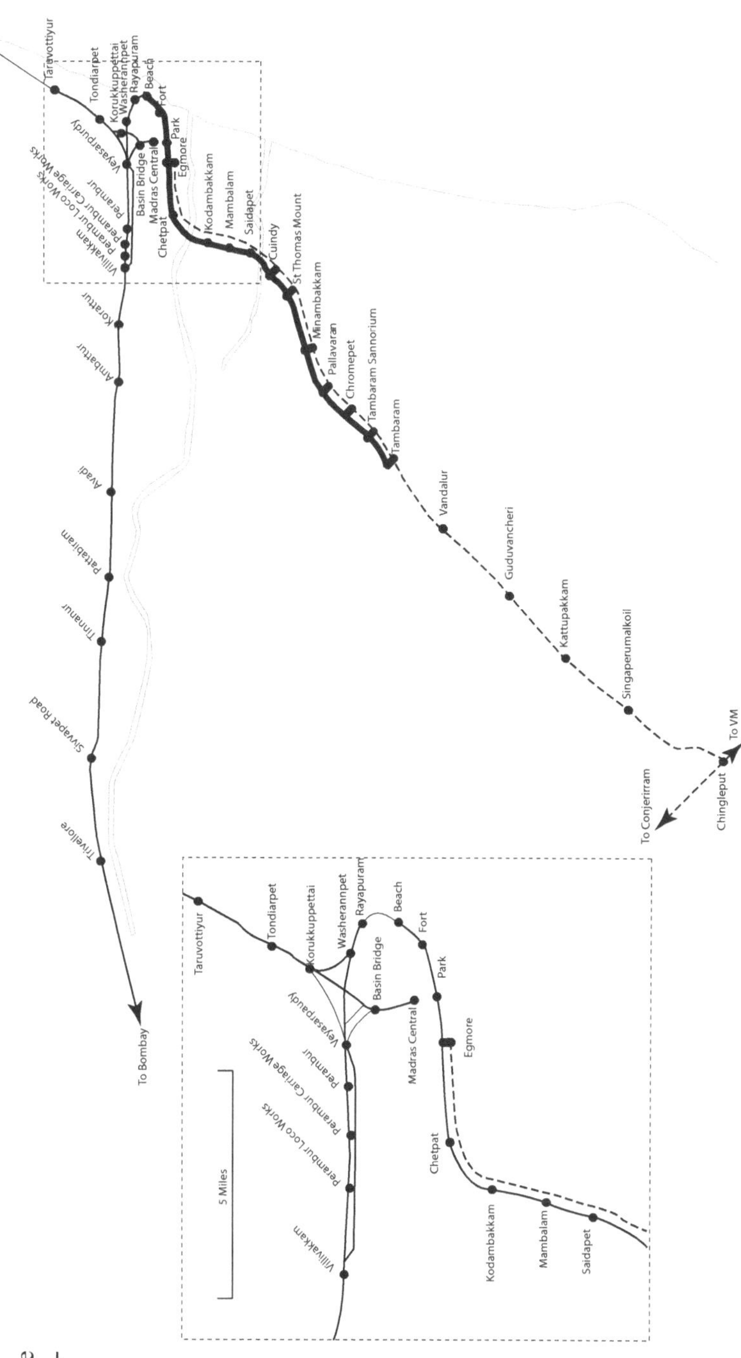

Madras Suburban Network in 1956 as Shown by the Overcrowding Enquiry Report

---

[1]   See EMU/MEMU paper

Calcutta/ Kolkata

Before World War 2, it was considered to be impractical to electrify the Calcutta suburban network due to the wide geographical distribution of urban areas. Economically, the proximity of the Bengal coalfields also favoured steam traction. However, the increase in the city's population over the war years and post-Partition put unprecedented strains on the suburban network. In the early 1950s it was decided to electrify services on both sides of the Ganges.

Electric suburban services commenced between Howrah and Seoaphuli to the north-west of the city on 14th December, 1957. It reached Bandel by 01/02/1957 and Bardhaman by 1963. This system differed from the Bombay suburban system in using 3,000V DC power.

The 3,000V DC experiment was short-lived: after consulting with French railway engineers, it was determined that using single-phase 25kV AC for electrification would dramatically reduce energy demand. When the electrification of Calcutta suburban services north from Sealdah started, they used the 25kV AC system, with the first lines opening in 1962 (Eastern Railway, Sealdah – Ranaghat Section, 1963).

The South Eastern Railway electrified its Howrah–Mecheda section of the Kharagpur division on 01/05/1968.

Conversion of the existing 3,000V DC lines to 25kV AC started in the early 1960s and was completed by 1967.

Calcutta Suburban Network in 1956 as Shown by the Overcrowding Enquiry Report

Other Electric Suburban Networks
Delhi

Delhi introduced its first suburban trains using ICF EMUs on Northern Railway Circular Ring Route from Nizamuddin to Nizamuddin in 1982. The Ring Route provides clockwise and anticlockwise services on a roughly circular route around the core parts of the city. Unfortunately, the line was not particularly successful due to poor placement of stations. It received a boost and some additional investment during the Delhi Commonwealth Games of 2010. This line has now been largely superseded by the Delhi metro and services have been reduced to 12 trains per day, with just 4000 passengers per day.

In the meantime, traditional suburban services from Delhi have increased with EMU and MEMU services to nearby cities, such as Ghaziabad, Palwal, and Sonepat.

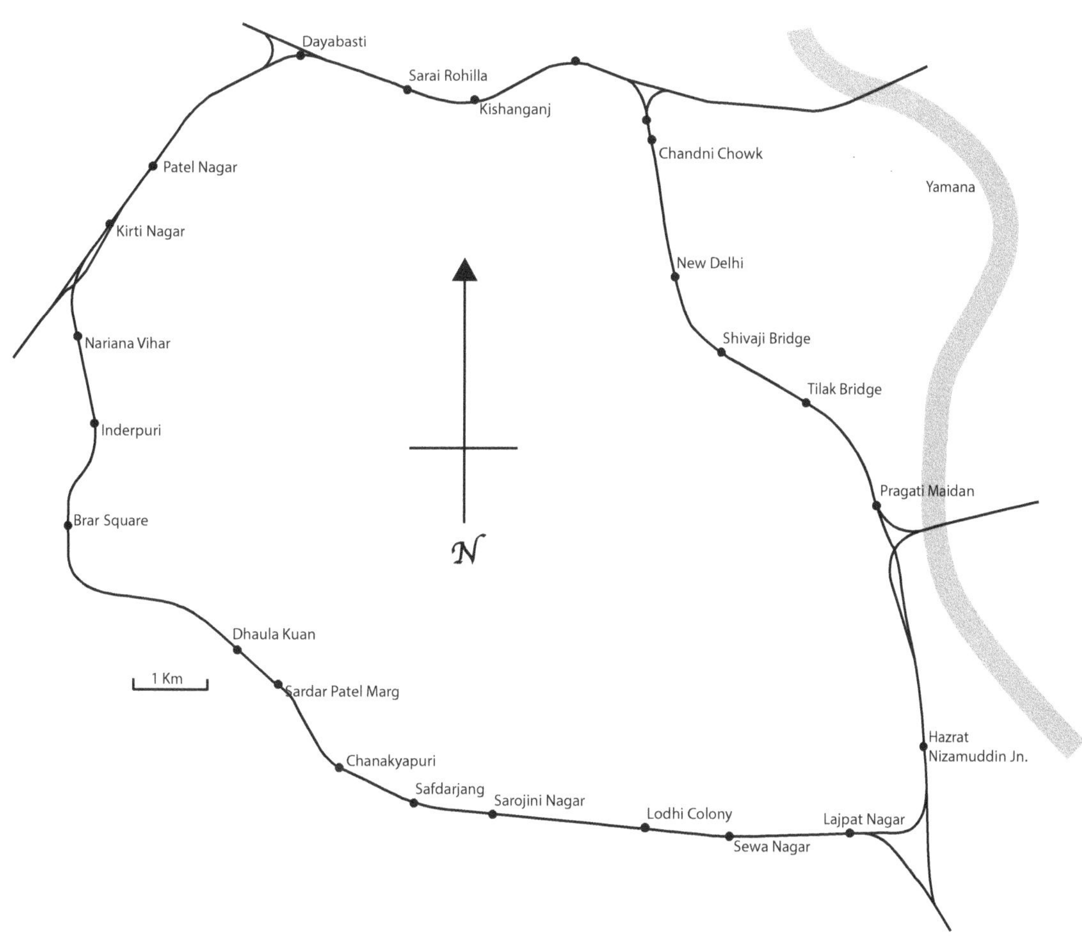

Delhi Ring Railway

Pune - Lonavala EMUs

EMUs started operating on the 63km stretch between Pune and Lonavala March 3rd, 1978. There are no exclusive tracks, and EMUs share the permanent way with long distance and freight trains. In 2009, all services were converted to 12-car rakes. Services start at Pune Junction; terminating points are Talegaon and Lonavala.

Bangalore

Karnataka Rail Infrastructure Development Enterprises (K-RIDE) plans a 148km network. This is not operational at the time of writing.

Hyderabad-Secunderbad

Hyderabad established its MMTS (Multimodal Mass Transit System) between 2000-2003. It initially served Lingampally-Hyderabad and Lingampally-Secunderabad and was later extended to Falaknuma and Ramachabdrapuram. This service uses existing Indian Railway lines.

Metros

Calcutta/Kolkata is home to the first metro to be constructed in India. Built with assistance from Russian and East German engineers, service on sections of the first broad gauge line from Dum Dum and Tollygunge started in 1984. The total system now consists of four lines (one of which is standard gauge) with a fifth under construction, and a total length of 39.6 miles.

In the 21st Century, railway developments in the major cities has concentrated on metro systems. While the older metro systems used broad gauge, there are generally no interchanges with Indian Railways and most newer lines use international standard gauge (1,435mm gauge). In addition to Kolkata, metros are now operational in Madras, Delhi, Bangalore, and Hyderabad. The Pune metro is under construction.

Liveries and Lettering

Colonial Era

The table below shows the observed liveries of railcars for the major railways of the colonial era.

Railway	Livery	Lettering
BBCIR	Suburban EMUs: red-brown overall with cream above the windows.	Yellow lettering on lower panels.
Barsi Light Railway	Red-Brown.	Script-style lettering, "Barsi Light Railway" on lower panels.
BNR	Sentinel railcars in overall maroon or red-brown.	Yellow or gold lettering on lower panels.
EBSR	Red-brown overall with two yellow stripes above the windows.	
EIR	Steam Rail Motor was possibly dark blue.	
GIPR	Red-brown (dark-red) lower panels and cream for upper; umber mouldings lined in cream. Suburban EMUs: dark brown with a cream band above the windows. The cream band may have been removed in later years.	Lettering in gold.
NSR	Drewry railcars were probably all green (similar to Malachite).	Yellow lettering above doors and windows; insignia on lower panel.
NWR	Steam Rail Motor was probably overall red-brown. KSR railcars were generally white. Ganz railcars were initially a two-tone scheme (red-cream?). Later (c. mid-1940s) they were white.	
SIR	Motor Rail petrol railcar was possibly cream with red-brown above the windows. Madras suburban EMUs were originally painted a mid-green. In later years they were silver.	

Independence Era

When replacement stock was provided to the Bombay suburban network in the 1950's it was generally painted silver. However, fairly soon afterwards, the standard EMU livery of red-brown with a cream band above the windows was adopted for most of the Indian regional railways. Post the period of this book, a variety of colourful new liveries have been adopted.

Diesel Multiple Units (DMUs) on the broad and metre gauge were generally painted red-brown with a cream band around the windows. On the narrow gauge, DMUs were generally light blue with a cream band around the windows - dark green with a cream band has also been observed.

Modelling

As discussed in previous volumes, Indian Railways have been modelled in a variety of scales and gauges. HO scale is a good choice because of general availability of scenery, track, and parts. Narrow gauge can be represented in HOe (9mm gauge track, which is good for 2' 6" lines). Metre gauge can be represented using HOm (12mm gauge track). Ideally, broad gauge should use 19.25mm gauge track in HO - British EM (18.2mm gauge) is the closest commercial gauge to this. Many modellers accept the compromise of using standard HO (16.5mm gauge) for broad gauge.

Selection of Plans

A selection of plans covering the major types used during the 20th Century have been provided. The biggest challenge has been finding good source material for these plans, since self-propelled equipment hasn't received the attention of the railway press and enthusiasts that locomotives have received.

Note: India adopted the metric measurement system in 1958, and some source material used that system. In all cases, the measurement system of the source material is used.

Note on Copyright

All materials in this book are copyright of the author or others where referenced. Copying is permitted for personal use during the construction of models. Contact the author if interested to use plans for commercial purposes, including construction articles for the modelling press.

Publication on the Internet is explicitly denied, and will be monitored closely

For narrow gauge, the larger 16mm/foot scale is becoming popular with availability of some Indian models.

In the past, Pegasus Designs has produced a 3D-printed model of a the YRD-1 metre gauge DMU in HO or OO. Hopefully, more will become available in future.

Scratch building self-propelled equipment is easier than building a steam locomotive. A variety of commercial chassis are available that will provide the necessary power, and the modeller need only provide the cosmetic external details.

There Will be Errors

In a book covering such a broad subject, it is virtually inevitable that there will be errors. The sources themselves vary greatly in quality, from very detailed works diagrams to sketch-like weight diagrams (and in a few cases, where noted, simply known dimensions and photographs). Even in the case of the most detailed sources, there were usually some assumptions required in order to prepare the diagrams. As a convention in the book, where a major dimension is indicated, then it is based on a known value - therefore the reader can work out what dimensions have been extrapolated.

If a reader becomes aware of any errors from their own research, the author would appreciate being informed - he can be contacted via email: glynthomas42@gmail.com . Corrections will be made to any subsequent editions of the book.

MSMR metre gauge railbus truck conversion, class YZZT, at Londa in 1947; there may have been 6 of these units [Kelland Collection, BRCT, 49130]

Steam Powered Vehicles

Gwalior Steam Railcars (2' Gauge)

Gwalior Maharajah's Steam Railcar as rebuilt with longitudinal boiler [Railway Gazette, 1916]

The Maharajah Scindia of Gwalior was enthusiastic about railways, and his state's Gwalior Light Railway (GLR) eventually became one of the largest 2'-gauge lines in the country. Several self-propelled vehicles were used by the line over the years.

The first railcar on the system was designed for the Maharajah's personal use. It was built by Kerr, Stuart and Co. (KS) as their works number 867 of 1904. This was fitted with a Merryweather's Improved Quick Steaming vertical boiler that could be fuelled by wood, coal, or kerosene. The power bogie could be removed for maintenance.

The luxurious interior was separated into men's and women's saloons by an arch with a silk curtain. The fittings were provided by Messrs Liberty and Co. Dark green Wilton carpets were provided. The women's compartment had a cabinet, bookcase and divan. The men's compartment had armchairs.

The Maharajah's car suffered from several severe issues in service. It was reported that the unit suffered from excessive vibrations at 20 mph and above, but this may not have been a serious problem because the line was rated for 15 mph operation. Problems with the boiler were clearly more serious. As early as November 1907, the Superintending Engineer of the Gwalior Light Railway wrote to the Consulting Engineer for Railways in Bombay, requesting a loading gauge infringement to permit a regular locomotive boiler to be fitted in the railcar and the infringement was permitted. The boiler was to be fitted laterally across the car, with the smokebox protruding 9" out-of-gauge. It is likely that this arrangement was required in order to fit the boiler into the existing engine compartment on the car, but it probably caused some operational issues, since the boiler would have largely blocked access to the compartment containing the generator and other equipment (plus fuel?). It is possible that the boiler used came from an 0-4-0ST built for the Maharajah's private line (KS, 851 of 1904).

The GLR ordered three additional railcars from KS - 1062/1908; 1172/1910; and 1351/1914. These were fitted out for general traffic, and used regular boilers fitted longitudinally instead of laterally. These cars resembled a regular locomotive (similar to Kerr Stuart's 'Skylark' class) permanently coupled to a coach[1]. Each car had first and third class compartments (for servants), plus lavatories. In service, they could haul separate third class trailers, which were probably built locally on the line.

On April 28th, 1916, Railway Gazette published an article about the Gwalior Light Railway, including photographs of its railcars at the time. By this time the Maharajah's steam railcar had acquired a larger longitudinal locomotive boiler. The running gear appeared to be a rebuild of the original railcar underframe, but with outside valve gear.

Gwalior Steam Railcar and trailer [Railway Gazette, 1916]

1 Railway Gazette, June 1916, provided by David Churchill

Maharajah's Railcar as Built

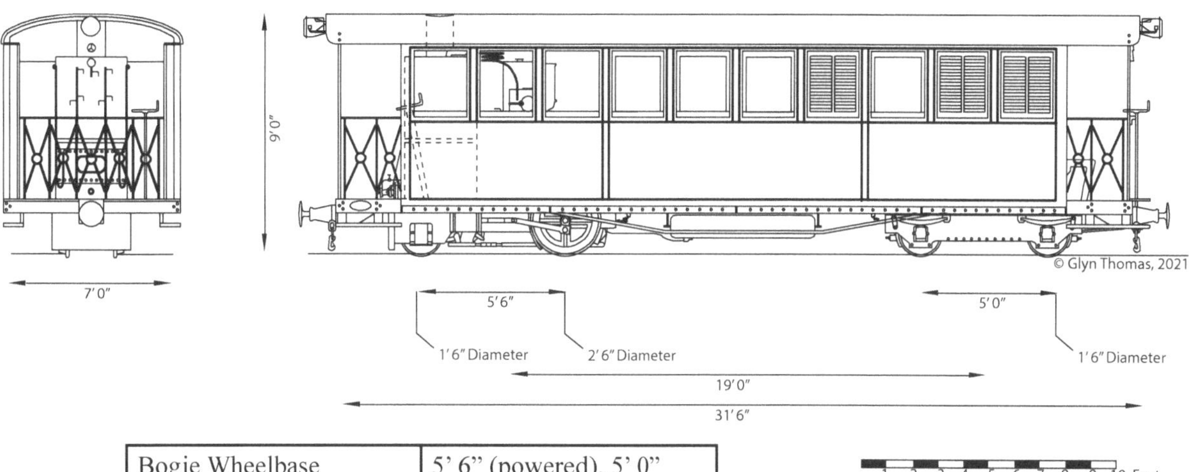

Bogie Wheelbase	5' 6" (powered), 5' 0" (trailing)
Pivot Centres	19' 0"
Wheel Diameter	1' 6"
Tare Weight	12 tons 7 cwt
Boiler Pressure	140 psi
Cylinders	6" diameter x 9" stroke

[Reference: Narrow Gauge and Industrial Railway Modelling Review 118 and Locomotive, Carriage and Wagon Review, 1905]

Maharajah's Railcar First Rebuild

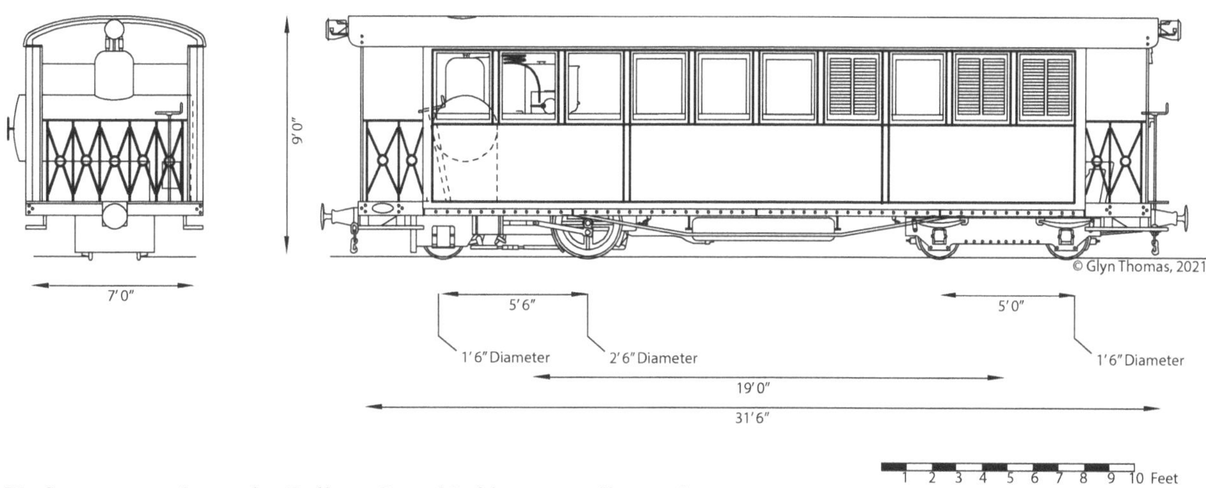

[References: as above plus Railway Board Infringement diagram]

Maharajah's Railcar Second Rebuild

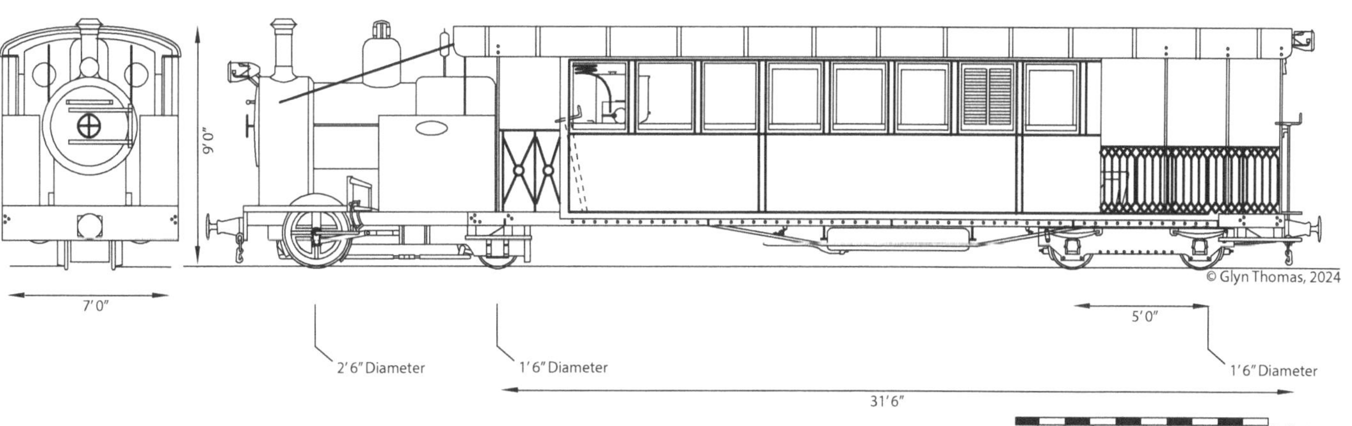

[References: as above plus photograph]

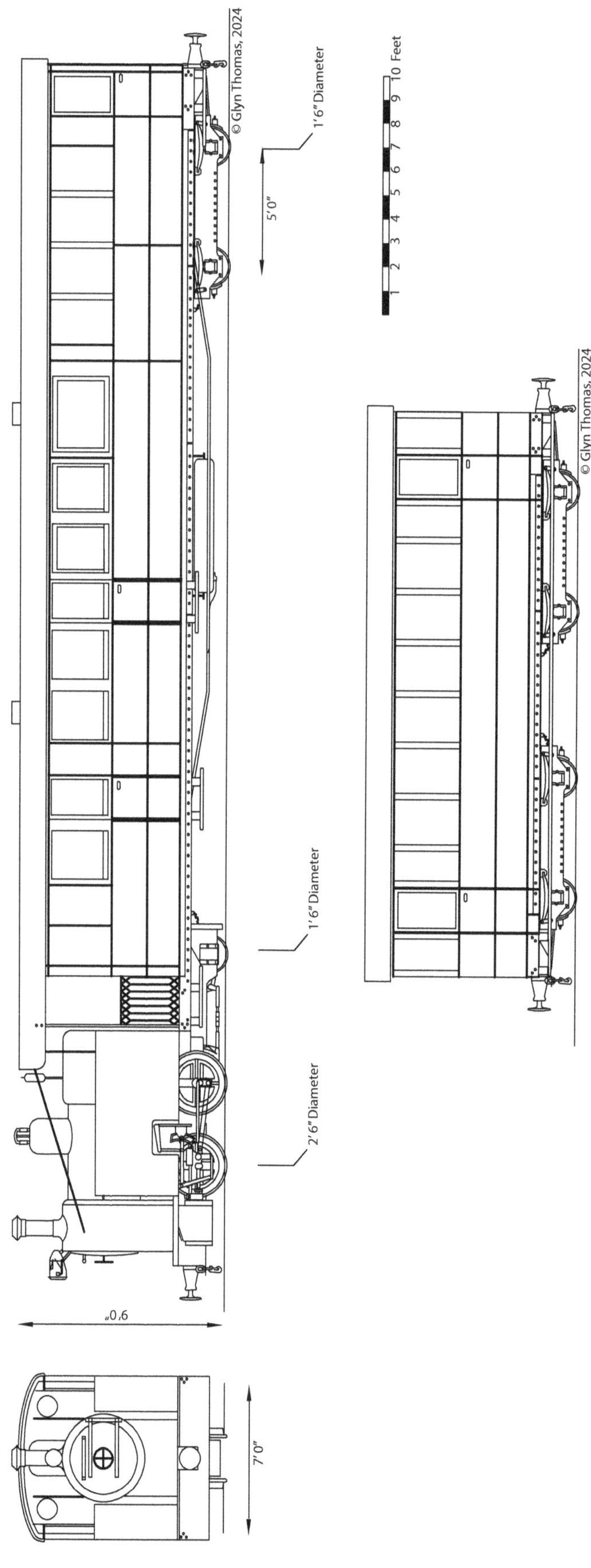

Gwalior General Service Steam Railcar

NWR Steam Motor Coach (Broad Gauge)

NWR Steam Motor Coach [Engineer, 1906]

In 1905, the North Western Railway (NWR) ordered a steam rail motor coach from Vulcan Foundry (VF).

The motor unit comprised of a 4-wheel bogie driven to the front axle only by outside cylinders with Walschaert's valve gear. The boiler was mounted horizontally with the firebox towards the front of the coach. Controls were provided so the motor coach could be driven from either end. The motor unit could be detached for maintenance.

The coach bodywork was built by the NWR and could accommodate 3 first-class, 3 second-class, 72 third-class passengers, and luggage at the motor end. On the line, the unit was numbered 1.

In 1906, Indian Engineering reported that the motor coach was tested successfully at Lahore. Top speed was 35 MPH.

NWR Steam Rail Motor, 1905

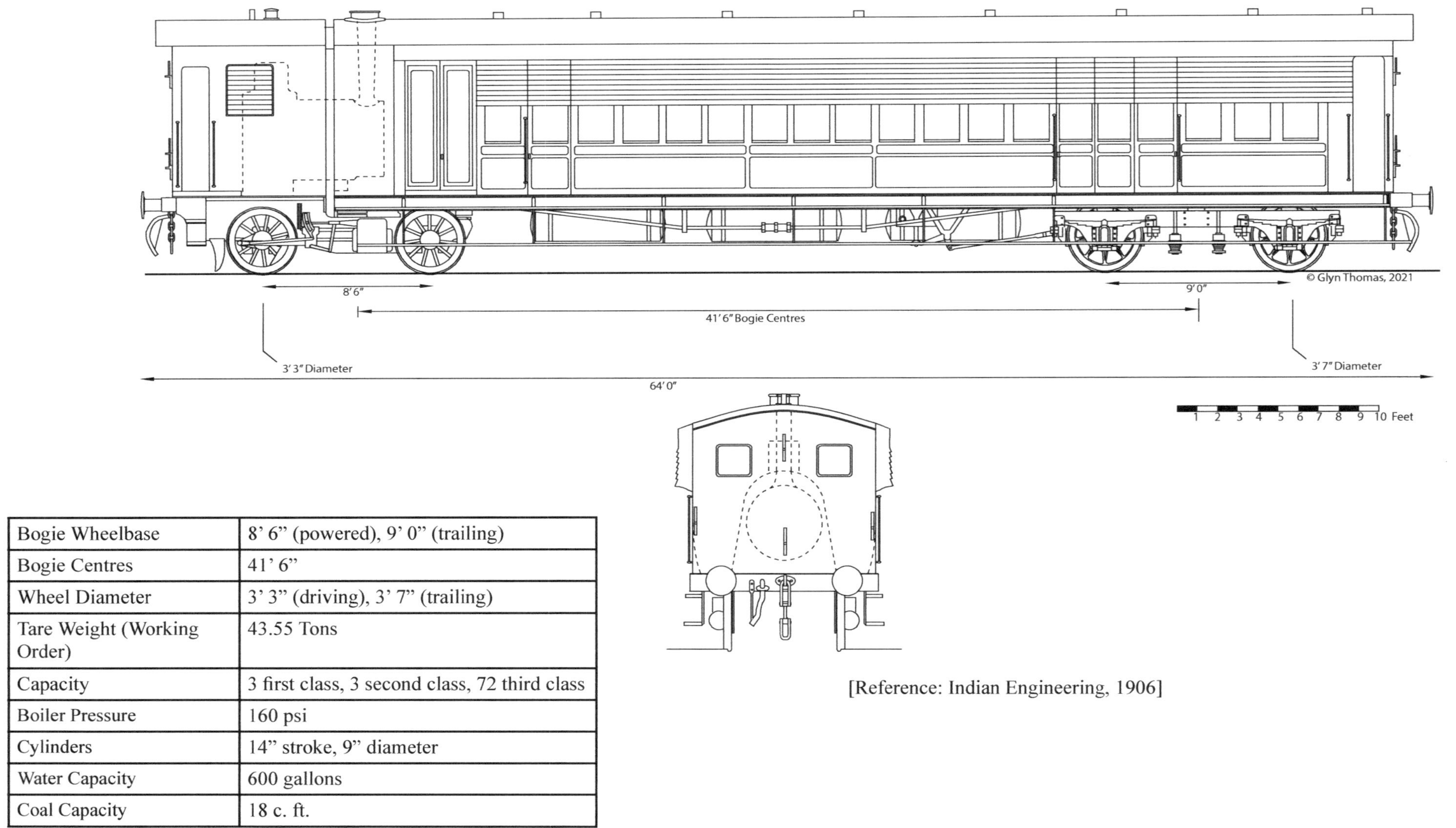

[Reference: Indian Engineering, 1906]

Bogie Wheelbase	8' 6" (powered), 9' 0" (trailing)
Bogie Centres	41' 6"
Wheel Diameter	3' 3" (driving), 3' 7" (trailing)
Tare Weight (Working Order)	43.55 Tons
Capacity	3 first class, 3 second class, 72 third class
Boiler Pressure	160 psi
Cylinders	14" stroke, 9" diameter
Water Capacity	600 gallons
Coal Capacity	18 c. ft.

GIPR Steam Motor Coach (Broad Gauge)

GIPR Steam Motor Coach [Locomotive Magazine, 1906]

In 1905, the Great Indian Peninsular Railway (GIPR) ordered a steam motor coach from Kerr, Stuart and Company (KS). The design used KS's patent, and was similar to steam motor coaches supplied by them to the Great Western Railway, Italian State Railways, the Buenos Aires Great Southern, and the Argentine Great Western Railways. GIPR intended to trial the unit on country branches and to supplement suburban services.

The motor unit comprised of a 4-wheel bogie driven to the rear axle only by outside cylinders with Walschaert's valve gear. The boiler was mounted laterally on the bogie. Controls were provided so the motor coach could be driven from either end. The motor unit could be detached for maintenance.

The coach bodywork was built at Parel workshops in Bombay and could accommodate 50 third-class and 6 first-class passengers. On the line, the unit was called Railmotor No. 1.

For comparison with the steam motor coach, Parel also built a composite trailer coach to be hauled by a small 0-6-0T. The trailer was constructed in just one working week, by a team of 180 workers[1].

While the result of the trials wasn't recorded in the railway press, it is notable that GIPR didn't repeat its order for steam rail motors. On paper, the design of EIR's steam motor coach (see next section) appears to be stronger, with more adhesive weight available for traction than in the KS design.

Parel's 0-6-0T and trailer could be seen as a precursor to steam push-pull sets, which ultimately superseded steam rail motors in Britain.

Bogie Wheelbase	9' 9" (powered), 10' 0" (trailing)
Bogie Centres	40' 9"
Wheel Diameter	3' 5" (powered), ' 6" (trailing)
Tare Weight (Working Order)	49 tons 1 cwt
Capacity	6 first class, 56 third class, plus luggage
Boiler Pressure	170 psi
Cylinders	15" stroke, 9" diameter
Water Capacity	550 gallons
Coal Capacity	30 c. ft.

1 Locomotive Magazine, 1906

GIPR Steam Motor Coach, 1905

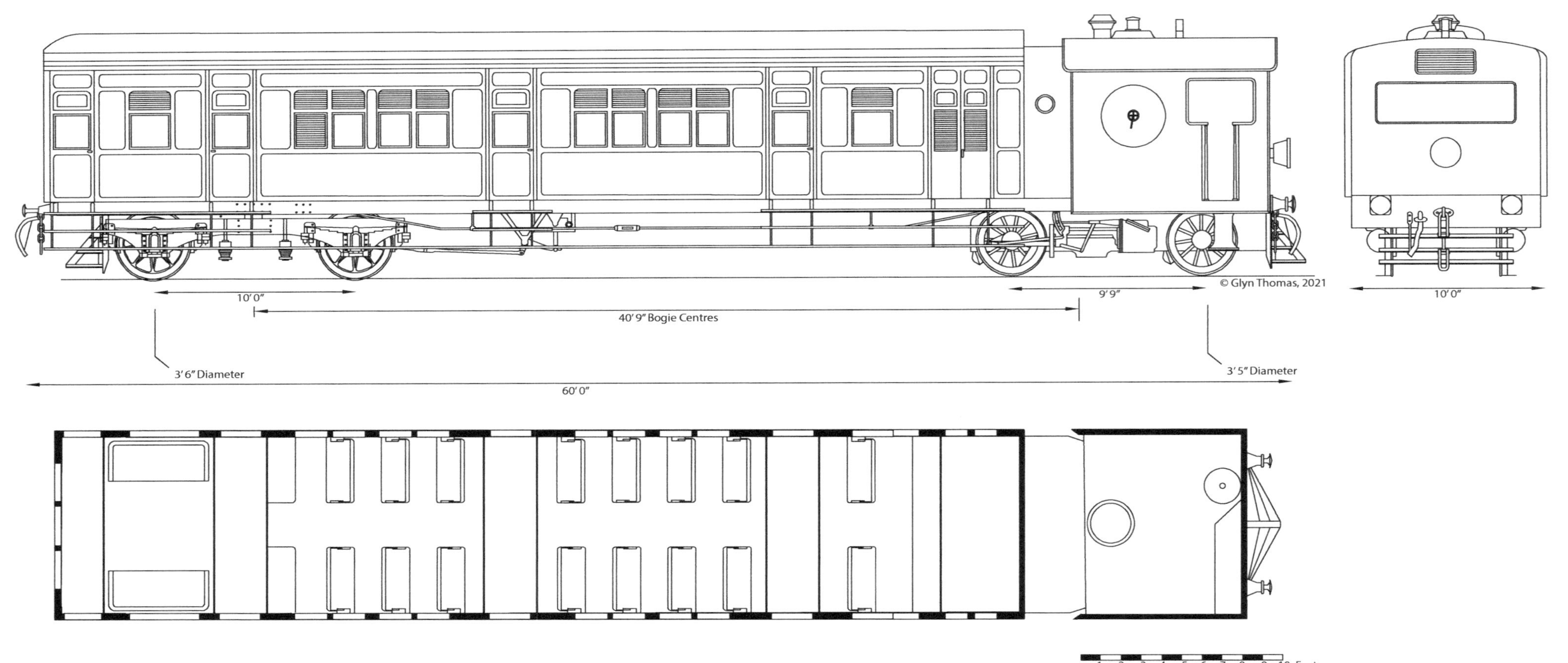

[Reference: Indian Engineering, 1906 plus photographs]

EIR Steam Motor Coach (Broad Gauge)

EIR Steam Motor Coach [Engineer, 1907]

In 1907, the East Indian Railway (EIR) ordered 5 steam railcars from Nasmyth, Wilson (NW). These were built to specifications provided by A.M. Rendel and F.E. Robertson consulting engineers of London. The design was based on a design by Whale, Chief Mechanical Engineer of the London and North-Western Railway (LNWR). The railcars were designed for operation on routes up to 51 miles.

The railcar consisted of a motor compartment, large third class compartment, and small first class compartment. Driving controls were provided at both ends.

The engine unit could be completely detached from the coach section for maintenance. It consisted of a horizontal boiler mounted on a 4-wheel coupled chassis. Drive was to the rear axle of the motor unit, with inside cylinders and Walschaert's valve gear.

The body was Moulmein teak, on a steel chassis. Coachwork construction was sub-contracted to Union Electric Car Company of Preston, England. Final finishing of the body was performed in India as part of erection.

On the railway, these were classified as class M and took numbers 1350-1354. Between 1927-1929, the railcars were rebuilt as 0-4-0T works shunters at Jamalpur works and named "Hercules", "Samson", "Phoenix", "Ajax", and "Atlas".

"Phoenix" has been preserved, and is now on display at the National Railway Museum in Delhi. "Hercules" is preserved an Varanasi Diesel Locomotive Works.

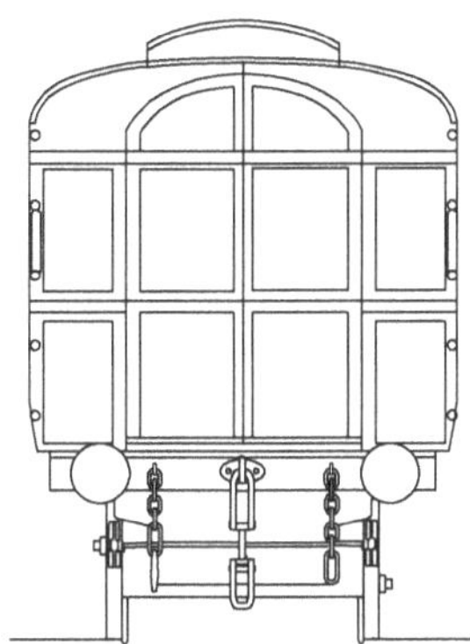

Bogie Wheelbase	35 c. ft.9' 0" (powered), 8' 0" (trailing)
Bogie Centres	40' 11"
Wheel Diameter	3' 7"
Boiler Pressure	160 psi
Cylinders	14" stroke, 9" diameter
Water Capacity	500 gallons
Coal Capacity	35 c. ft.

EIR Steam Motor Coach, 1907

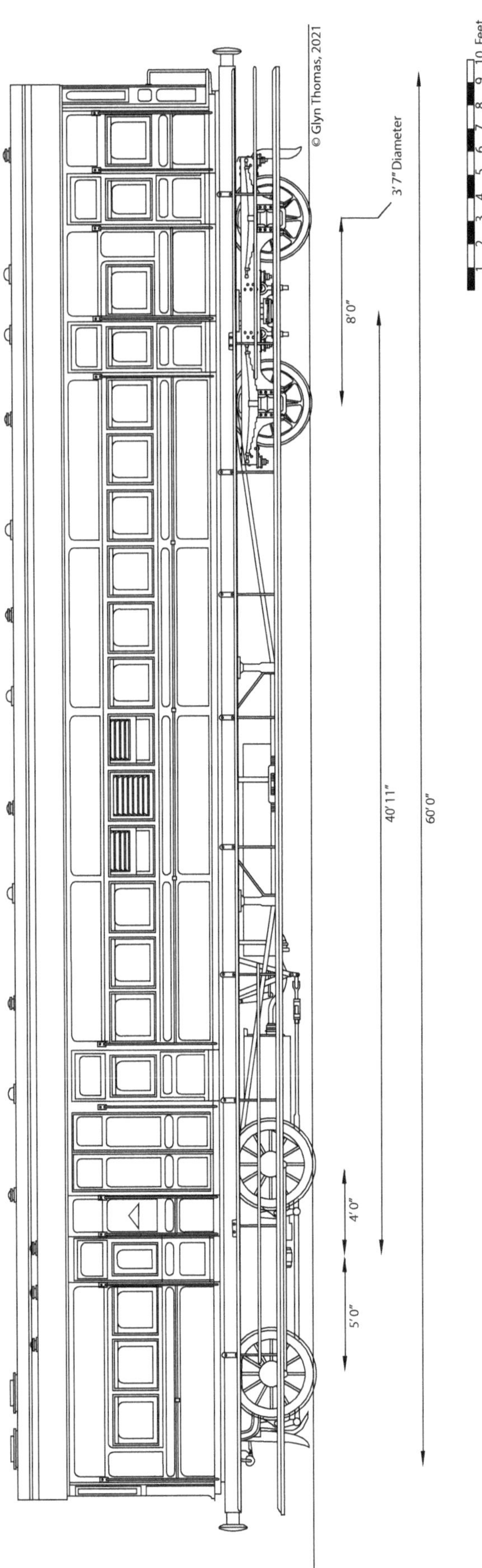

[Reference: The Engineer, 1907]

Sentinel Railcars, 1925-7 (2' 6" Gauge)

BNR Sentinel at Kharagpur in the 1930's [Kelland Collection, BRCT, 50055]

BNR, 1925

The Bengal Nagpur Railway (BNR) experimented with Sentinel railcars around the same time as the BLR. In 1925, they ordered three sets for the narrow gauge and two sets for the broad gauge. The design was overseen by A.C. Carr, Consulting Engineer to the BNR. Externally, the broad gauge and narrow gauge sets looked very similar - an articulated unit, with the engine over a central bogie.

The units were built in 1925-1926. Broad gauge works numbers were 6009 and 6128, narrow gauge works numbers were 6104, 6126 and 6127. Sentinel Cammell exhibited the 6104 set at the Wembley Exhibition of 1925 before sending it to India.

The narrow gauge units were designated the SPC Class, and used on Satpura Lines numbered 1-3. The broad gauge units were numbered 4 and 5.

The engine unit from one of the BNR broad gauge Sentinel railcars was eventually converted to a 4wGT shunting locomotive named "Miss Muffet", for use around Jamalpur works. This locomotive survived into preservation and after a period of static display, was returned to steam at the works in February 2021.

Barsi Light Railway, 1927

The Barsi Light Railway was one of the best-known Indian narrow gauge lines due to it's association with its Consulting Engineer, E.R. Calthrop, and his influential designs. The overall line ran from Miraj, through Kurdavadi to Latur Town - a distance of 202 miles - the longest continuous narrow gauge route in India. The line was originally owned by the Barsi Light Railway Company of London. It was taken into Indian Railways ownership in 1954. The entire line was converted to broad gauge starting in the 1990's and completed in 2008.

Two Sentinel railcars were introduced in 1927 after Calthrop had left the railway (he resigned as Consulting Engineer in 1925 and died in 1927). They were bought for 3,995 GBP each[1]. On the railway, they carried numbers 27-28 and were used for short-hauls on the Pandharpur-Kurduwadi-Barsi Town sections. Three 4wVB Sentinels with Leeds Forge coaches also bought as a comparison.

---

1 See Hughes

Bengal Nagpur Railway Sentinel

Bogie Wheelbase	8' 0" (powered), 5' 6" (outer)
Pivot Centres	25' 10"
Wheel Diameter	2' 6"
Tare Weight	22 tons
Capacity	6 first-class, 31 third-class passengers
Boiler Pressure	274 psi
Cylinders	$6\frac{3}{4}$" diameter x 9" stroke

[Reference: Locomotive, Carriage and Wagon Review, 1925]

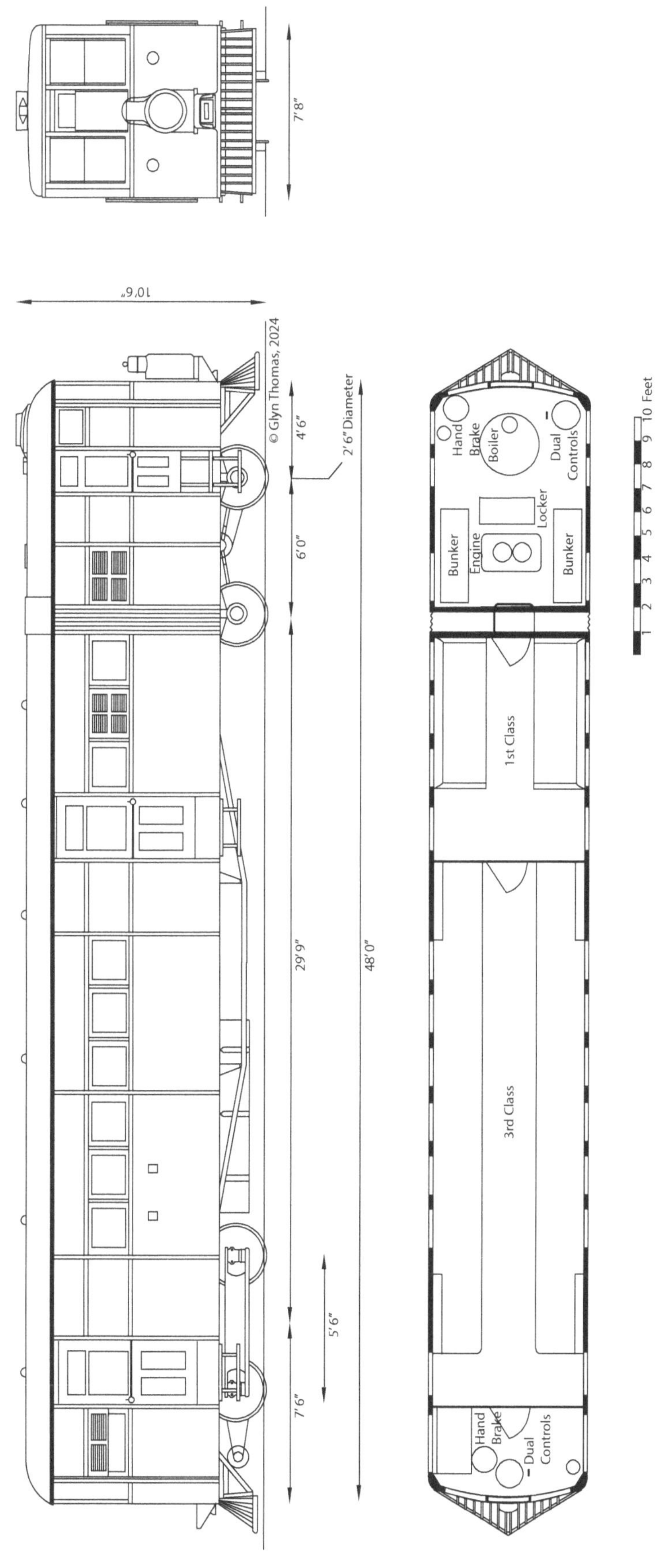

Bogie Wheelbase	6' 0" (powered), 5' 6" (trailing)
Pivot Centres	29' 9"
Wheel Diameter	2' 6"
Tare Weight (Working Order)	21 tons 15 cwt 0 qtr
Capacity	6 first class, 20 third class

[Reference: builder's diagram in the Mike Satow collection at the British Library]

Internal Combustion Vehicles

Gwalior Railcars, 1905-1987 (2' Gauge)

Gwalior Railcar 798, 9/11/1978 [Laurie Marshall, DHRS Collection]

Following its early experience with steam railcars, Gwalior State Railways continued to experiment with railcars for both the Maharajah's and public use. Petrol railcars started to appear in 1912 with orders from Drewry (some placed via Kerr Stuart). The first order was for a 6-seat 10 hp car, works no. 451[1], for the railway management, and a 12-seat 20 hp car. works no. 445[2], for the Maharajah's fleet (probably for use by his entourage).

In 1913, Gwalior returned to Drewry for a larger 20 hp chassis (works no. 526[3]) to be used for the Maharajah's private car. This provided a 9-seat railcar with bodywork by René Breteau of Paris. At a later date, after 1915, this was fitted with a radiator from an early Rolls Royce Silver Ghost (possibly the 1907 car, chassis 60576, called "The Pearl of the East"[4], which had been brought to India by Frank Norbury to compete in the annual Motor Union of Western India Bombay-Kholapar Trial of 620 miles in 1908; he won category V and the car was subsequently sold to the Maharajah). This railcar is now preserved at the Jai Vilas Palace in Gwalior[5].

A second 'Rolls Royce' railcar was converted from the 1909 40/50 hp automobile chassis no 1113. This had originally been supplied to the Viceroy and later sold to the Maharajah. It was illustrated as a railcar in a 1928 Rolls-Royce Bulletin and must have been converted to a railcar at some time between 1915 and 1928. This was an open car with basic seating, so it probably wasn't for the Maharajah's personal use.

The Wickham 4wDM railcar, which later became Indian Railways No 798, may have been intended for use by railway personnel as an inspection car. Its bulbous ends were very distinctive and made the car popular with railfan photographers. It was ordered by Heatley and Gresham of Bombay, through the agency of William Bayliss. Wickham's order number was 7850, works number 1646 to type R1046 with a Ford BB engine. It was dispatched to India on 21/12/1934[6]. This car appeared to still be in good condition in 2008.

In 1947 Gwalior purchased an open sided 11-seat railcar from Wickham for the Maharajah's entourage that was otherwise similar to the 1934 railcar, works no. 4550, order no. 19631, engine Ford V8 BB18F, engine No. 7158961, dispatched 18/8/1947, may have originally had running no. 11[7]. This car is also now preserved at Jai Vilas.

In 1986-7 (IRFCA) or 1988-9 (Narrow Gauge World, 2021), the railway acquired eight[8] 4wDM railcars that were designated NRD1 by the railway. They were built at the Southern Railway workshop at Mysore and were powered by an Ashok Leyland 680 engine, rated at 156HP. Their axle load was rated at 6 tons + 3%. Numbers were 1001-1008. No. 1003 had a slightly larger nose section and this may have been a common modification after the first unit(s). These initially operated with two trailers plus a brake-trailer. Soon after entering service the rules were adjusted to permit running with three regular trailers. They operated on the Gwalior to Bhind (83 km) and Gwalior-Sheopur Kalan (200 km) sections and may generally have run with the passenger section unoccupied as a 'power car'. Maximum permitted speed was 35 kph. Narrow Gauge World in April 2021 reports that they didn't see much service. They were certainly stored out of use by 2008.

---

1 Bg 2-cylinder engine, 90x130mm cylinders; weight, 17 cwt; 5' 6" wheelbase

2 Bg 4-cylinder engine 90x130mm cylinders;; weight, 1 ton, 12 cwt

3 Bg 4-cylinder engine 90x130mm cylinders;; weight, 1 ton, 17 cwt, 10' wheelbase

4 John Fasal, "Rolls Royce and Bentley in British India", plus his personal notes provided to Roger West

5 Jai Vilas claims this is a Rolls Royce vehicle from 1906

6 The Wickham Works List, Keith Gunner and Mike Kennard

7 The Wickham Works List, Keith Gunner and Mike Kennard

8 Only 1001 to 1003 have been observed in photos, so the series may have been curtailed

*Gwalior 20HP Drewry railcar (445/1912). This may have been intended to carry the Maharajah's entourage
[Railway Gazette, 1916]*

Gwalior Maharajah's Drewry Railcar (526/1913) [Railway Gazette, 1916]

Drewry Maharajah's Railcar in its final form with Rolls Royce radiator

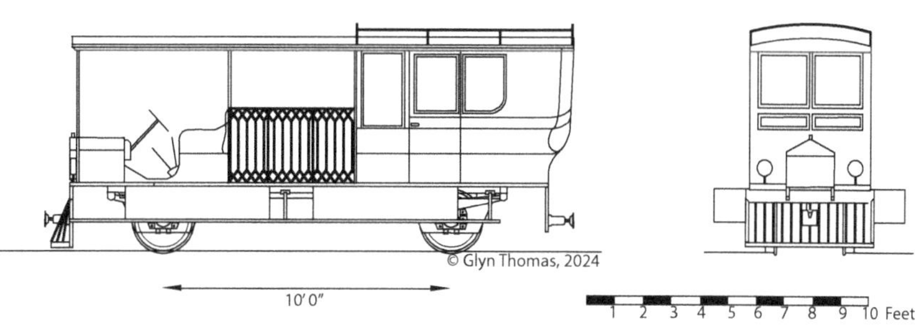

[Reference: Photographs and know dimensions]

Gwalior Wickham railcar 4450/1947 for the Maharajah's entourage as preserved at Jai Vilas Palace
[Roger West]

Gwalior Maharajah's Drewry railcar (526/1913) as preserved at Jai Vilas Palace. Note the addition of the
Rolls Royce radiator [Roger West]

Wickham Railcar 798

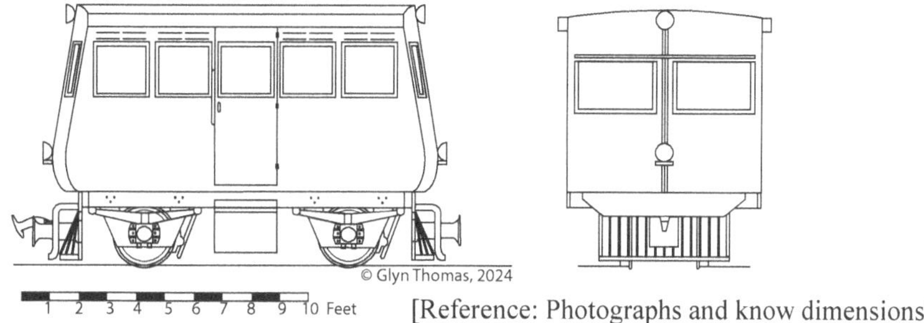

[Reference: Photographs and know dimensions]

NRD1 Varitions

NRD1 no. 1001 at Gwalior, 29/11/1989. These were cleared to operate with up to three trailers
[Fuzz Jordan, DHRS Collection]

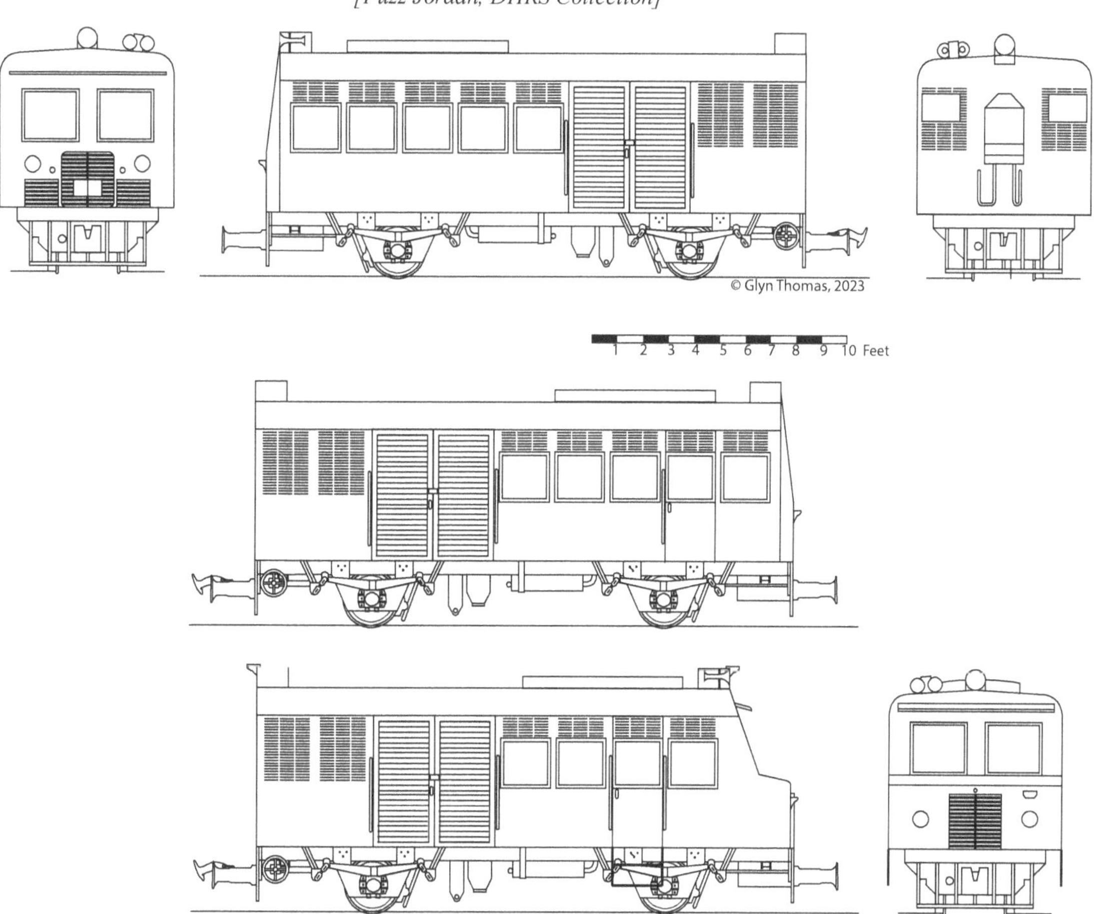

[Reference: Photographs and know dimensions]

NRD1 no. 1001 at Gwalior, 25/2/2000 [Fuzz Jordan, DHRS Collection]

NRD1 no. 1003 at Gwalior, 27/2/1999 [Fuzz Jordan, DHRS Collection]

Matheran Railcars, 1909-1930s (2' Gauge)

Matheran Railcar No. 2 of 1928 [David Churchill Collection]

The Matheran Light Railway acquired its first 8-seat petrol-me-chanical railcar in 1909. This was an small railcar from Drewry (built by BSA). The car was designed with a slight slope to the floor to compensate for the predominant grade on the line. It was lettered with the railway's name, implying it was used in public service (possibly for an on-demand first class service):

THE MATHERAN STEAM LIGHT
TRAMWAY COY LIMITED
SIR ADAMIEE PEERAHOY AND SONS AGENTS

The technology available when the Drewry railcar was built was too lightweight to make a significant impact on the railway's traffic, and World War 1 and its aftermath intervened before Matheran further experimented with self-propelled vehicles. In 1928, Brookville provided a 4wPM railcar, works number 1202. This was also a small vehicle with capacity for about 6 passengers and a driver, and may have been intended to replace or supplement the Drewry car. Although Hughes lists this as a locomotive, Brookville's Type D were generally railcars fitted with Ford engines. It weighed 2 tons.

Matheran also received a larger railcar, built around a Dodge Brothers chassis in 1928. It was reported to seat 14 passengers and was numbered 2.

Drewry Railcar

Two railcars based on Dodge truck chassis were present on the line in the 1930's. Indian Railway no. 899 is preserved at the Delhi museum where it's claimed to have been bought from "Grashame"[1] in the 1930's. In is likely that "Grashame" was a dealer or broker in Britain or the US and the original builder was probably Koppel Industrial Car and Equipment Co. of Koppel, Pennsylvania, USA[2]. Jeff Scherb produced a good diagram of 899 for Narrow Gauge and Short Line Gazette, May-June 2005 It's possible that 899 is a rebuilt body on the chassis of the 1928 railcar no. 2.

Under Indian Railway ownership, the Dodge railcars were num-bered 898 and 899 and classed FZZ. They differed in hood de-sign and wheel arrangement and it's likely that 898 is the newer car (possibly 1932 and 1934). 899 has a 2-APM wheel arrange-ment, while 898 was a 2-A1PM (assuming that the rear axle wasn't powered). At some point, 898 was rebuilt with a Perkins P6 diesel engine, which developed 85hp - these engines were available new from 1937 through 1960.   898 was last seen at Neral and may still exist.

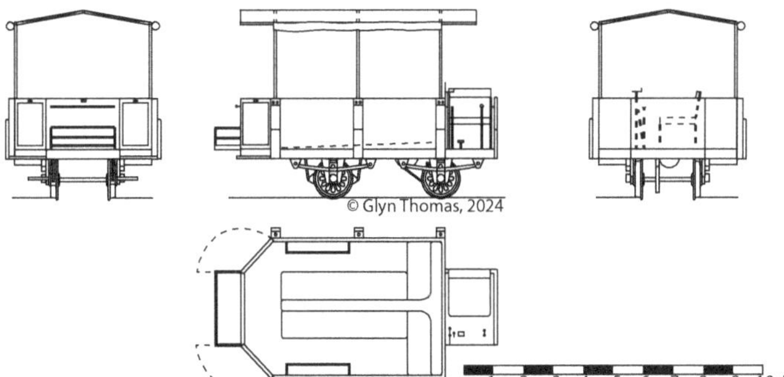

[Reference: Photographs and known dimensions]

1 David Churchill offers potential explanations for the Greshame provenance indicated by the Delhi Railway Museum- - either (or perhaps both) of the following -
(a) Graham Brothers of the US who built trucks in the 1920s and were taken over by Dodge in 1925 and Chrysler in 1928 with some trucks still branded as Graham until the early 1930s. 899 at Delhi has a Graham Bros plate on the engine.
(b) Heatley and Gresham of Letchworth, Herts and Bombay who were agents supplying railway equipment to India. 899 at Delhi appears to be right hand drive which may indicate it was supplied via Dodge in the UK.
2 Via David Churchill - between 1933 and 1938, Koppel built a range of rail-cars utilizing Dodge truck chassis (see "Koppel Industrial Car and Equipment Co. (Koppel)" on page 148)

Brookville Railcar

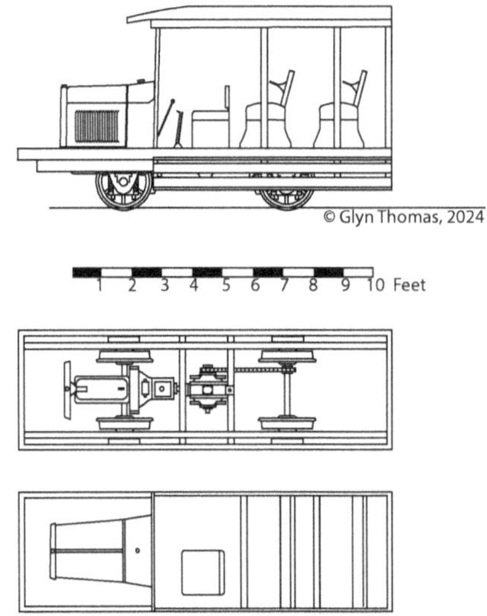

[Reference: Speculative - based on Brookville Type D plans in
"Brookville Locomotives - Then and Now"]

Dodge Railcar No. 2

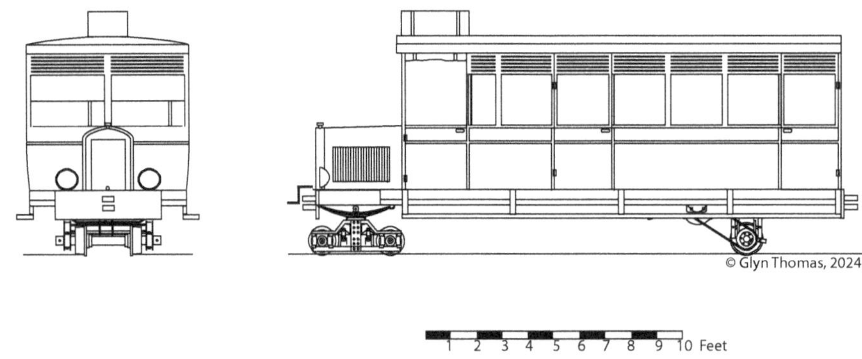

[Reference: Photographs and Dodge Light Repair Truck dimensions]

Matheran Railcar 899 at National Railway Museum, Delhi, 18/12/1988 [Author's photo]

Railcar No. 898

Railcar RM 898 at Neral, 21/11/1980 [Laurie Marshall, DHRS Collection]

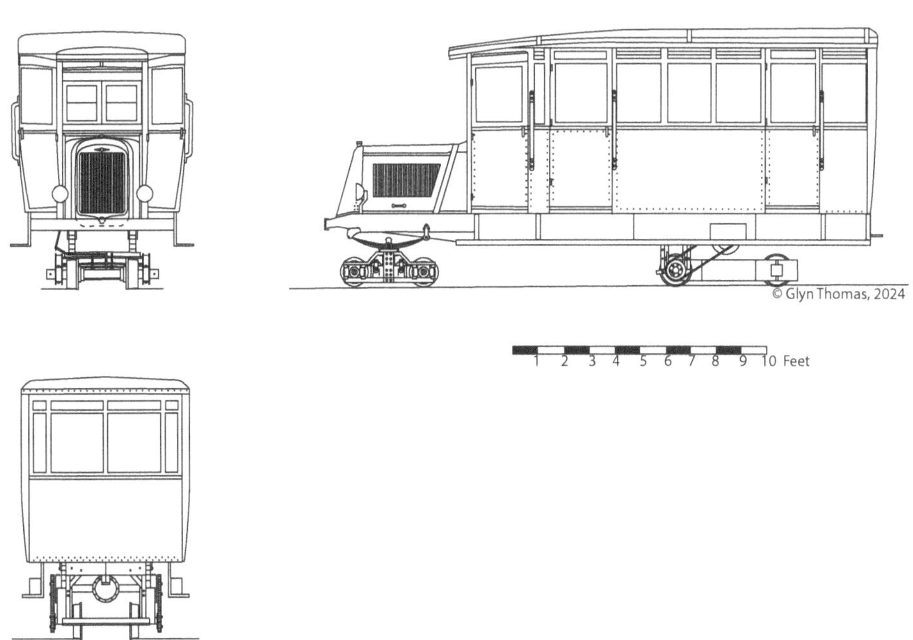

[Reference: Jeff Scherb's diagram of 899 plus photographs]

Rao of Cutch Shooting Car, 1910 (2' 6" Gauge)

Rao of Cutch Shooting Car [Locomotive Magazine]

Cutch was a small princely state on the coast north of Bombay. Local rail services were provided by the 2' 6" gauge, Cutch State Railway that was established by the state in 1901. The line from Tuna to Anjar was opened in 1905 and it was subsequently extended to Bhuj in 1908. A link to Bhachau was added in 1912 and a further link to Kandla in 1932. The final overall length was 72 miles. Cutch State Railways were merged into the Western Railway in 1951.

The Rao of Cutch, Maharao Khengarji Bawa, was responsible for the funding and development of the railway. In 1910, he ordered a petrol-driven railcar for use by private shooting parties in the state. As an early example of a petrol-powered railcar, this received attention from the international railway press[1].

The car was supplied by McEwan, Pratt & Co. of Wickford (their works number 13) to the specification of E.R. Calthrop & Partners. It was powered by a 27 HP petrol engine with 4" x 5" cylinders. A 3-speed gearbox permitted speeds of 10, 20, and 30 mph in each direction with the engine running at 900 RPM. It had capacity for 8 passengers and 4 cwt of luggage.

Inside, the engine compartment was in the centre of the car with storage for game and equipment above it. Luxurious passenger compartments were provided on each side, furnished with horse-hair seats upholstered in buffalo leather.

The car appears to have been a success because it continued to be illustrated in the makers catalogue of 1921.

Interestingly, the World Survey of Foreign Railways lists the Cutch State Railway as owning 7 railcars in 1939, although many of these may have been inspection vehicles.

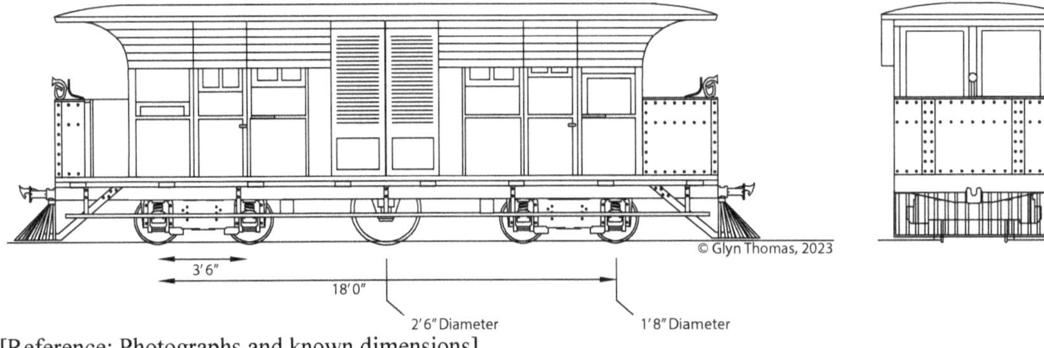

[Reference: Photographs and known dimensions]

---

1 See Locomotive Magazine, September 1910

Kalka-Simla Railcars, 1911-1933 (2' 6" Gauge)

Kalka-Simla Railcar No.3 driven by LP Hughes in 1929 [https://shankardubai.tripod.com/louishughes.htm]

The North Western Railway (NWR) was an early operator of railcars on the Kalka-Simla Railway (KSR), and these have continued to be used up to the present day. Simla was the summer capital of the government during the colonial era, requiring large amounts of mail and many first-class passengers to be transported during the summer months.

The first three railcars (numbers 1-3) were supplied between 1911 and 1913 by Lloyd and Plaister Ltd., a British engineering company better known for building fire engines. No. 1 was a mail car with capacity for 2 passengers and ½ ton of mail. Nos. 2 and 3 had capacity for 10 passengers, with a wheelbase of 6' 6". Hughes reports that these cars were rebuilt in 1914 with new engines, but rode roughly due to the long wheelbase. These were possibly fitted with White and Poppe engines (during the rebuild?).

NWR was undeterred by their early railcar experience and followed up with an order for two petrol railcars from Drewry Car Company (DrC), numbered 5-6 in 1921 (the missing no. 4 was an inspection car on a NWR's Jacobabad-Kashmore line). These cars had the unusual wheel arrangement of 2-4-2. As with most equipment supplied to the KSR, there were initial difficulties in operation, in this case due to wear on the trucks. Once these problems were overcome with local modifications, these railcars ran successfully in service.

DrC also provided a conventional 40HP 4-wheel railcar in 1927, number 7. DrC 1628 0-4-0PMR 38/40hp, Bg(4) engine, 9 seats, ex. works 27/8/27, SS Branksome Hall to Karachi[1].

DrC followed up with its most successful design for the KSR - a bogie railcar with capacity for 14 passengers and mail, or 16 passengers. Four were built between 1925 and 1930 and numbered 8-11. The motor on these cars was fixed over the front bogie, so these were essentially articulated cars.

In 1931, NWR went to D. Wickham and Co. for a small railcar, numbered 12. Its works number was 494, built to order no 4186, Wickham type KS, fitted with a Meadows EPC, engine no. 7296, and body by Creasey[2]. This car was dispatched on 29/1/1932 and shipped via Karachi[3]. This car has subsequently been preserved at the National Railway Museum.

The final colonial iteration on the railcar design was an Armstrong, Whitworth and Co. diesel-electric bogie railcar, built in 1933 and numbered 14. This car had capacity for 14 passengers. It had a teak body that was painted white for use on the railway with a varnished Venesta interior. It proved to be more economical in service than the petrol railcars. This car is also preserved at the National Railway Museum.

1 The Railway Products of Baguley-Drewry Ltd and its Predecessors, Allen Civil and Roy Etherington

2 Creasey were a well known vehicle body builder based in Knebworth, Hertfordshire

3 The Wickham Works List, Keith Gunner and Mike Kennard

Railcars 8-11 have the longest and most varied history on the line. During World War 2, these car were re-built with General Motors diesel engines due to severe rationing of petrol. The bodywork also underwent modifications over the years. In around 1980, Indian Railways performed a major rebuilding of the cars and renumbered them 1-4. At least one of these (no. 2) was fitted with a clear fibreglass roof before 2004. By 2012, these cars were out of service, and were refurbished for the 2013 season with improved interiors and air brakes. By this time, all the cars were fitted with clear roofs. At least one of these cars is still in service in 2021.

In recent years, KSR has introduced a new luxurious railcar, RA-100, for charter service. This has capacity for 8 passengers, air-conditioning and a kitchen. This may also be a rebuild of an older railcar.

In service, the railcars make the trip from Kalka to Simla in 4 ½ hours, which is faster than locomotive-hauled trains, and hasn't changed since the railcars were first introduced.

Kalka-Simla Railcar No.6 [Kelland Collection, BRCT, 50139]

No. 5-6

Note that photos show various detail differences from the plan, which was based on builder's diagrams. There appears to a higher floor level in the back 2 compartments which was glazed; this was probably a mail compartment. There was also more pronounced beading on the body.

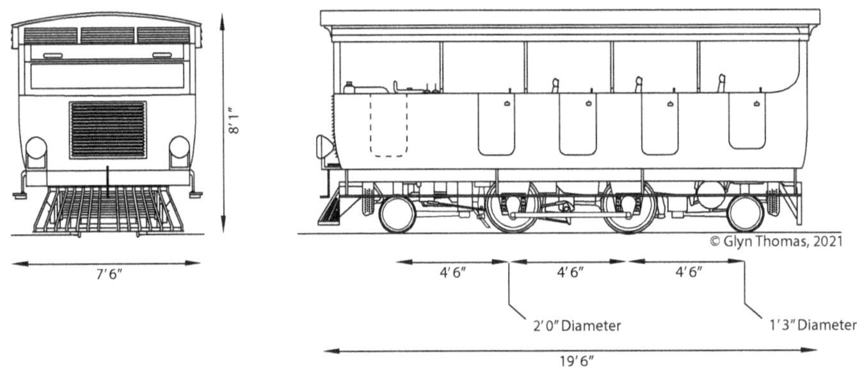

Powered Wheelbase	4' 6"
Overall Wheelbase	13' 6"
Wheel Diameter	2' 0" drivers, 1' 3" pony trucks
Power	45-50 HP
Cylinders	4 ½" diameter, 5" stroke
Capacity	16 passengers (19 maximum)

[Reference: The Engineer, 1921]

No. 7

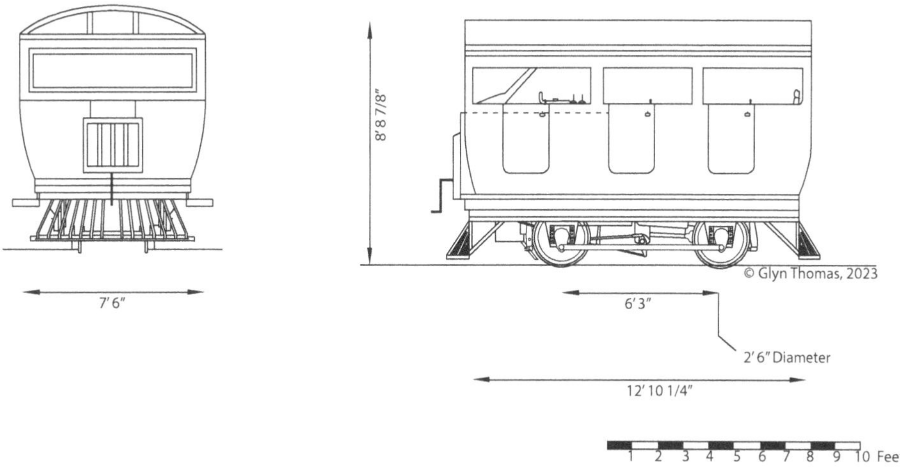

Wheelbase	6' 3"
Wheel Diameter	2' 6"
Capacity	8 passengers
Power	40 HP
Empty Weight	4.45 Tons
Cylinders	4
Stroke	3 3/4" x 6"
RPM	1,000

[Reference: NWR diagram book, Mike Satow collection at the British Library]

Kalka-Simla Railcar [Drewry advert via Grace's Guide]

Nos. 8-11 as built

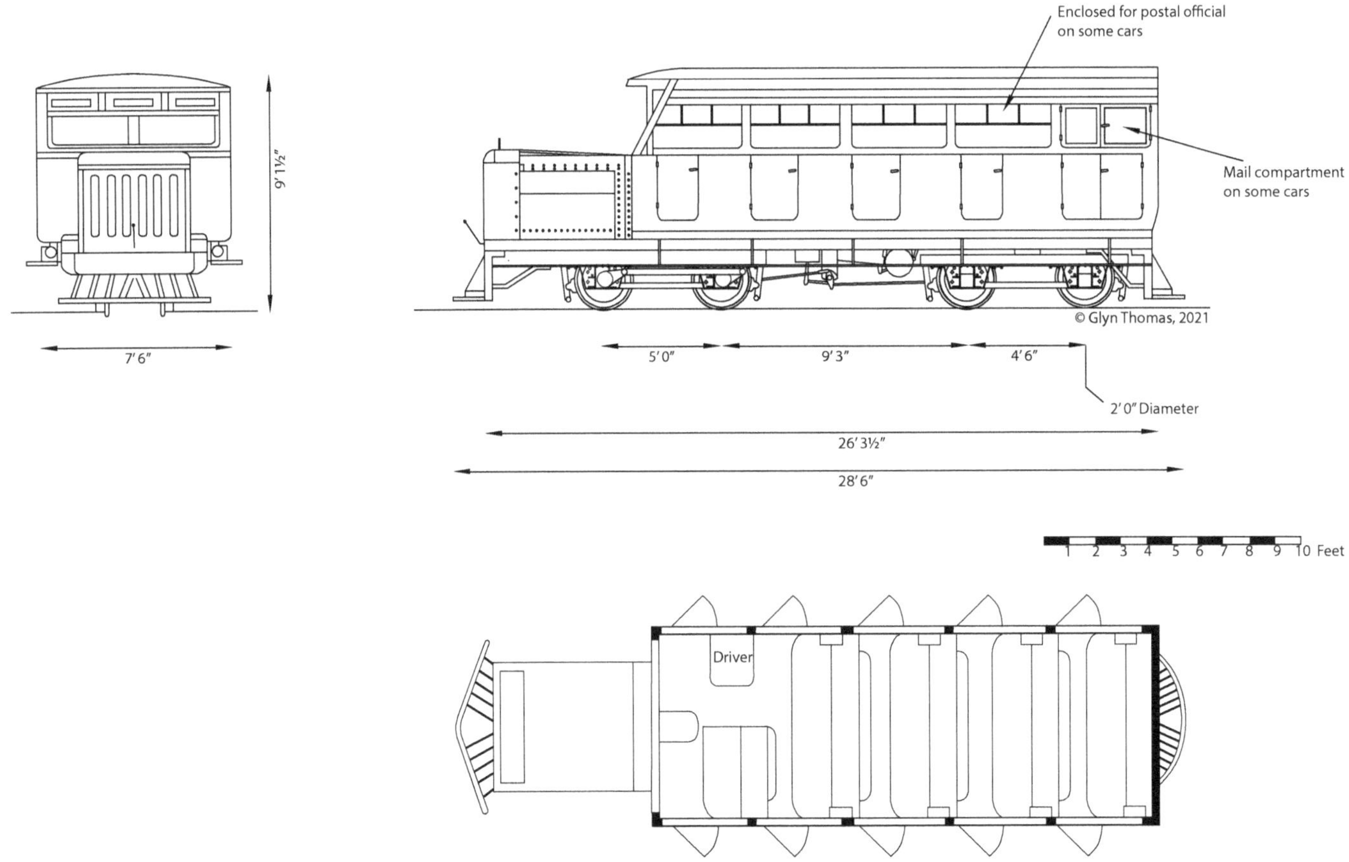

Bogie Wheelbase	5' 0" powered, 4' 6" trailing
Bogie Centres	14' 0"
Wheel Diameter	2' 0"
Capacity	14 (8-10), 16 (11) passengers

[Reference: NWR diagram book, Mike Satow collection at the British Library]

Railcar no. 8 at Kalka, 30/11/1979 [Laurie Marshall, DHRS Collection]

Railcar no. 11 at Kumarhati, 30/11/1979 [Laurie Marshall, DHRS Collection]

Rebuilt Kalka-Simla Railcar No. 1 near Simla, 21/10/1994 [John Tolson, Transport Treasury, JMT13250]

Nos. 1-4 (rebuild of 8-11)

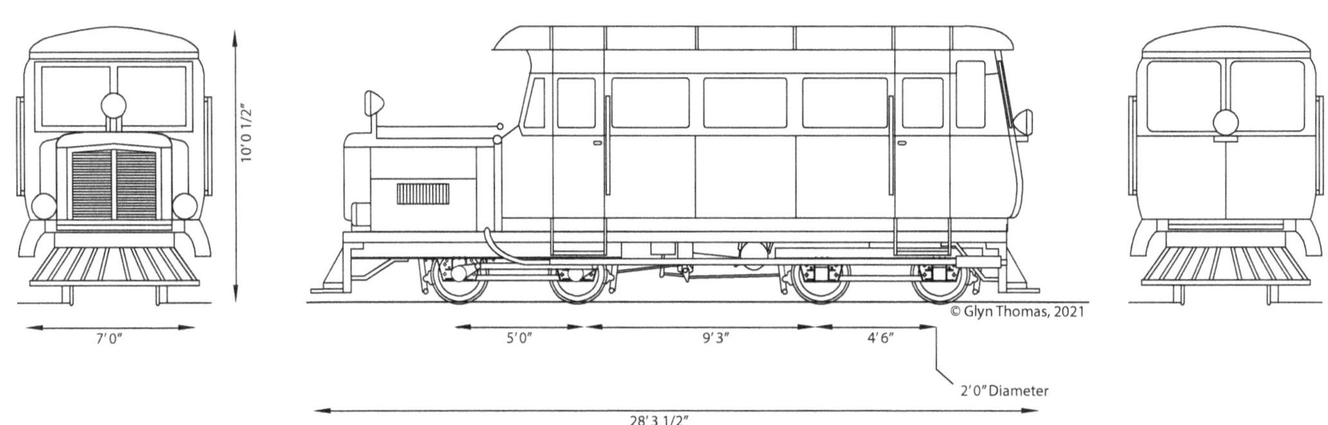
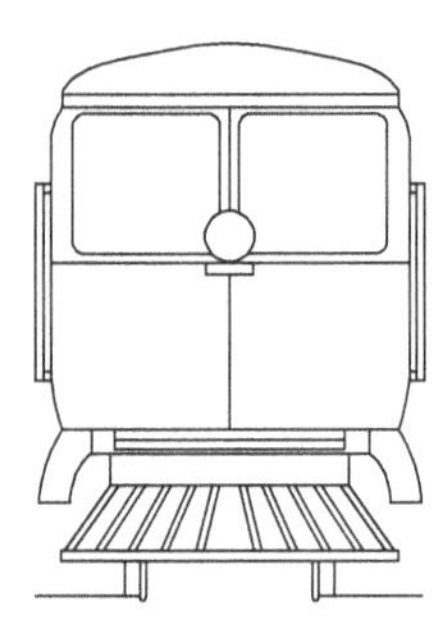

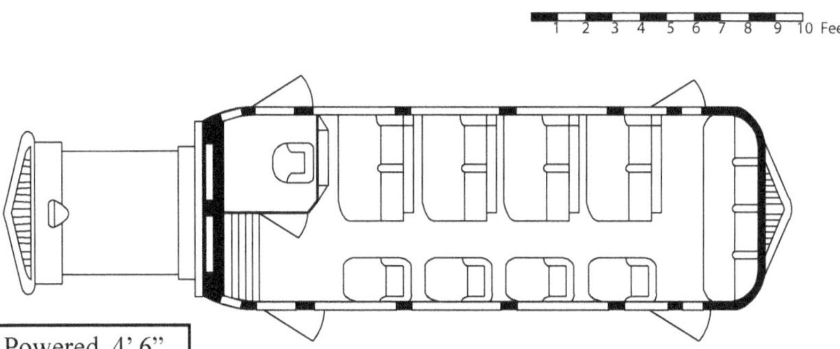

Bogie Wheelbase	5' 0" Powered, 4' 6" Trailing
Bogie Centres	14' 0"
Wheel Diameter	2' 0"
Capacity	16 passengers
Power	85 HP
Empty Weight	9.7 Tons
Cylinders	6
Diameter and Stroke	5½" x 6"
RPM	1,000

[Reference: NWR diagram book, Mike Satow collection at the British Library and photographs]

Note: diagram is based on Nos. 1-3. No. 4 had some variations, including brake gear exposed along the running boards, and the left-hand rear door blocked off. Refer to photographs for detail differences. It appears that the last 2-3 rows of passenger seats were reversed in No. 4 and possibly other cars.

Kalka-Simla Railcar no. 12 at Delhi Railway Museum, 16/10/1994 [John Tolson, Transport Treasury, JMT13199]

No. 12

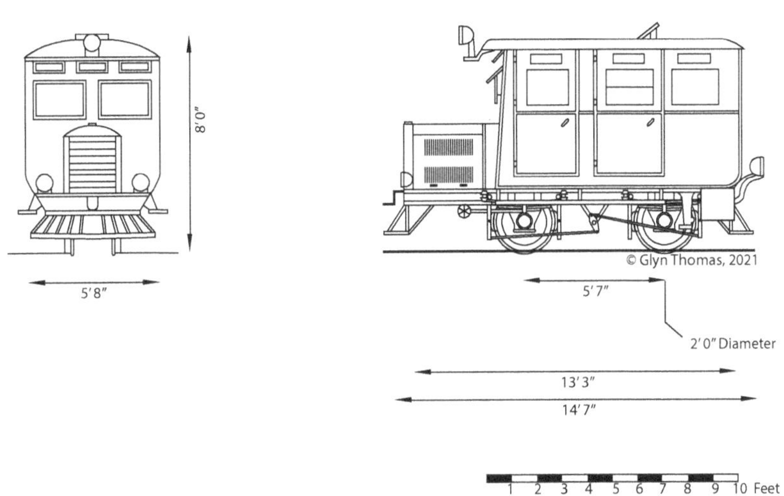

Wheelbase	5' 7"
Wheel Diameter	2' 0"
Capacity	4 passengers
Power	58 HP
Empty Weight	2.5 Tons
Cylinders	6
Stroke	3" x 4 3/4"
RPM	2,000

[Reference: NWR diagram book, Mike Satow collection at the British Library]

Kalka-Simla Railcar No. 14 at Delhi Railway Museum, 16/10/1994 [John Tolson, Transport Treasury, JMT13162]

No. 14

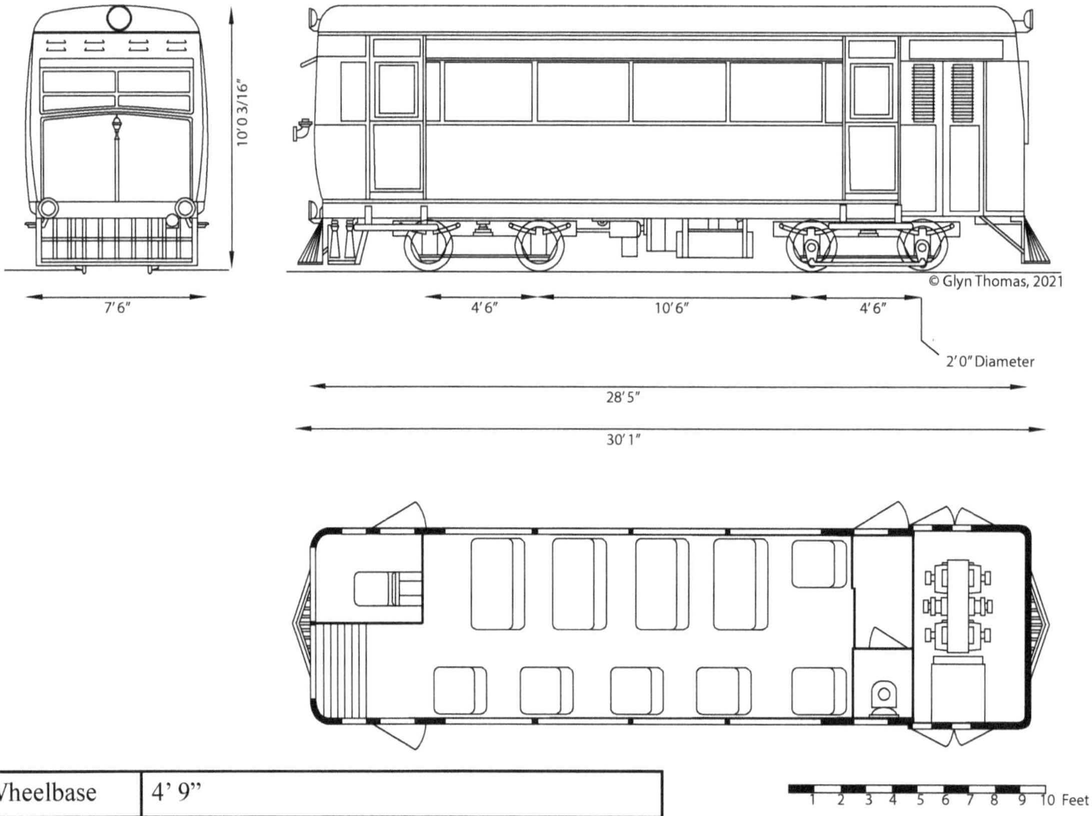

Bogie Wheelbase	4' 9"
Bogie Centres	15' 0"
Wheel Diameter	2' 0"
Capacity	14 passengers and 4 cwt mail or 16 passengers
Power	90 HP
Weight	13.07 Tons
Cylinders	6
RPM	2,000
Gears	5, 10, 20 MPH forward or reverse

[Reference: NWR diagram book, Mike Satow collection at the British Library]

Darjeeling Railcar, 1920 (2' Gauge)

Motor Rail Railcar for the DHR [Builder's Photo]

From the earliest days of the Darjeeling Himalayan Railway (DHR), passengers were sometimes offered the option of "gravity cars" - unpowered trolleys with just a brake, for downhill travel.

However, the steep grades and tight curves of the line made the construction of railcars that could make a successful round-trip over the entire line a challenge. The first attempt was a Motor Rail 4wPM car with a 40HP engine provided in 1920. This doesn't appear to have been very successful because further cars weren't ordered, although it remained on the line until at least the 1940s.

In his books on the DHR, Terry Martin mentions that "rail-taxis" - locally produced trolleys with a petrol engine and 6-seats, were operated out of Kerseong on the upper section of the line during the late colonial period.

A second railcar was listed in Railway Board returns between 1927 and 1942, but details of this car have not been found[1].

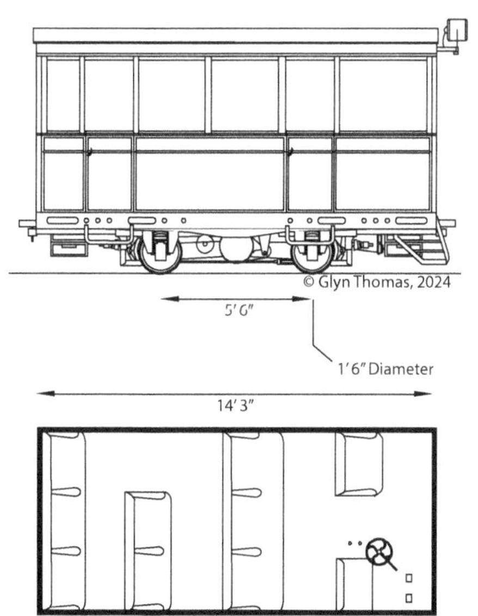

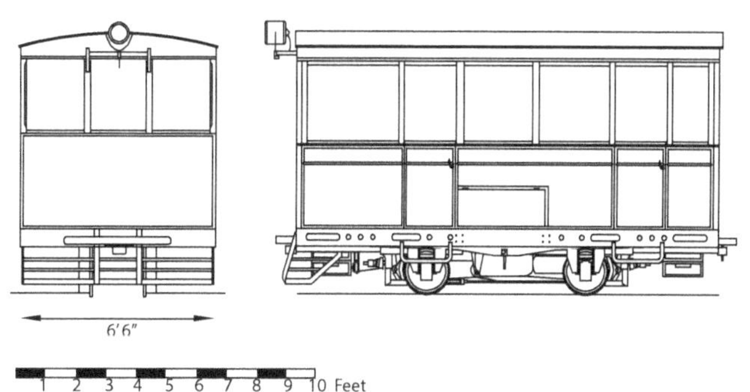

[Reference: Diagram in The Early Years of the Motor Rail & Tram Car Company 1911-1931, by W.J.K. Davies and photographs]

---

1 From David Churchill

Nilgiri Drewry Railcars, 1922 (Metre Gauge)

Nilgiri Railway 1922 railcar on trial at Drewry's works [Works Photo]

Drewry provided two small 4-coupled railcars to the Nilgiri railway in 1922. Their works numbers were 1324-5. These had duplex patent transmission and then chains to one axle. Before sending to India, they were tested on an 8% grade at Drewry's works for "starting power". Hand cranking was used to start engine. Hand brakes were the primary brakes, and an emergency rack brake wheel was fitted that usually ran freely on one axle.

These railcars were not initially successful in operation due to transmission problems caused by the unique operating conditions of the Nilgiri railway. 1324 was returned to Burton for modifications in 1925 and once modified returned to the railway with parts to remediate the second railcar as well[1].

The later history of these units is unknown.

Wheelbase	6'
Wheel Diameter	25"
Power	100 HP
Engine	Baguley 4 cylinder petrol, 6" diameter, 8 ½" stroke
Gearbox	3-speed
Tare Weight	8 tons 8 cwt
Capacity	8 seat and 1½ tons mail or luggage

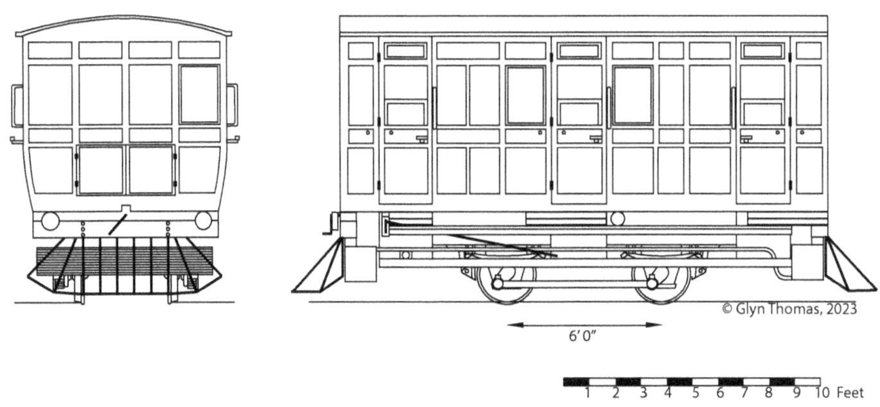

[Reference: photographs and known dimensions]

---

1 See "The Railway Products of Baguley-Drewry Ltd and its Predecessors"

GBSR Armstrong Whitworth Railcars, 1932 (2' 6" Gauge)

Amstrong-Whitworth Railcar no. 104 for GBSR [David Churchill Collection]

In 1932, Armstrong Whitworth provided four diesel railcars for the Gaekwar's Baroda State Railway, where they were numbered 103-106[1]. These were fitted with their patented A.B.E. transmission. The 80-95HP Saurer engine was at the front of the car with the weight carried on a bogie. The drive operated via a carden shaft and drove a fixed rear axle via a worm gear.

One of these units was trialled, without its body, on the Leek and Manifold Railway in the UK before being dispatched to India.

The railcars were divided into first- and second-class compartments, and it appears that they could be driven from either end.

David Churchill provided 1930's photographs of units 102 and 104 in service. By this time, 104 has gained a tubular device over the roof of the main driving compartment. This is likely to be part of the water cooling circuit, exposed to air flow to reduce overheating.

The AW railcars were rebuilt to first-class saloons with seating capacity 14 persons in 1943-45. They retained the single (former driving) axle and bogie.

No. 102 as photographed shows a totally different design - maybe nos. 101 and 102 were locally built? A driver's compartment is provided at one end with the remainder turned over to third-class and second-class compartments. It may have been possible to drive from controls in the second-class compartment too, because there is a horn and bell at that end as well. It is equipped with a self-contained turntable, which would allow the vehicle to be turned at the end of the line so that the driver's compartment faced forward.

Engine Compartment of Amstrong-Whitworth Railcar no. 104 for GBSR[David Churchill Collection]

Coach 14, rebuilt from an AW railbus was at Pratapnagar in 1980. Tare 8.1 tonnes [The late Peter Bawcutt courtesy of Peter Tiller]

---

1 The numbering of these railcars seems to be uncertain – Hughes has 103-106 whereas Brian Webb has them as 101 to 104.

GBSR Railcar as Built

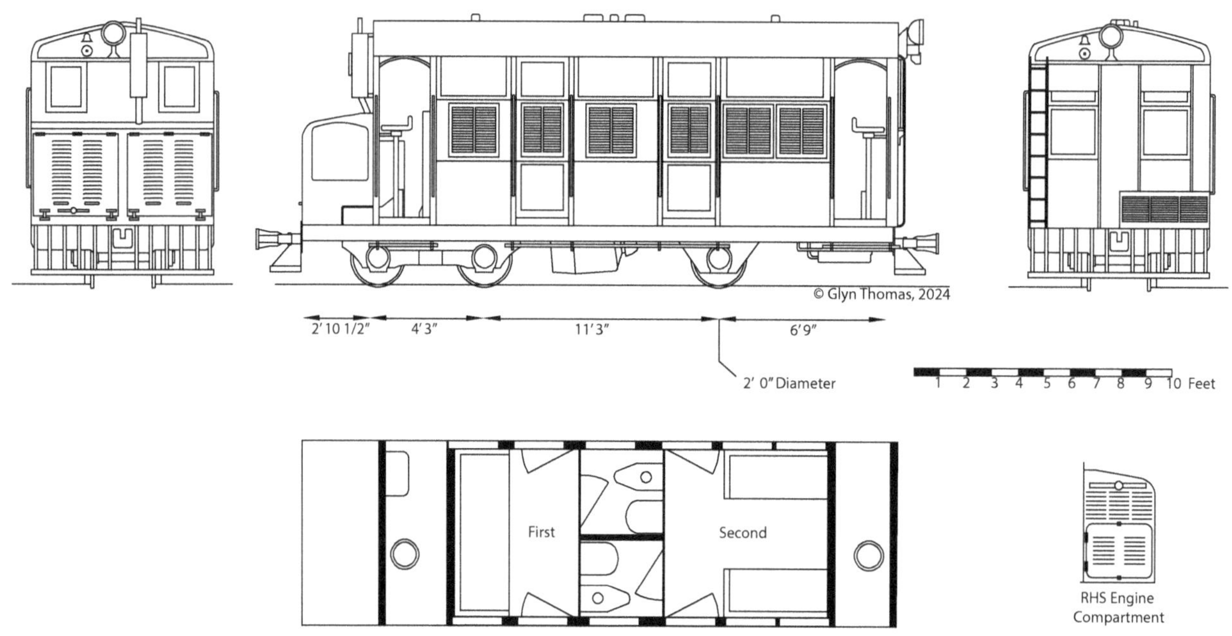

[Reference: GBSR blueprint and John Lacey's diagram for the Indian Railways Study Group]

GBSR Railcar as Running from around 1938 Onwards

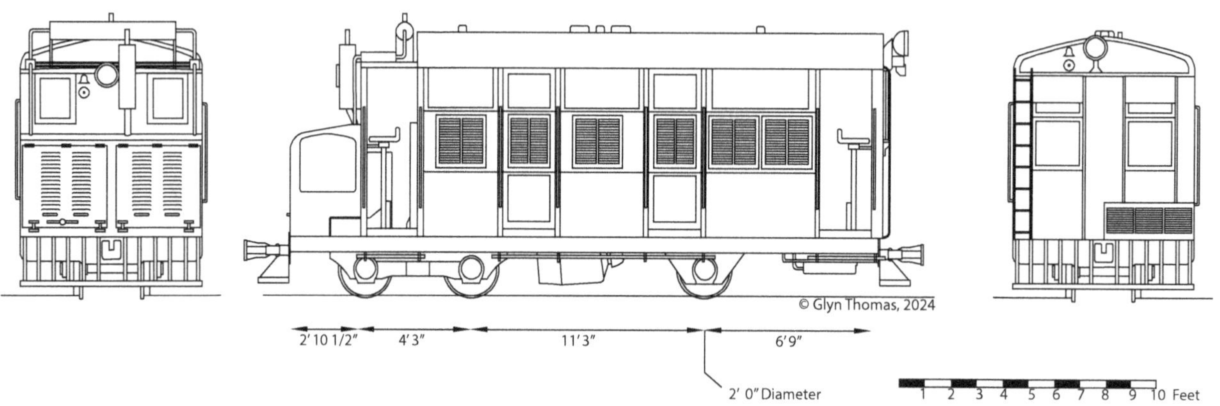

GBSR no. 102

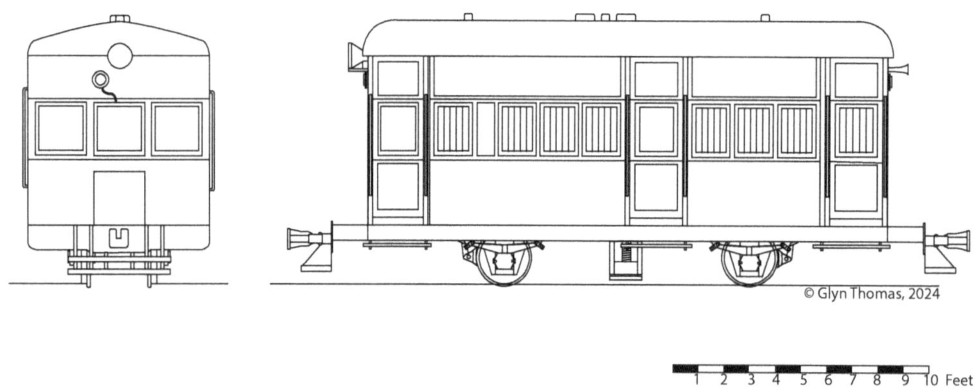

GBSR no. 102, the solebars are marked "Return 7 1939", which dates the photograph. Unfortunately the builder's plate is illegible, but it is not AW [David Churchill Collection]

GBSR no. 102 [David Churchill Collection]

Western Railway and its Predecessor's Railcars

Ford and Chevrolet Railcars at Jaipur [The late Peter Bawcutt courtesy of Peter Tiller]

In an uncharacteristic vague caption in Hughes' Indian Locomotives Part 4 - Metre Gauge 1941-1990', he comments that 'the Western Railway had quite large number of these makeshift units [diesel railcars], especially in the Saurashtra area'. It has been possible to track down some records of these railcars, but it may never be possible to tell the full story without access to the original records. See "The Ones That Got Away" on page 151 for more details on identified cars.

These railcars share a number of common design features. In general, they use standard production road truck engines, chassis, and transmissions. In the most basic form, the road wheels were replaced with rail wheels and a railcar body built on the truck bed. A more advanced version, which may have been more common, was to mount the engine and transmission inside a regular railway coach body - this resulted in a higher ground clearance than a road truck, so the final drive was usually connected from the truck's driving axle to a rear railway axle using chains. In these versions, the front of the coach had large windows for driver's visibility and ventilation grates to provide cooling for the engine.

The first (metre-gauge) example below is based on the photo on Peter Bawcutt's photo taken at Jaipur in 1970. The Ford railcar appears to be based on a standard 1937 truck chassis with relatively few modifications. The design was obviously fairly successful, since it appears to still be operational in 1970. Its running number was RMC1195.

Roderick Smith photographed a second metre-gauge type at Dhola Junction on the Bhavnagar to Ahmedabad line in 1977, towing two standard 4-wheel coaches as trailers. This appears to be similar to the Chevrolet design below. In the photograph, the chain guard is missing (if it was ever fitted) and it is interesting to consider what modern safety inspectors would say about operating an open chain drive next to crowded low-level platforms.

The third metre-gauge example is based on a railcar that appears in the Bawcutt photo and was also photographed by LG Marshall derelict at Jaipur shed in 1985. Marshall states that this used a Chevrolet engine and was built for the Johdpur State Railway in the 1930s. Its running number was RMC1194.

Following Independence, the Western Railway operated a fleet of approximately 10 locally-built chain-driven narrow gauge railbuses in the Bhavnagar area. These cars divided into at least three distinct classes - no. 51s had a Chevrolet 30hp engine and a 1-A wheel arrangement; no. 53s had a Leyland 75hp engine, retaining the general appearance of the earlier type; nos. 59s and 60s used a 1-1A wheel arrangement and a larger 95hp Leyland engine. It isn't clear what the full breakdown between the types was. The larger cars were capable of pulling several small trailer cars. The best record of this type that has come to light so far is a series of photographs taken by Peter Bawcutt in 1969.

David Churchill has a 1976 photo of 60s by an unknown photographer. A very similar photo by Lou Johnson of 59s was taken in 1978.

The heyday for these units was probably from the late 1930s into the 1950s - a period that wasn't well documented by photographers for geopolitical reasons. By the 1960s, most of these units would have been end of life, and more robust designs based on standard railway practice were starting to become available.

Ford Railcar (metre-gauge)

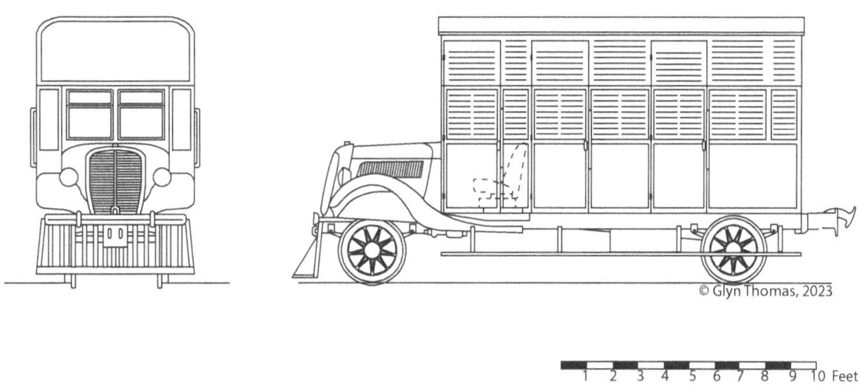

[Reference: Ford 1937 truck plans and photographs]

Bhavnagar Railcar (metre-gauge)

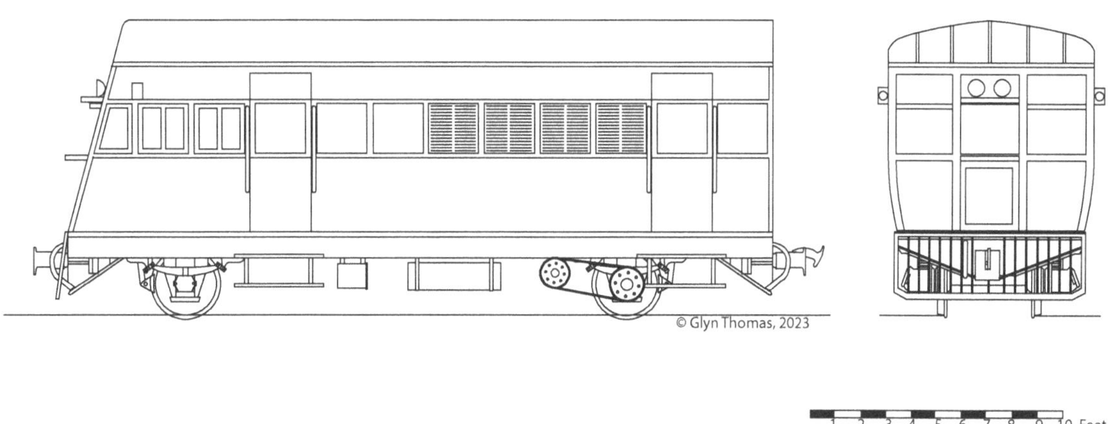

[Reference: WR coach plans and photographs]

Chevrolet Railcar (metre-gauge)

Chevrolet Railcar at Jaipur, 17/11/85 [Laurie Marshall, DHRS Collection]

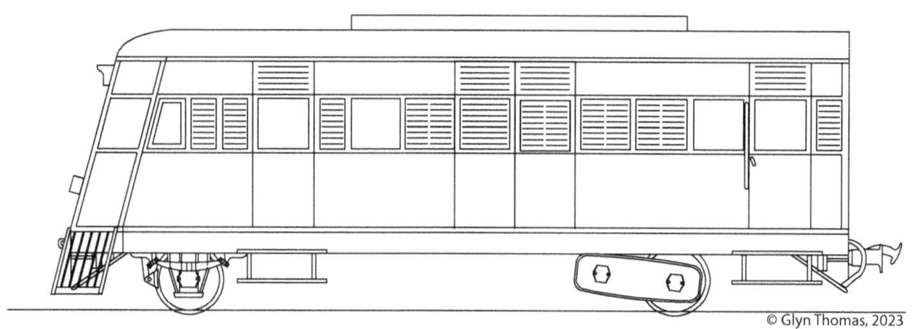

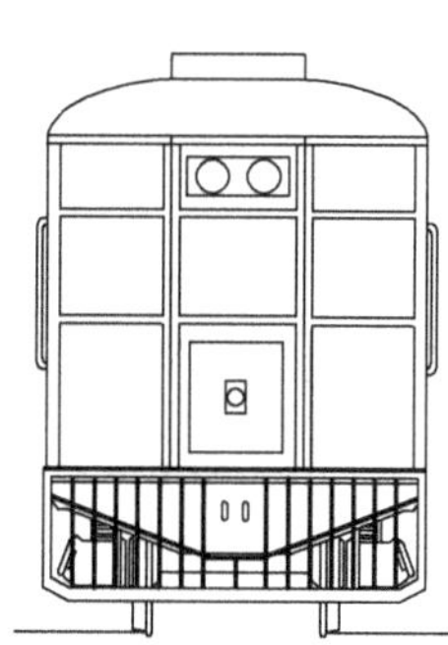

[Reference: Scaled from photographs]

Bhavnagar Railcar (narrow-gauge)

Railcar 60s at Bhavnagar, 1976 [David Churchill Collection]

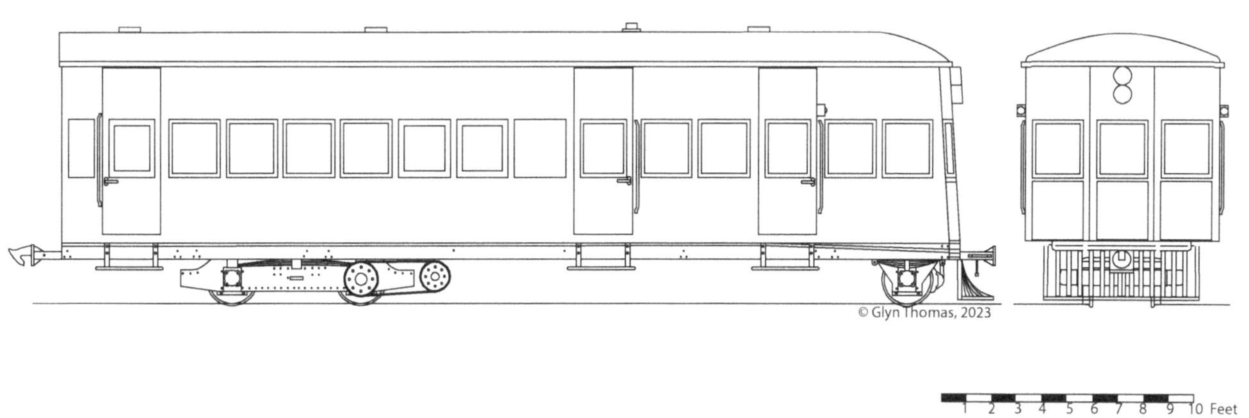

[Reference: Photographs and known dimensions]

WR 53s equipped with a Leyland 75hp diesel engine. [The late Peter Bawcutt courtesy of Peter Tiller]

Two of the three pairs of daily trains were worked by 'rail motor units' hauling trailers. In 1969, 493 Mahuva-Bhavnagar RM Passenger comprising rail motor unit 60s with three four-wheeled trailers, approaches Bhavnagar Terminus. The journey time was about 1½ hours less than by steam-powered 499 Mixed [The late Peter Bawcutt courtesy of Peter Tiller]

WR 60s rail motor equipped with a Leyland 95hp diesel engine. Seating capacity 33 passengers [The late Peter Bawcutt courtesy of Peter Tiller]

WR trailers 195s and 194s. [The late Peter Bawcutt courtesy of Peter Tiller]

MSMR Railcars, 1934 (Broad Gauge)

MSMR Railcar c. 1947 [Kelland Collection, BRCT, 48074]

During the 1930's, diesel technology matured to the point that it could be considered for use in full-scale railway vehicles. Self-propelled passenger vehicles offered the perennial promise of reduced staffing costs, potentially higher service speeds, and faster turnaround times at terminals. Diesel railcars and multiple were also popular with the traveling public due to their sleek modern appearance and (usually) upgraded interiors.

In 1934, Armstrong Whitworth provided six large railcars to the Madras & Southern Mahratta Railway (MSMR). These were numbered 1-6 and classified YZZT. The cars were equipped with Armstrong-Saurer 6BXD engines, rated at 160HP. and Laurence, Scott & Electromotors electrical equipment. The railcar bodies were supplied by the (MSMR) workshops, and provided seating for 110 passengers[1].

Delivery of all six vehicles took place between February and August 1935, initially to Madras, but eventually all vehicles operated on the Cocanada (Kakinada) to Kotipalli line, which had originally opened in 1929 with steam traction. The halts on this line were Karapa, Aratlakatta, Velangi, Ramachandrapuram, Draksharamam, Gangavaram and Somagundam. The railcars reduced the run time from 99 minutes to 87 minutes and were also able to add 7 additional halts (a total of 14 halts). The railcars operated twice daily to connect with a slip coach from the Howrah-Madras mail train, and average daily mileage for all six vehicles varied between 830 and 860 miles with one railcar held in reserve. They could operate in multiple with themselves but were not used with trailer vehicles. The cars were maintained at Cocanada Port station and also went for heavy maintenance to Perambur. The Kotipalli line closed in 1942 and these units were probably out of use at that time[2].

These cars were still in storage at the time of the introduction of the Comeng DMUs in 1958, and one of the engineers cannibalised the units for parts to repair KSR 14.

MSMR Railcar c. 1947 [Kelland Collection, BRCT, 48073]

---

1 Derby-Sulzer Website

2 Indiarailinfo.com

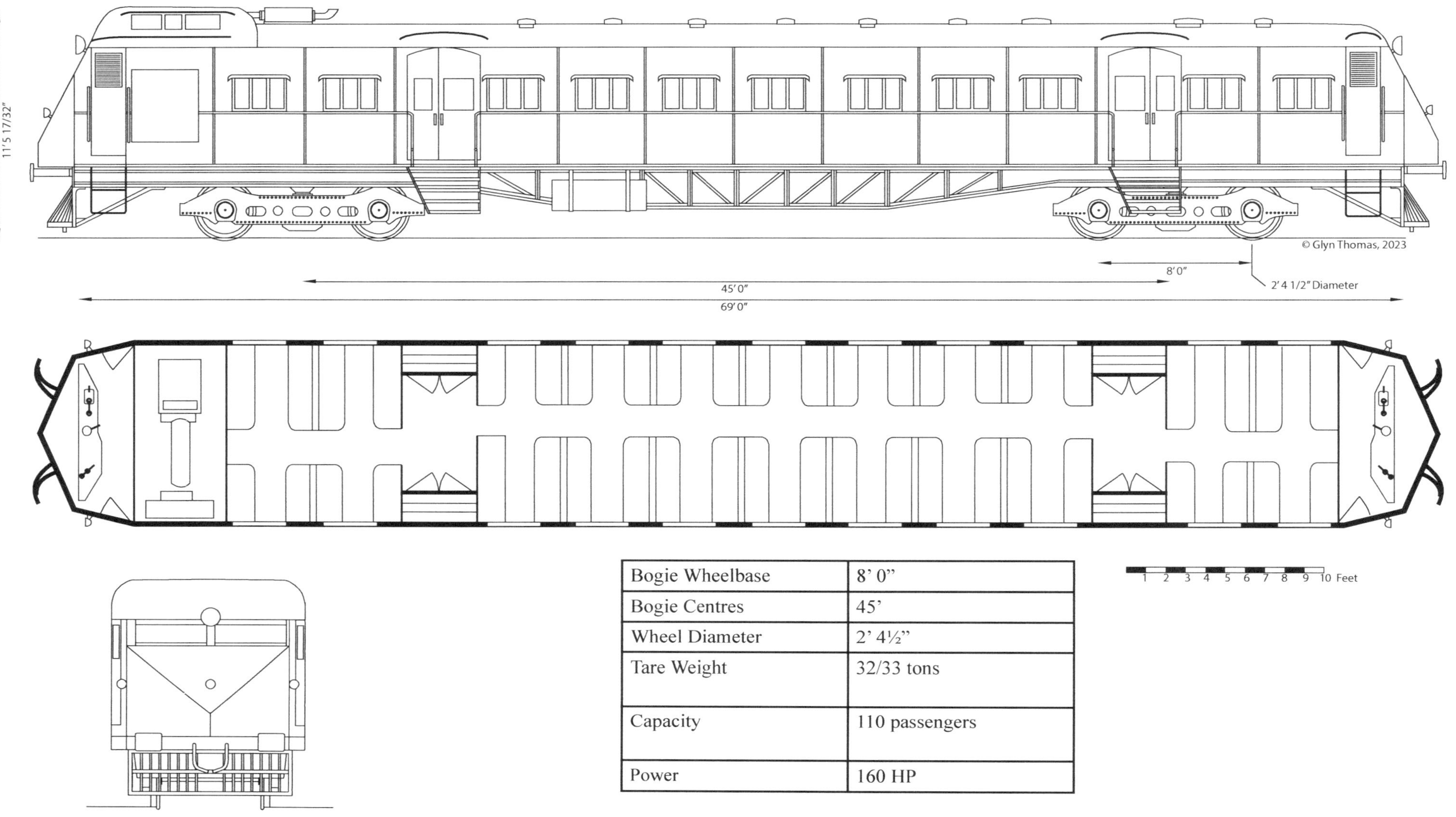

Bogie Wheelbase	8' 0"
Bogie Centres	45'
Wheel Diameter	2' 4½"
Tare Weight	32/33 tons
Capacity	110 passengers
Power	160 HP

[Reference: Plans in Armstrong Whitworth A Pioneer of World Diesel Traction book and observations from photographs]

Martin and Co. Railcars, 1935-1952 (2' 6" Gauge)

Railcars out of use at Arrah on 6/12/1978. The foreground car is RC3. Judging by the detail differences, the rear car is probably RC1. On the ASLR, these cars were painted white above light blue with a red separation line and sliver roof. [Julian Rainbow Collection]

Martin and Co. operated a number of 2' 6" and 2' gauge lines in Northern India. From the early days, these lines struggled to make money on passenger traffic, so Martin was an early adopter of diesel railcars to reduce costs. These lines operated on the plains without significant gradients or sharp curves, so they were kinder to the under-powered early railcars.

The **Shahdara-Saharanpur Light Railway** (SSLR) introduced its first railcar, RC1, built by Wickham, in 1935. It was provided as a 30-seater chassis for the body to be built locally. The order came from William Bayliss. order no. 9450. Its works no. was 1986, type R1092. It was fitted with a Ford BB petrol engine no. BB5311430[1]. The petrol engine was replaced with a Mercedes Benz diesel engine in 1959[2].

RC1 was followed on the SSLR by two locally-built railcars. These were probably built at Martin's Howrah Amta Light Railway workshops at Bankra in 1959 and 1961. They were fitted with Mercedes Benz diesel engines and numbered RC2 and RC3.

By 1969, these diesel railcars were hauling daily passenger trains in each direction between Baraut and Saharanpur. A PJ Bawcutt photo shows RC2 operating with three conventional bogie coaches as trailers at Saharanpur. Rob Dickinson photographed one of these railcars on a Rampur-Manhyaram train around 1970.

The SSLR closed around 1970, and the railcars were transferred to Martin's **Arrah–Sasaram Light Railway** (ASLR), where they remained until that line closed in 1978.

Martin's **Baraset-Basirhat Light Railway** (BBLR) chose Walford Transport Limited of Calcutta for its first railcar, which was reported in Railway Gazette of July 1938 and Foreign Railway News of October 1938. This car used a 13' Commer truck chassis with 7' wheelbase. Power was provided by a 55 HP Perkins Leopard engine mounted centrally. The car had a Borg and Beck clutch and 4-speed gearbox driving an open propeller shaft, with final drive to the rear wheels via chains. This car was 4-wheeled, and was fitted with Cowdrey drum air brakes. Outer panels were of hardened Masonite, lined with Venesta board. The roof interior was teak frames with steel sheet and covered with waterproof canvas. The car body had glass windows all round - only the windows on the doors and rear windows opened, but an open grill at the front of the car provided ventilation.

The Walford prototype was obviously reasonably successful, because a further 3 units had been supplied to the BBLR by 1940 and were used to provide an expedited railcar service on the line[3]. From the Railway Board Reports, there was probably also an additional railcar delivered in this period.

David Churchill collated data from Railway Board Reports and gives the following numbers for the BBLR: 1 railcar from 1938-9; 5 railcars from 1940-2; 7 diesel locomotives from 1943-52 (this probably included reclassified railcars, plus at least one steeple-cab locomotive - see "Additional Photographs"[4]). The BBLR closed around 1955-6.

While not mentioned in Hughes or the railway press, the **Bukhtiarpur-Bihar Light Railway (BuBLR)** also operated railcars similar to the BBLR design, and these were probably built by Walford. One of these is preserved at the Birla Technology Museum in Kolkata, where it was measured by David Churchill and Samit Roychoudry. It was powered by a Perkins 6-cylinder in-line engine that delivered 75 HP, and had conventional brakes on the rear wheels. The preserved example is numbered JLT-1 and only has a single bench behind the driver (3-4 passenger capacity), so it's debatable whether this qualifies as a railcar.

David Churchill's review of Railway Board Reports notes the Bukhtiarpur-Bihar line having 1 petrol and 3 diesel locomotives from around 1940 (definitely by 1946) though 1956. JLT-1 is probably one of the diesel locomotives, and the other two were likely of the same design.

Based on a Railway Board infringement request, David also determined that the BuBLR operated a bogie railcar built by Burn & Co. briefly between 1940-2. This had a 45' long body, with 5' wheelbase bogies on 30' centres. It had a Ford V8 engine driving just one axle via mechanical transmission. The car could be driven from either end and was fitted with vacuum and hand brakes. It was designed to carry 58 passengers, but the Board reduced this to 54.

[See also "HALR Railcar, 1951 (2' Gauge)" on page 70]

---

1 Wickham Works List, Keith Gunner and Mike Kennard

2 Hughes in Railway Magazine, September 1969

3 See Locomotive Magazine, 1942

4 David Churchill identified an infringement request from May 1942 for a Walford bogie diesel fitted with a 110 HP GM diesel engine, running at 2000rpm; a photo in his collection shows this to have a steeple cab

Shahdara-Saharanpur Light Railway RC2-3

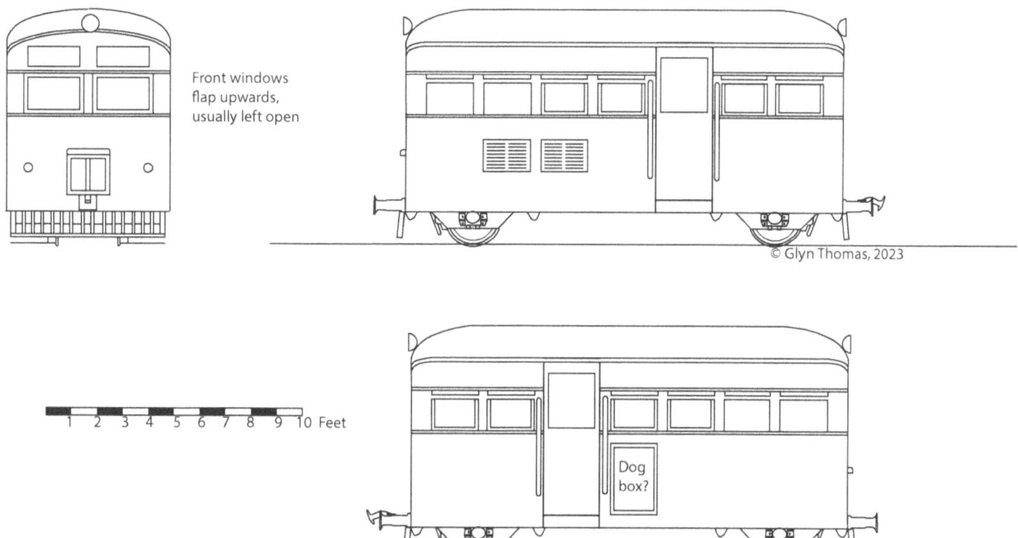

[Reference: Photographs and known dimensions]

Bukhtiarpur-Bihar Light Railway JLT-1

Bukhtiarpur-Bihar Light Railway JLT-1 [Alamy]

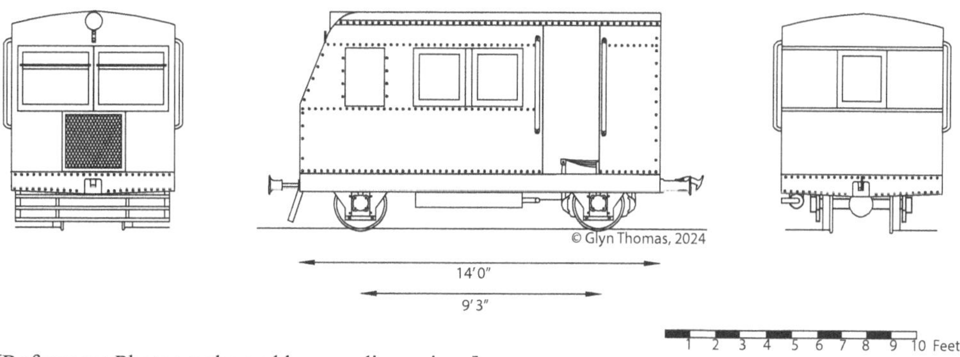

[Reference: Photographs and known dimensions]

Assam-Bengal Railcar, 1938 (Metre Gauge)

Railcar for Assam-Bengal Railway by Wickham of Ware, 1938 [David Churchill Collection]

In 1937, the Assam Bengal Railway placed an order with Wickham of Ware for two four-wheel petrol railcars. These were delivered in February, 1938 (works numbers 2379-80) and were numbered 1 and 2 on the line. Soon after arrival they were modified at Dibrugarh with extra radiators on the centre of the roof, and particulars were then as follows :—

Diam. of wheels 2ft. 0½in.

Wheelbase 13ft. 2in.

Overall length 25ft. 11 in.

Overall height 11 ft. 3in.

Overall width 8ft. 6in.

Tare weight 4.25 tons[1]

The power unit was a Ford V8 30HP engine capable of giving a running speed of 35 to 40 m.p.h. The engine was mounted in the centre of the car under the middle seats, and was water-cooled with a fan-cooled radiator, and a four-speed gearbox. There were four longitudinal seats accommodating 32 passengers, and the equipment included electric light and mechanical ventilation. The railcar could be driven from either end, with the driver's position on the car's axis, separated from the passengers by roller blinds. Both Westinghouse air brakes and a manual brake were provided. The body was constructed of welded steel

These vehicles were used by the military during World War 2, when the ABR was on the front-line in the battle for Burma. They were of particular value in 1942 when thousands of refugees from Burma crossed the Patkoi Hills to Tipong and were then taken by rail to a reception station at Lekhapani[2].

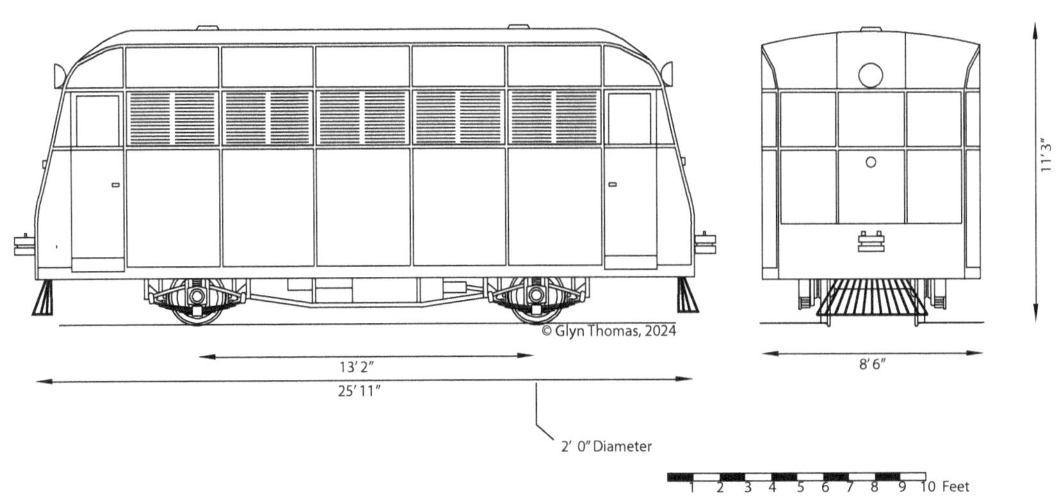

---

1 Dimensions from Locomotive magazine, 1953; "Wickham of Ware" has slightly different dimensions

2 Locomotive Magazine, 1953 via David Churchill

NSR Drewry Railcar, 1939 (Broad Gauge)

NSR Diesel-Mechanical Rail Car [Administrative Report for Indian Railways, 1939]

In 1939, Nizam's State Railway received four double power-bogie railcars, class DB, and a spare power-bogie from Drewry Car Co. These were ordered in 1937 and were inspected by Sir Douglas Fox and Partners. They were fully air-conditioned using equipment by J. Stone and Co. They were powered by a Gardner 6LW engine with 6 cylinders of 4¼" diameter and 6" stroke, with Vulcan-Sinclair fluid coupling, and a Wilson epicyclic gearbox. The EE Preston works numbers were 1110-4, and DrC works numbers were 2131-5 of 1937-8.

These units appear to be a stretched version of very successful units supplied to the Buenos Aires Southern Railway in Argentina around the same time. While the Argentine units had a single power bogie, the NSR units had two power bogies. These units were probably the most advanced diesel railcars provided to India between the wars.

According to the Railway Board Annual Reports[1], for the years ending March 1940 through to March 1946, the four cars averaged approx. 150,000 miles per annum between them. Their history following independence hasn't been determined.

In the early years these cars were painted in an attractive two colour scheme, probably either green and cream or two-tone green.

NSR Diesel-Mechanical Rail Car at Kazipet Station [Drewry Advert via drewry.net]

---

1 Research by David Churchill

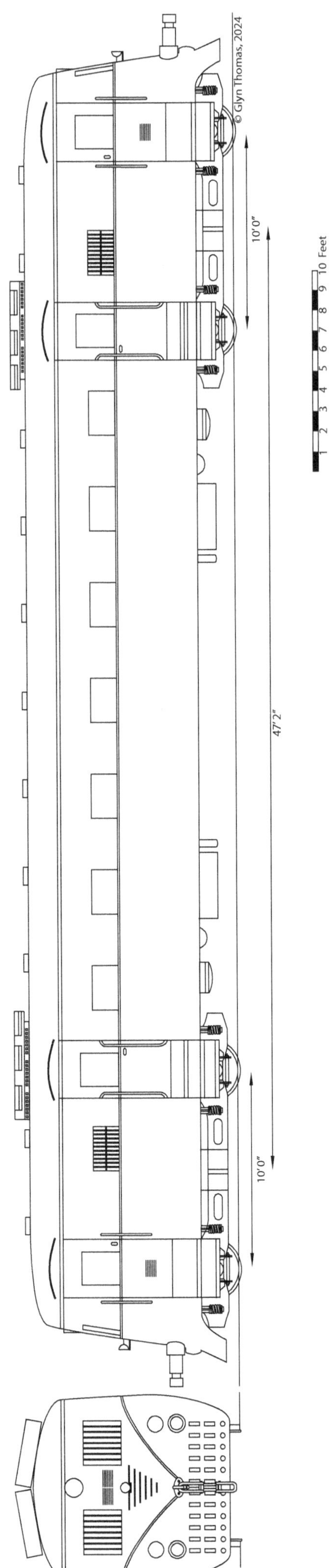

[Reference: Argentine diagrams in Railway Gazette, photographs and known dimensions]

Bogie Wheelbase	10' 0"
Bogie Centres	47' 2"
Tare Weight	37.5 tons
Power	2 x 108 HP engines, der-ated to 89 HP

NWR Ganz Railcar, 1939 (Broad Gauge)

Ganz Diesel-Mechanical Railcar (all white colour scheme) [IME Paper, 1944]

In 1937, in an attempt to recover traffic from road competition, the NWR sought tenders for diesel railcars for use in the Punjab. The specification required a railcar capable of operating at 45 mph against a 5 mph headwind. It was also required that the cars should be available 18 hours/day for 320 days/year. Ganz of Budapest won the order with the lowest bid - 11 railcars and two spare power bogies for Rupees 14,99,273 (GBP 112,445). Ganz was also contracted to service the vehicles with an India-based team.

The cars were delivered to Karachi in January of 1939 and deadheaded to Lahore. Their first three months of operation was used for retraining steam locomotive drivers to the new equipment. Subsequently, the units were based at Jullundur, which was a centre for several branch lines. The new service was introduced on 15th May, 1939 requiring 8 cars to be in service each day. Average daily mileage per car was 346.8, and the schedule required 45 mph top speeds and 27-30 mph average speeds.

Very limited outdoor maintenance facilities were provided at Jullundur. In addition, several routes required cars to overnight at the far terminus, requiring a run of about 700 miles between each maintenance check. Inevitably, reliability suffered and on 11th November services needed to be reduced to 6 cars in service each day. By 18th November, there was a further service reduction to require only 4 cars in service each day. The entire service was withdrawn on 14th December 1939.

The cars were reconditioned through the first half of 1940, incorporating numerous repairs and improvements. A 4-car service was reintroduced at Jullundur on 1st October 1940. Following the reconditioning, the cars' reliability was much improved.

Meanwhile, two Ganz cars and a spare were transferred to Karachi in 1941 to operate a 26-mile route with 16 stops, substituting for bus services that had been suspended due to petrol rationing. Although the railcars weren't ideally suited for this traffic the main issues in service were spring failures due to heavy overcrowding. This service lasted seven months after which the cars were returned to Jullundur. Unfortunately, it proved impossible to increase the service there to a 6 cars due to difficulties with obtaining spare parts during war time.

At Partition, these railcars were allocated to Pakistan where they continued to operate services in the Lahore area. By this time the teething problems had been resolved and the units were reasonably reliable. In the railway press at the time, these units were often touted as an example of successful railcar operation. A photograph in Overseas Railways for 1962 shows a unit leaving Lahore.

Ganz Diesel-Mechanical Railcar - it appears that a two colour scheme (red-cream?) was adopted in service initially.
This was probably delivered around January 1939 [Administrative Report for Indian Railways, 1938-9]

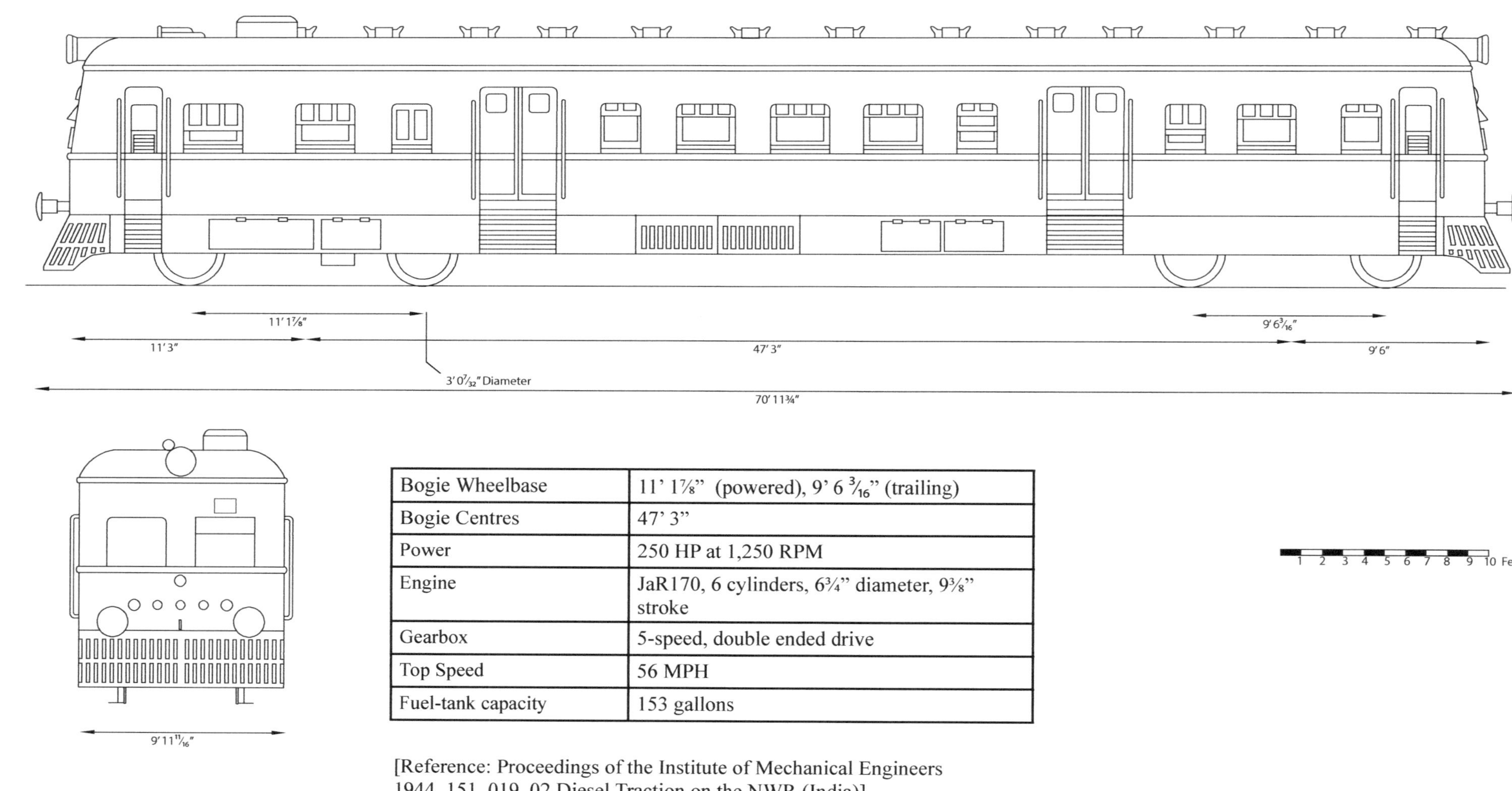

Bogie Wheelbase	11' 1⅞" (powered), 9' 6 3/16" (trailing)
Bogie Centres	47' 3"
Power	250 HP at 1,250 RPM
Engine	JaR170, 6 cylinders, 6¾" diameter, 9⅜" stroke
Gearbox	5-speed, double ended drive
Top Speed	56 MPH
Fuel-tank capacity	153 gallons

[Reference: Proceedings of the Institute of Mechanical Engineers 1944_151_019_02 Diesel Traction on the NWR (India)]

Morvi Maharajah's Railcar, 1941 (2' 6" Gauge)

Morvi Maharajah's Railcar, 1941. Note the salon windows engraved with the state's herald [LM 1941]

The Maharajah of Morvi, Lakhdhirji, and the Yuvraj (heir apparent), Mayurdhwaj, were frequent users of the state's railways. In 1941 they commissioned a luxury railcar for use between Morvi and Rajkot (Headquarters of the Western India States Agency) or Navlakhi (the region's major port). Before introducing the railcar, state coaches were attached to regular passenger trains or specials with resulting delays and expense. Each of these journeys could be achieved in about an hour with the new railcar.

Despite its luxury, the design appears to be a standard Indian adaptation of a commercial truck chassis. In this case a 27.34 HP Dodge six-cylinder engine was used, with most of its original transmission and what appears to be a chain drive from the truck chassis' rear axle to the rear axle of the railcar. The Locomotive Magazine article plans even shows the truck's hood and steering column still in place, although these were presumably removed in practice. The railcar was able to travel at 45mph in each direction. However, no driving controls were provided in reverse and the guard would communicate with the driver via a speaking tube from an observation compartment.

Inside, the interior was finished in lustre grey with silver grey embellishments of sporting scenes and peacocks (whose Sanskrit name was considered the origins of the state's name). Furniture and fittings were from Luxton. While the external colour isn't mentioned, it appears to also be lustre grey with state heralds on the sides. The passenger compartment windows appear to have been frosted with a pattern of the state's herald for privacy.

The design and specification for the car was by the Locomotive and Carriage Superintendent, Mr. C.O.B. Morgan. The car was built at the railway's Kathiawar workshops.

In addition to this railcar, the Morvi State Railway operated a number of railcars in regular service. Railway Board reports (from David Churchill) note the following numbers, which may include the Maharajah's car - 1 railcar from 1931-1933, 2 in 1934, 3 from 1935-1936, 2 from 1937-1938, 3 from 1939-1941. 4 from 1942-1946. Bradshaw for Jan 1944 has a Rail Motor Service of two trains in each direction (25/26, 27/28) from Wankaner Jn-Rajkot, 1 to 1½ hours.

[Reference: Diagrams in Locomotive Magazine, June 1941]

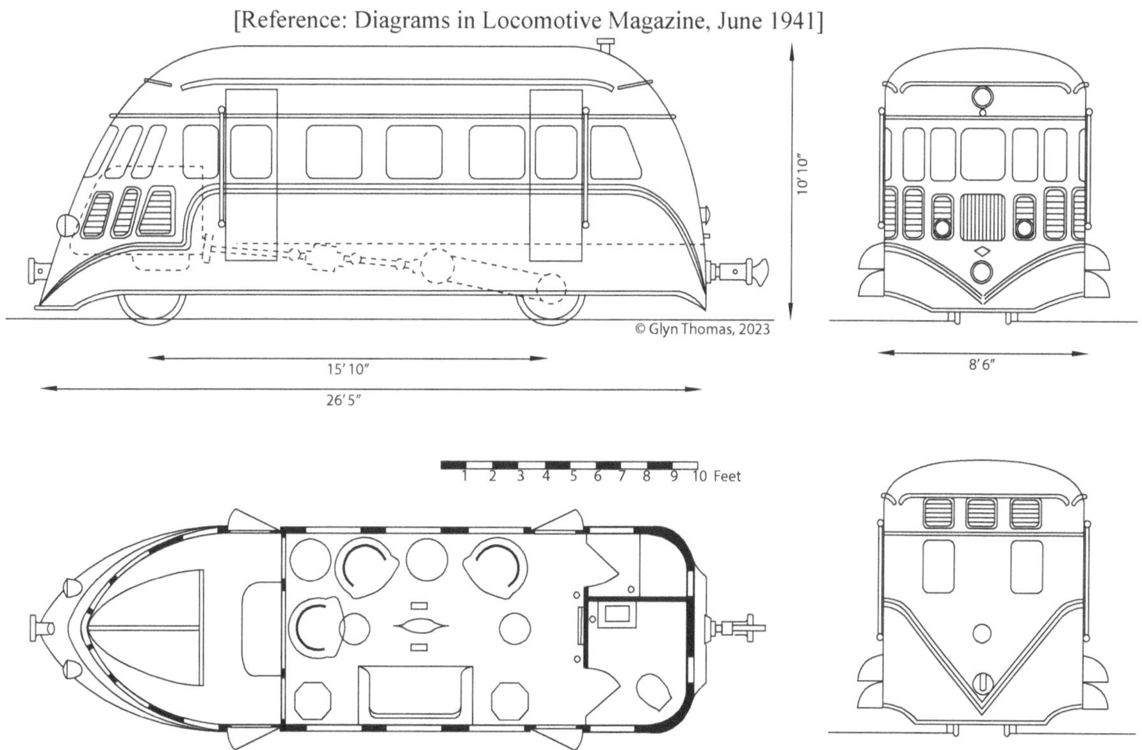

HALR Railcar, 1951 (2' Gauge)

HALR RC1 at Howrah Maidan, 1965[The late Peter Bawcutt courtesy of Peter Tiller]

As discussed in "Martin and Co. Railcars, 1935-1952 (2' 6" Gauge)" on page 62, Martins and Co. had an interest in operating railcars on its lines. In 1951, it built a small railcar for the 2' 0"-gauge Howrah-Amta Light Railway. It was fitted with a 90hp engine and numbered RC1. It can't have been particularly successful in its initial form because it was rebuilt in 1958.

The subsequent history of this car is uncertain, but it was photographed by PJ Bawcutt on the line in 1965.

Although often described as a railcar it appears that this vehicle was actually used as a locomotive.

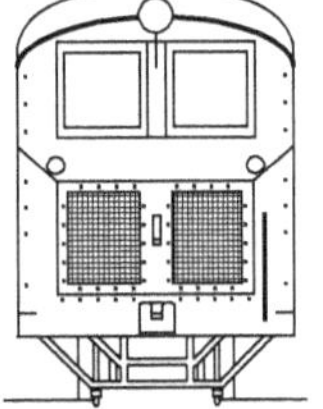

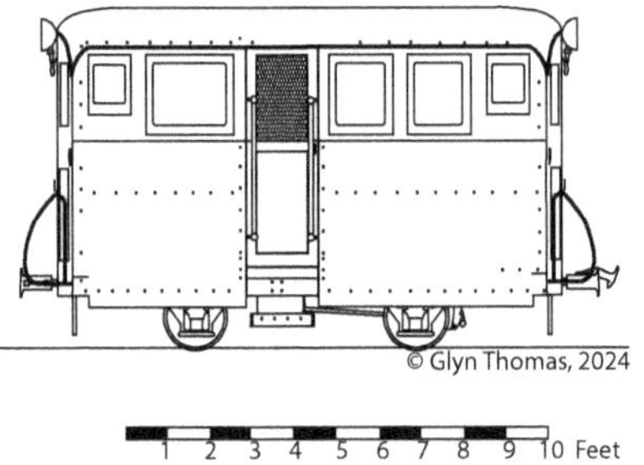

[Reference: Photographs and known dimensions]

HALR RC1 at Howrah Maidan, 1965[The late Peter Bawcutt courtesy of Peter Tiller]

YRD-1 DMU, 1955 (Metre Gauge)

Fiat YRD1-Class MG DMU units 1001 and 1004 at Lucknow, 27/02/1979 [David Churchill]

In 1955, Fiat provided 12 two-car metre gauge diesel multiple units to India under the Colombo Plan. These units were tested in Italy on the Biella-Cossato-Valle Mosso line, and many publicity photos were taken there.

Each unit was fitted with an under-floor 400 HP flat-6 diesel engine with mechanical transmission through a five speed gearbox. The railcars were slow to accelerate but easily reached speeds up to 60 kph. The two cars could collectively seat about 100 people. With only one power bogie per car they lacked traction, and could have trouble starting when overcrowded. There are reports of passengers and crew being asked to push the train to get it started.

Six of these units went to the Northern Railway for use on the Delhi-Rewari-Loharu route. These were maintained by Shakurbasti shed in Delhi, and appear to have been adopted enthusiastically. The other six units may have been assigned to Mayuram initially but records are incomplete.

Severe reliability problems started with the Fiat engines almost immediately. As early as 1958, Northern Railway requested designs for the replacement of the engines with an Ashok-Leyland O.900 engine, although it's not clear whether this was ever acted on[1].

In Oct. 1977, the following routes of North Eastern Railway (NER) had diesel railcar service:

- Brahmavart - Kanpur Central
- Lucknow Jn. - Sitapur Jn
- Kanpur Anwarganj - Lucknow Jn.
- Sitapur Jn. - Mailani Jn.

"Trains were well patronised on the Lucknow - Kanpur route but not so much on the Lucknow - Sitapur route. This was partly because they had limited stops and charged mail/express fares (only second class accommodation though) and also due to the odd timings they ran between Lucknow Jn. and Sitapur Jn.

The railcars continued to operate on the NER until the mid-1980s and ended their working days on the Mathura Jn.–Brindavan route. The last reported sighting was in 2002 near the shed at Mathura Cantt. where units were observed lying decrepit in a siding.[2]"

1 Macfarlane, The Australian Railcar Project, via DHRS

2 Direct quote from IRFCA - Harsh Vardhan, V. Anand, David Churchill, John Lacey, G. Swaminathan and Yogesh B.K

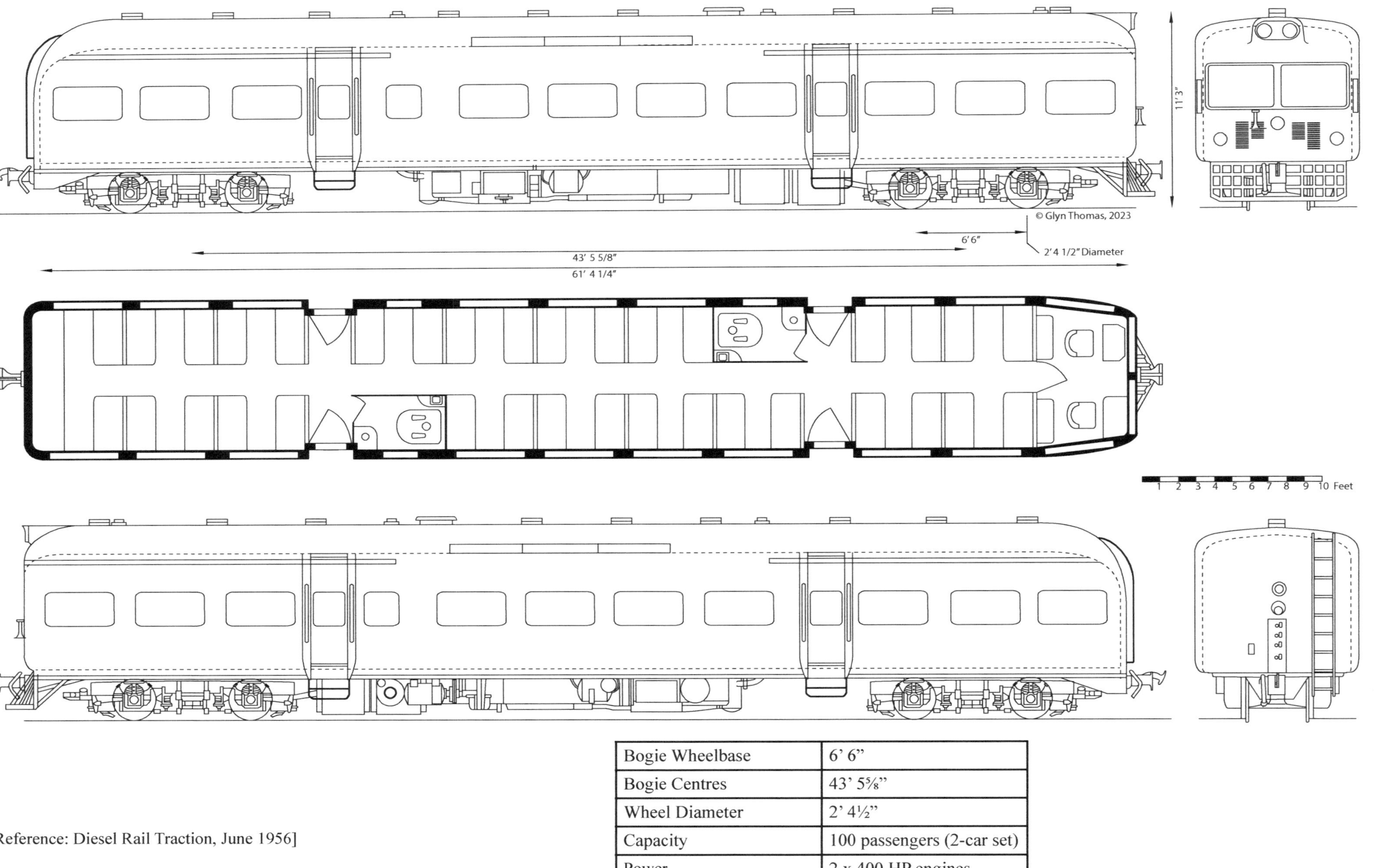

[Reference: Diesel Rail Traction, June 1956]

Bogie Wheelbase	6' 6"
Bogie Centres	43' 5⅝"
Wheel Diameter	2' 4½"
Capacity	100 passengers (2-car set)
Power	2 x 400 HP engines
Maximum Speed	60 kph

Commonwealth Engineering Railcars, 1958 (Broad Gauge)

RC 1016 with an inaugural train on the Northern Railway, 1958 [BUT photo, David Churchill Collection]

Indian generally bucked the worldwide trend towards using Diesel Multiple Units (DMUs) for short distance passenger traffic in the steam-diesel transition years. With lower car ownership, the country didn't see the rapid reductions in passengers that other world railways experienced. Even so, with reliable DMUs becoming available for import, some DMUs were acquired for branch line service.

In 1958, 24 broad gauge DMUs were ordered from Commonwealth Engineering Co. Ltd. of Australia under the Colombo Plan[1]. Each car was powered by two Leyland B.U.T. 0.900 engines specially designed for railway use and built at the Albion plant in England, with mechanical transmission. The engines were six-cylinder horizontal units with 20" fluid flywheels, rated for 2,000 HP at 1,800 RPM. The power plant was similar to contemporary British Railways DMU designs[2].

These units were built at Commonwealth Engineering's Bassendean plant in Western Australia, which was originally established to assemble covered vans. The completed units were transferred by rail (on temporary 3' 6" gauge bogies) to Fremantle, and then via two shipments to India (one shipment was via the Belship, "Belkarin").

In service, 12 cars were initially assigned to the Tuni-Tadepalliguden section and its branches on the Southern Railway. The remaining units were assigned to the Northern Railway for its lines between Lahore and Ludhiana and from Ambala Cantonment.

An enthusiast's tour in 1980 visited the DMU shed at Rajahmundry on the Southern Railway, which operated several of these units. The DMUs appeared to be in good physical condition, but the shed was apparently finding it difficult to obtain spare parts to keep them in service.

The railcars were 70 ft. long over headstocks, had 48 ft. 6 in. bogie centres and a bogie wheelbase of 9 ft. 6 in. They had a full-width driver's cab at one end and a half cab at the other[3].

---

1 The Colombo Plan, established in 1950, is an international plan led by the US to provide technical, educational, and capital aid for the development of South and South-East Asia. Other original participants included Britain, Australia, Canada, Japan, and New Zealand. It still exists today with a wider membership and remit.

2 "The Indian Railcar Project" by Eric Adam, Australian Railway Historical Society Bulletin, December 1989

3 Locomotive Magazine, 08/58

RC 1012 on the Southern Railway, 1958 [BUT photo, David Churchill Collection]

RC 3996 at Rajahmundry on 1/2/1980. By this time the rear compartment (probably for women) had acquired window bars to prevent unauthorized access. The units were out of service waiting for spare parts. [Mike Tisdale]

Commonwealth Engineering DMU, 1958

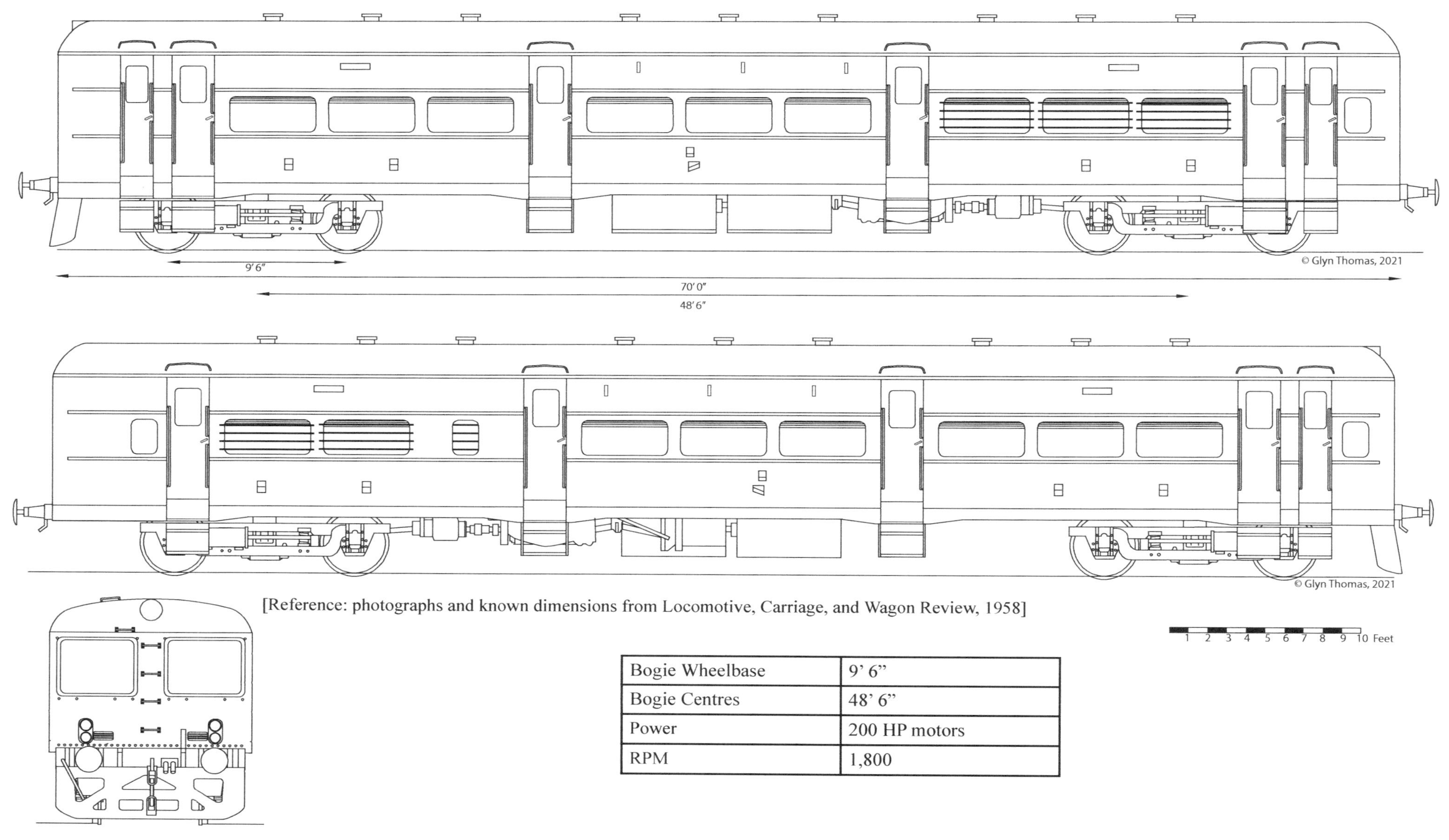

[Reference: photographs and known dimensions from Locomotive, Carriage, and Wagon Review, 1958]

Bogie Wheelbase	9' 6"
Bogie Centres	48' 6"
Power	200 HP motors
RPM	1,800

ICF DMU, 1964 (Metre Gauge)

ICF DMU no. 128 at Charbagh on train to Lucknow, 01/12/1982 [Trevor Davis, Transport Treasury, TD-PIN764]

As part of the drive to become self-sufficient in building of railway rolling stock, ICF collaborated with Ashok-Leyland on the production of a 2-car DMU for the metre gauge. The Railway Research Design Standards Organization (RDSO) produced the design. A prototype DMU with two underfloor Ashok Leyland RE680 "power plus" engines was introduced for use on the Southern Railway in October 1964. SR intended to use it for suburban service on the Tricky division. The engines ran at 2,200 RPM and the car's top speed was 80 kph. Ashok-Leyland provided the engines on a sale or return basis. The two cars were coupled together with a hook and yoke automatic centre coupler and KHEOPS jumper connections plus two air connections for brakes. There was also a vestibule gangway between cars. Transmission was via a Cardan shaft to the inner end of the outer bogie, and an air-operated mechanical gearbox. The units were fitted with a Serck-Behr cooling system with roof-mounted radiator and hydraulic fan. Electrical equipment was provided by J Stone (Deptford) Ltd[1].

The bogies were welded steel with SKF roller-bearings and quick-acting Westinghouse air brakes.

Each car had 83 seats and a toilet, arranged as three open saloons. The interior was hardwood lined with two-tone vynatile sheeting. The prototype's exterior finish was blue/cream with gold stripes.

While the prototype unit was obviously satisfactory in service, only five more 2-car units were built by ICF between 1968 and 1971[2]. Starting in the 1990's, Indian Railways returned to producing similar railcars and DMUs, although since they don't appear in ICF reports, these were probably built or converted at regional workshops.

---

1 See Indian Railway Gazette, October 1964; Railway Gazette, November 1964; Railway Gazette, May 1965

2 See ICF Annual Report, 2017-8

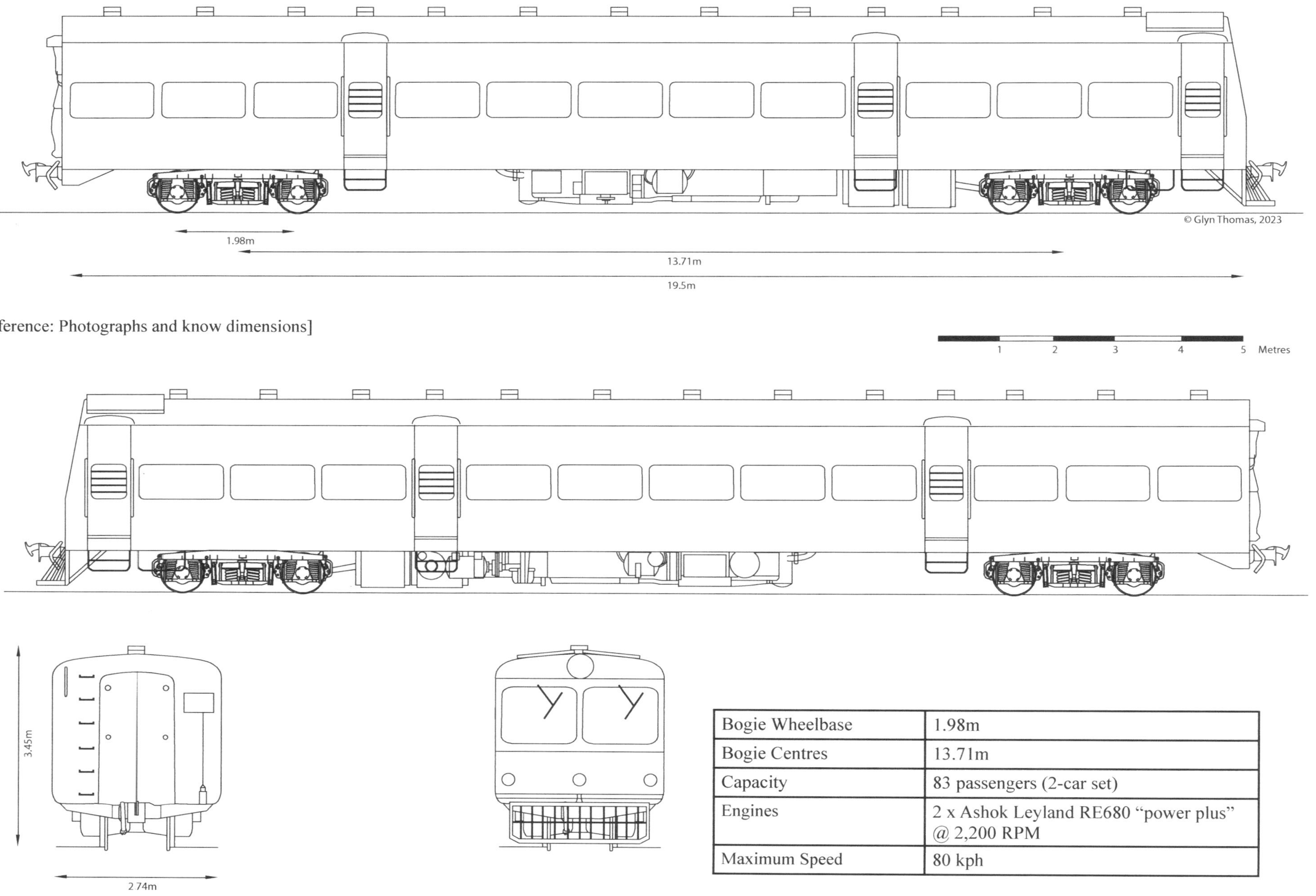

Bogie Wheelbase	1.98m
Bogie Centres	13.71m
Capacity	83 passengers (2-car set)
Engines	2 x Ashok Leyland RE680 "power plus" @ 2,200 RPM
Maximum Speed	80 kph

Standard Railbus, 1966 (2' 6" Gauge)

Lightweight Diesel Railcar for Ahmadpur-Burdwan [Railway Gazette, July 1968]

McLeod's Light Railways was a private company that operated a number of narrow gauge lines in Northern India. The company wasn't absorbed into Indian Railways immediately following independence and survived as a separate private entity. Some of its lines were closed in the 1950's, and by the 1960's reduction in traffic had made the company's financial situation critical. Indian Railways decided to absorb the remaining lines in 1966-7.

To improve the economics of the former McLeod's network centred on Katwa, with lines to Ahmadpur and Bardhaman (Burdwan), Indian Railways designed new lightweight diesel railcars for passenger service, derived from road truck engines and transmissions. Initial versions used an Ashok Leyland COP 350/1/1 water-cooled engine similar to those used in Comet trucks. These railcars had a 4-wheel single-ended power car, designed to haul several 4-wheel trailers (2 straight coaches and 2 coaches with guard's compartments). At end stations, the power car needed to be detached and turned around on a turntable. The first cars were build at Eastern Railway workshops (Jamalpur?) with prefabricated aluminium car parts from Hyderabad Allwyan Metal Works. The power cars and trailers were classified EZZT (later EZZS) and guard trailers were EZZR.

Each branch from Katwa was about 50km in length. The Bardhaman line saw 5 round trips per day, taking about 3 hours per trip. No. 7000 of the original design was observed on the network in January 1985 and was already looking well worn. Other numbers associated with Katwa include 7002 and 7038. This network never received enough railcars to eliminate locomotive-hauled trains, and some trains remained steam-hauled into the 1990's.

It isn't clear how many of the early units were built, but their longevity and the fact that the class was continued suggests a successful design.

It is likely that several railway workshops built varations of this design. Trailer ESSR 7040, preserved at the Motibagh (Nagpur) museum was reportedly built at Mysore Workshop in 1977. ICF, Rail Coach Factory, Bangalore (RCF - later operated by BEML), and Izatnagar Works have all been mentioned as potential suppliers of this equipment, and it is possible that each produced some. Multiple builders could explain the numerous differences in design details across the class, and it's also likely that rebuilds were performed during their lifetime, For example, Santipur's power car 7041 was delivered with large windows, but has smaller windows in more recent photos (as well as an updated cab design.)

In service, the accommodation in the power car was initially intended for the train crew, but was subsequently downgraded for regular passengers use. In later years, the power cars were fitted with ugly cages over the windscreens and lights to protect from stone throwers.

The Katwa system received new ZRB railcars in the early 2000's (see later). It is likely that the early power cars were withdrawn from service at that time. Several earlier trailers remained in service.

Railbus no. 7000 on the Katwa Line, January 1985 [Brian Manktelow, International Steam]

Wheelbase	4,476mm
Tare Weight	5.9 tons
Capacity	26 passengers (power car)
	42 passengers (coach)
	38 passengers (coach/guard)
Average Speed	21 kph
Length	8.13m
Width	2.2m
Built	1968-c. 1985
Manufacturer	Various
Max speed	50kph

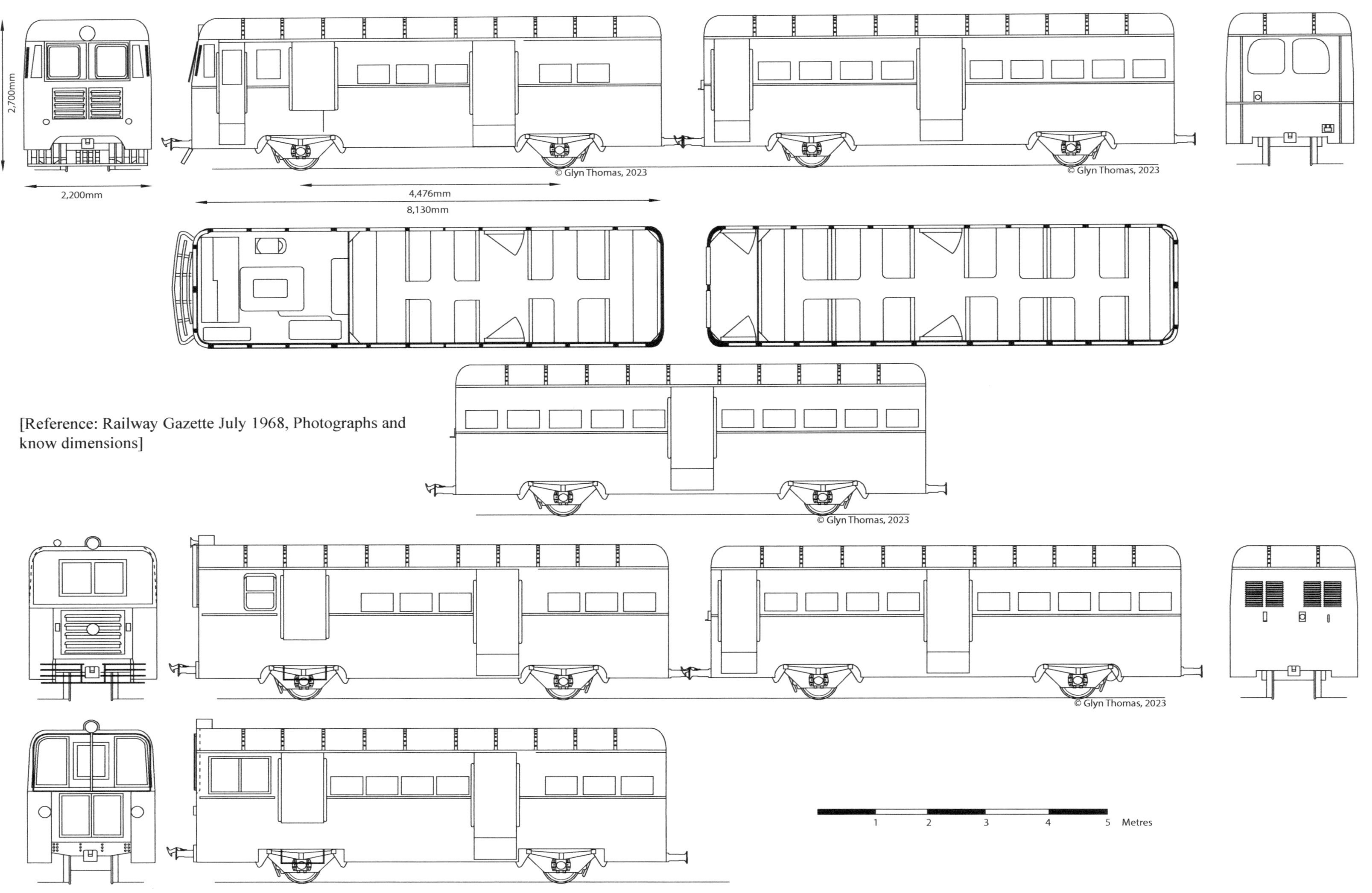

[Reference: Railway Gazette July 1968, Photographs and know dimensions]

Updated Standard Railbus, 1980s (2' 6" Gauge)

ZRD Railbus at Santipur in 1980 [David Churchill]

In the early 1980's a second iteration of narrow gauge railbus design started to appear and expanded the modernization beyond the Katwa network. The class used a similar power plant to the earlier EZZx cars and generally similar dimensions, with updated cab and larger windows. On the Southern Railway, entire sets were labelled ZRD (class) with a set number. A power-car and three trailer consist of ZRD-001 was photographed by Sumit Sharma on the Yelahanka-Kolar Gold Fields-Bangarpet line in 1980. This unit had the Ashok Leyland logo etched into its cab windows and was probably the demonstrator unit for the updated design. Eventually, the Yelahanka line received four units, which may have been sufficient to eliminate steam passenger services there. On the Yelahanka line, these units were numbered sequentially (1, 2, 3, etc.) with power car and trailers in the same sequence.

The Santipur-Nabadwip Ghat line, only 27km long, also received the newer ZRD sets. David Churchill photographed a unit there in 1980, although it was officially allocated to Katwa; it appears to have stayed on the line. A January 1985 photo shows two new power cars (7041 and ????) plus three trailers (7042, 7043, 7044). The Yelahanka-Bangarpet section closed for gauge conversion in the late 1990's, and its railbuses were re-gauged to metre gauge and sent to the Shimoga-Talaguppa line (see next section).

It appears that most of these units were rebuilt in later years and most were fitted with smaller windows like the earlier design. No. 7041 ran in this form until the closure of the Santipur-Nabadwip Ghat line for gauge conversion in 2010.

Several of these railcars have been preserved:

- Chennai railway museum: 7002 power car and 7038 trailer (both small windows)

- Motibagh (Nagpur) narrow gauge railway museum: 7041 power car and 7040 trailer (both small windows)

- Dhanbad Heritage Park: 7031 power car, classified EZZS (large windows).

Railcar 7041 at Santipur 23/01/2003 [Protik Maitra]

Rear headlight on power car only
[Reference: Railway Gazette July 1968, Photographs and know dimensions]
© Glyn Thomas, 2023
© Glyn Thomas, 2023
1 2 3 4 5 Metres
In later years, end windows were plated over, sometimes with visible rivets

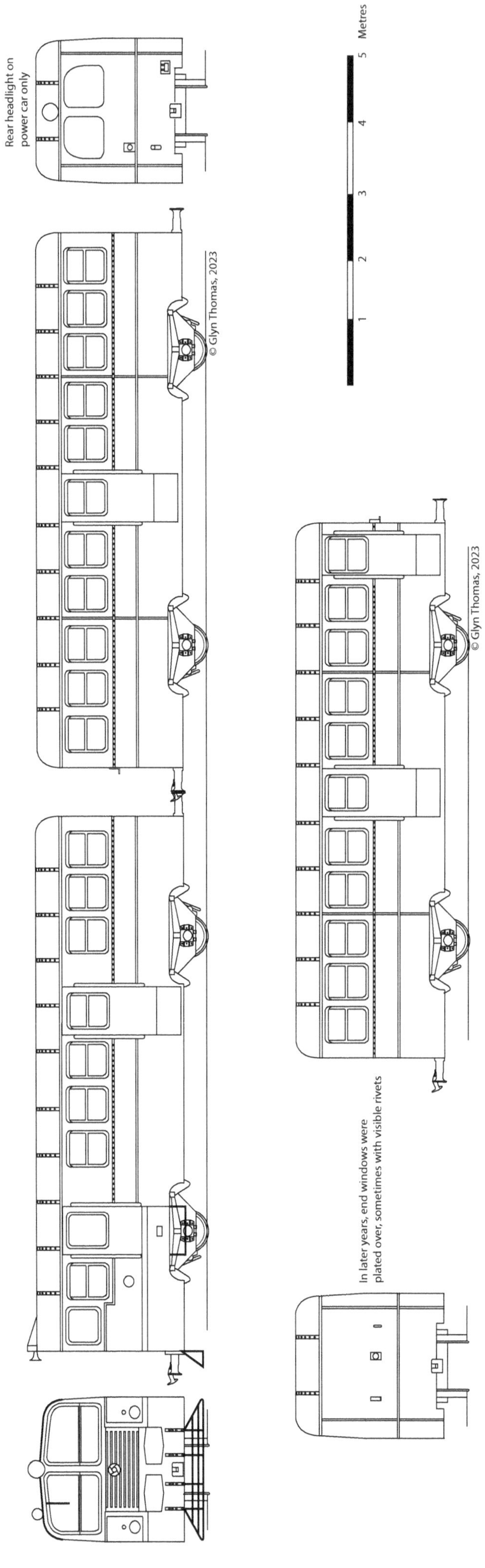

Burdwan ZRD Railcar 7036 13/12/1981 [Wilson Lythgoe]

Burdwan railcar arriving and another departing 13/12/1981 [Wilson Lythgoe]

YRD Railcars, rebuilt 1990s (Metre Gauge)

YRD MG Railbus on the Shimoga-Talguppa line [Deepak Ra - Creative Commons License]

As documented on page 81, four new ZRD railcar sets were supplied to the narrow gauge Yelahanka to Bangrapret line in the early 1980's. When that line closed for gauge conversion in the late 1990's, these railcars were converted to metre gauge, reclassified as YRD and sent to work on the Shimoga-Thalaguppa line. Indicative of the variability of this class, the railcars at Thalaguppa display at least three design variations, as shown in the drawings. Observed numbers are: YRD, YRD/2, and YRD/3.

Shimoga-Thalaguppa was converted to broad gauge in 2007. One of the railcars was subsequently used at the Heritage Railway Bridge over the Kapila River at Sujathapuram. When the heritage operation finished there, it was brought to the Mysuru (Mysore) museum for display[1]

YRD MG Railbus on the Kabini Bridge tourist line 26/11/2010 [Aravind Gundumane - Treks and Travels Blog - aravindgundumane.com]

---

1 Mysuru Railway Museum website

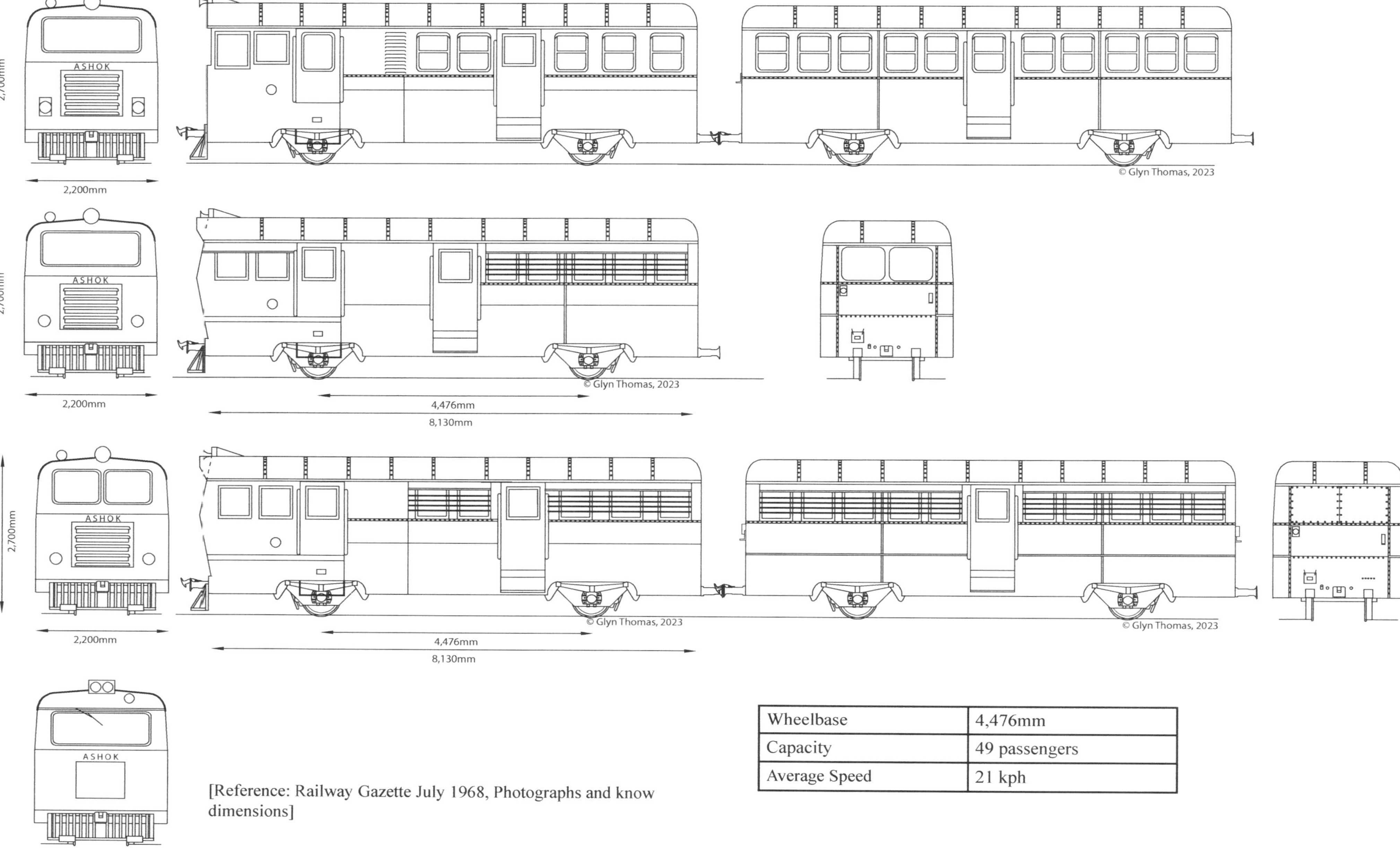

Wheelbase	4,476mm
Capacity	49 passengers
Average Speed	21 kph

[Reference: Railway Gazette July 1968, Photographs and know dimensions]

4-Wheel Railbus, c. 1993 (Metre Gauge)

MG Railbus on the Adraj Moti to Vijaypur line, [Indian Rail Road on YouTube]

With gauge conversion gathering pace in the 1990's it would have been difficult to justify investment in metre gauge rolling stock. However, there was logic in having smaller railbus designs that could pick up remaining passenger traffic on stubs of the former MG network.

In 1993, RDSO published updated specifications for metre gauge railbuses. Two designs were proposed - a small version, that was probably intended as the specification for the YRD type discussed previously (even though these were rebuilds) and a larger version that was based on the broad gauge WRB design.

A number of these larger MG railbuses are known to have been built:

- At least 2 at Vijaypur-Ambliyasan line (42km long) on the Western Railway, one number 10102 (years built 1994-1998)

- At least 1 on Siliguri Junction-Bagdogra on the NFR, number 10000, built 1996. Withdrawn 2016.

At the time of writing there is a proposal to use some of these railbuses on the Nilgiri Mountain Railway (presumably on the section between Coonoor and Udhagamandalam).

MG Railbus 10000 on the Siliguri Junction-Bagdogra line [Aakash Sharma via IndiaRailInfo]

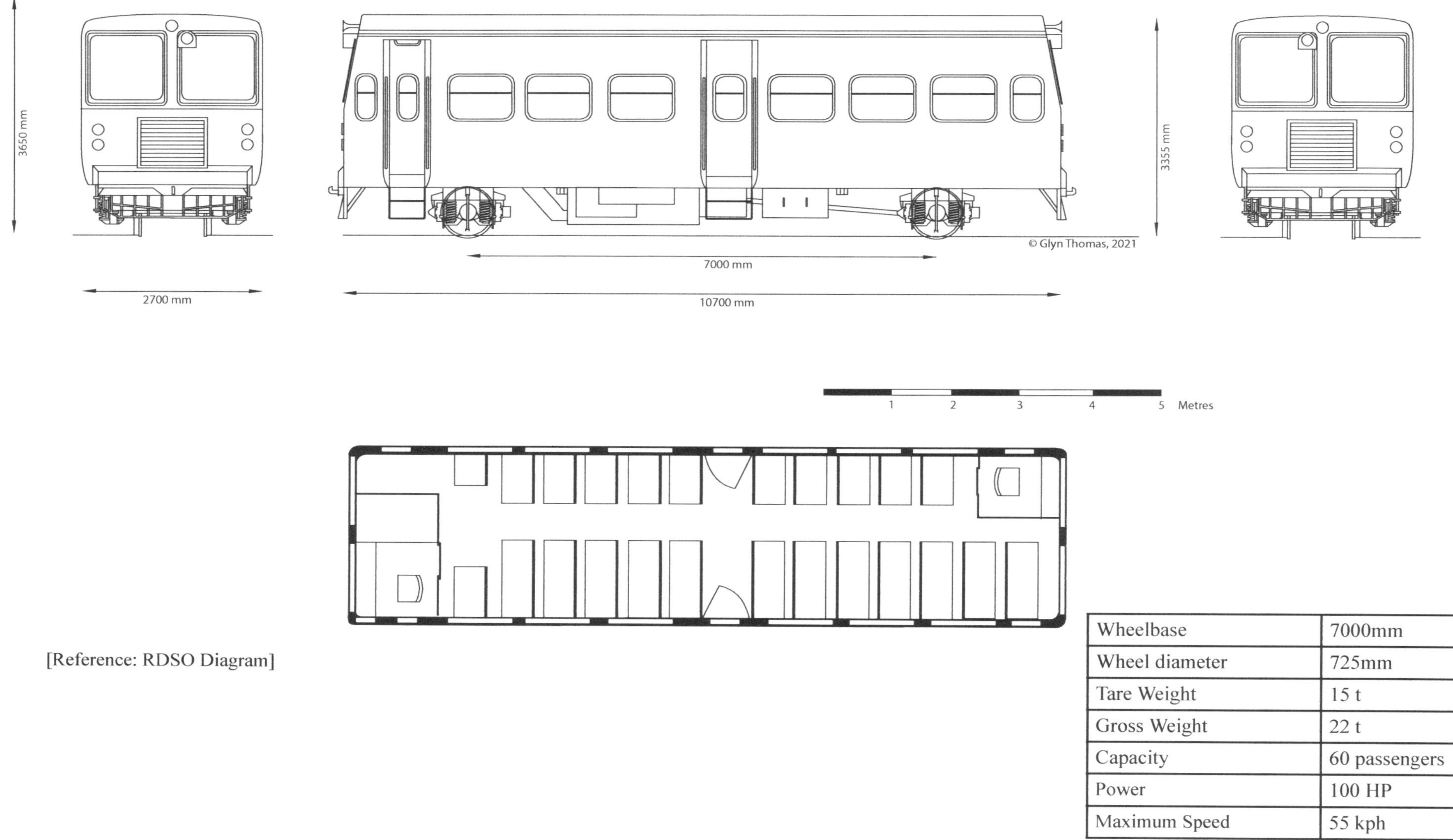

[Reference: RDSO Diagram]

Wheelbase	7000mm
Wheel diameter	725mm
Tare Weight	15 t
Gross Weight	22 t
Capacity	60 passengers
Power	100 HP
Maximum Speed	55 kph

YRB Bogie Railcar, 1996 (Metre Gauge)

Metre-gauge bogie railcar, on the Mathura Jn-Virndavan line [Adobe Stock]

In 1996, RDSO published a specification for the conversion of metre gauge ICF coaches into 75-seat double-ended railcars. At least 10 of these were built and appear to have been quite successful in service. Numbers observed include 10001, 10002, 10006, 10009, and 10010. While the design can probably be linked back to the ICF DMUs of the 1960's, these cars don't appear on ICF production numbers, so they were probably converted by regional railway workshops.

Lines known to have received this include:

- Vijaypur to Ambliyasan
- Mathura Jn-Virndavan
- Indara Jn-Dohrighat
- Thiruthuraipoondi-Agasthampilli

The most famous of these operations was the Mathura Jn-Virndavan line. Units 10006 and 10009 were observed there, but others may also have been used. The passenger service was discontinued around 2019 due to the COVID pandemic. Service resumed on November 18, 2021.

There were operational issues between Mathura Jn and Virndavan because the railcar was under-powered and there are several instances recorded of passengers needing to push the car to get it moving. In 2022, the Ministry of Railways announced the introduction of a more powerful railcar for the line, which was similar in appearance to the older cars[1]

Photographs from Mehsana taken in the early 2000s show several 3-car DMUs (two single-ended driving motor cars with a central trailer) following a similar design. One motor car number was 29352A. A 2014 photo taken at Bikaner shows trailer 202154 being transported on a broad gauge flatcar. It is not clear how many units of this type were placed in service or where they operated.

---

1 Economic Time, August 19, 2022; railcar no. ??3105

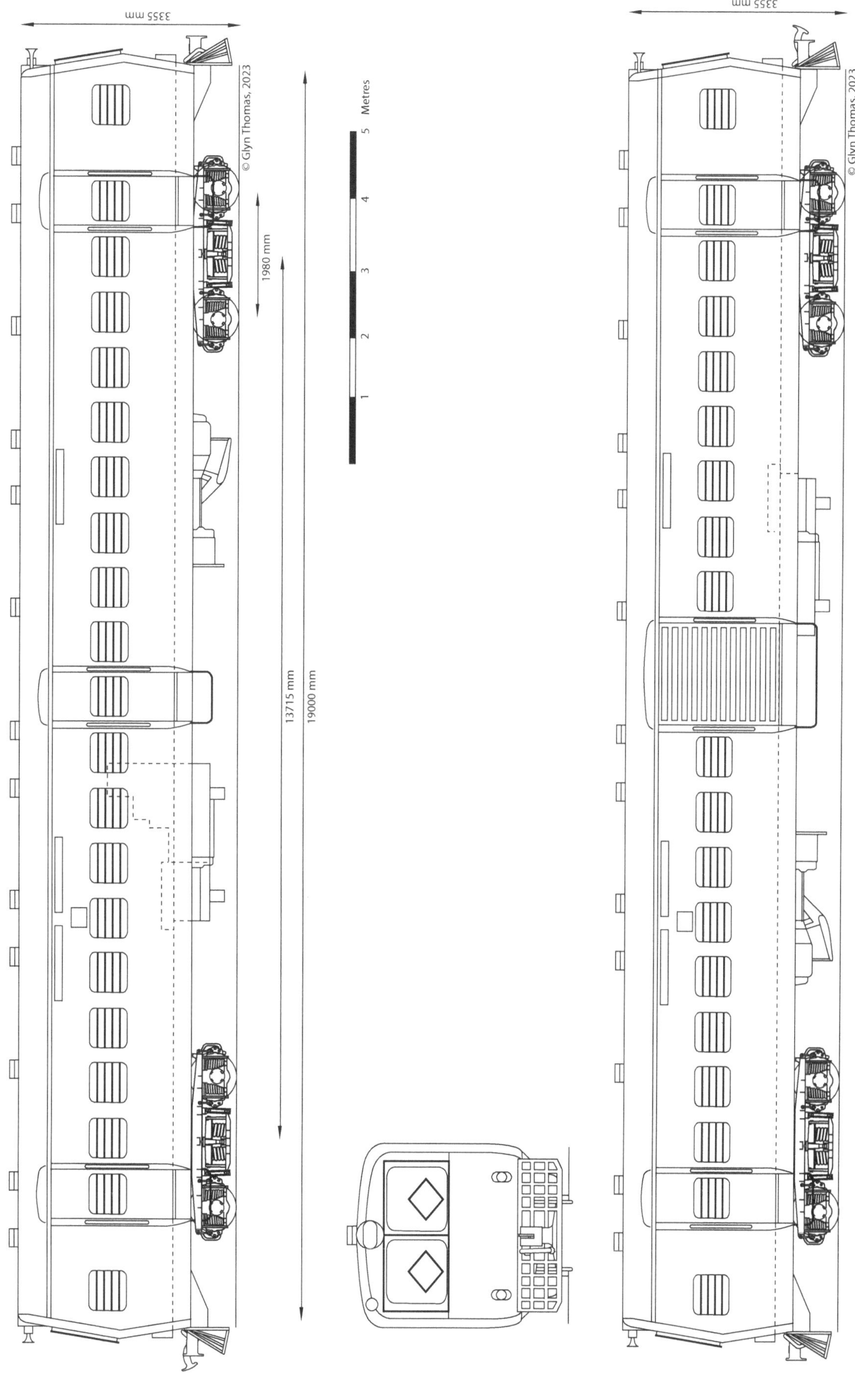

[Reference: ICF coach plans and known dimensions]

BEML Railcar, 1997 (Broad Gauge)

BEML Railcar 30006 on 506 Kolar-Bangarpet train [Jay Balakrishna Video - You Tube]

Bharat Earth Movers Limited (BEML) is a domestic manufacturer of railway equipment. In 1997, they introduced a lightweight 4-wheel railcar for use on broad gauge lines with low traffic. Overall, 20 of the class were constructed, consisting of two sub-classes on Indian Railways, WRB and WRB1. These used an Ashok-Leyland diesel engine for power.

WRB 30006 was one of the best known examples of this class. It was introduced on the Bangarpet-Kolar line in 1997, following conversion of the line from narrow gauge. The railcar was busy during rush-hours when commuters used to connect with trains from Kolar to Chennai, Tirupati, and other destinations. In 2016, the railcar was replaced by a DEMU on this service. WRB 30006 was subsequently transferred to the Yeshwantpur-Nelamangala, but never attracted enough passengers to justify the services, and it was withdrawn in 2017. In service, there were reports of reliability problems, and also that the engine sound was over-powering in the passenger compartment.

Routes reported to have used the BEML railcars include:

* Silchar-Jiribam

* Junagagh-Dhari

* Tiruturaipundi-Agastiampalli

* Banmankhi-Bihariganj

* Shimoga-Talaguppa

* Ambliyasan-Vijapur-Adraj Moti

* Bangarpet-Kolar - mentioned in RailNews

* Mathura-Vrindavan

* Goindwal-Beas, Bobilli-Salur (WRB1)

* Yeshwantpur-Nelamangala

* Kakinada-Kotiaplli (WRB1)

* Merta Road-Merta City (WRB1)

* WRB allocated to Krishnarajapuram on the SWR

WRB1 30018 is preserved in Mumbai (Heritage Gully), soon to move to a new heritage location at Lonavla.

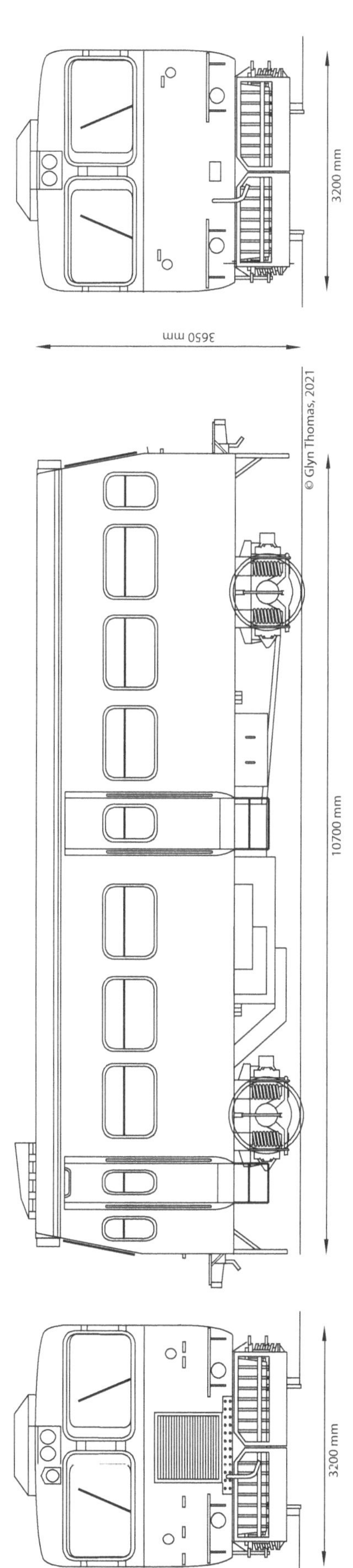

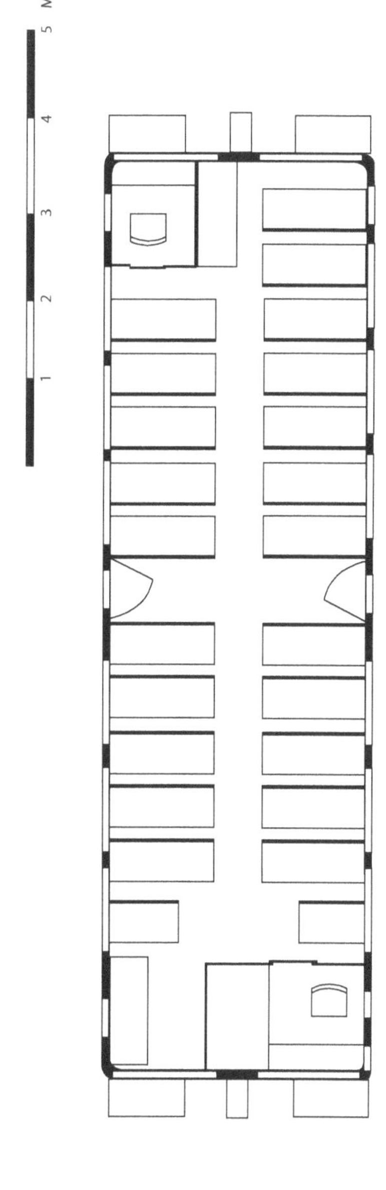

[Reference: RDSO Diagram]

Wheelbase	7,000 mm
Wheel Diameter	915 mm
Tare Weight	16 tons
Gross Weight	24 tons
Capacity	72 Passengers
Power	175 HP motor, 6 cylinders
Maximum Speed	60 kph

ZRB Railbus, c. 1999 (2' 6" Gauge)

Railcar 10607 at Katwa on the Ahmadpur service, December 2004 [Samit Roychoudhury]

The ZRB railbus design of c. 1999 appears to be a direct update of the 1980 ZRD railcar sharing many dimensions and was probably intended to provide replacement units for life-expired railcars on the Katwa network.

An official photo from Golden Rock workshop in 2002 shows a three-car set (power car 10604 and two coaches without guards compartments). This train was subsequently seen on the Katwa line. It is possible that other workshops also built some units. There is no evidence that coaches with guards compartments were built in this series.

In service, trains were often composed as a mix of the new trailers and older ZRD trailers.

The Shakuntala Railway from Murtajapur Junction to Yavatmal and Achalpur was the last remnant of the Central Provinces Railway Company and remained in private ownership until 2016, although Indian Railways operated the passenger trains on the line. Simon Mortimer photographed ZRB power car 10607 with three trailers at Murtajapur Junction in 2002 and observed that they were out of use, so they were likely tested there and not suited to the line's traffic needs. 10607 was subsequently seen in use at Katwa. The Shakuntala Railway closed for gauge conversion in 2019-20.

Running numbers observed on the Katwa network include power cars 10601, 10604, 10607, 10610 and trailers 10603 and 10612. 10601 was observed with two different cab fronts - large windows which were probably original, and smaller windows, probably as a result of a rebuild.

Rear view of railcars 10607 and 10610 at Katwa, c. 2009/10 [Fuzz Jordan, DHRS Collection]

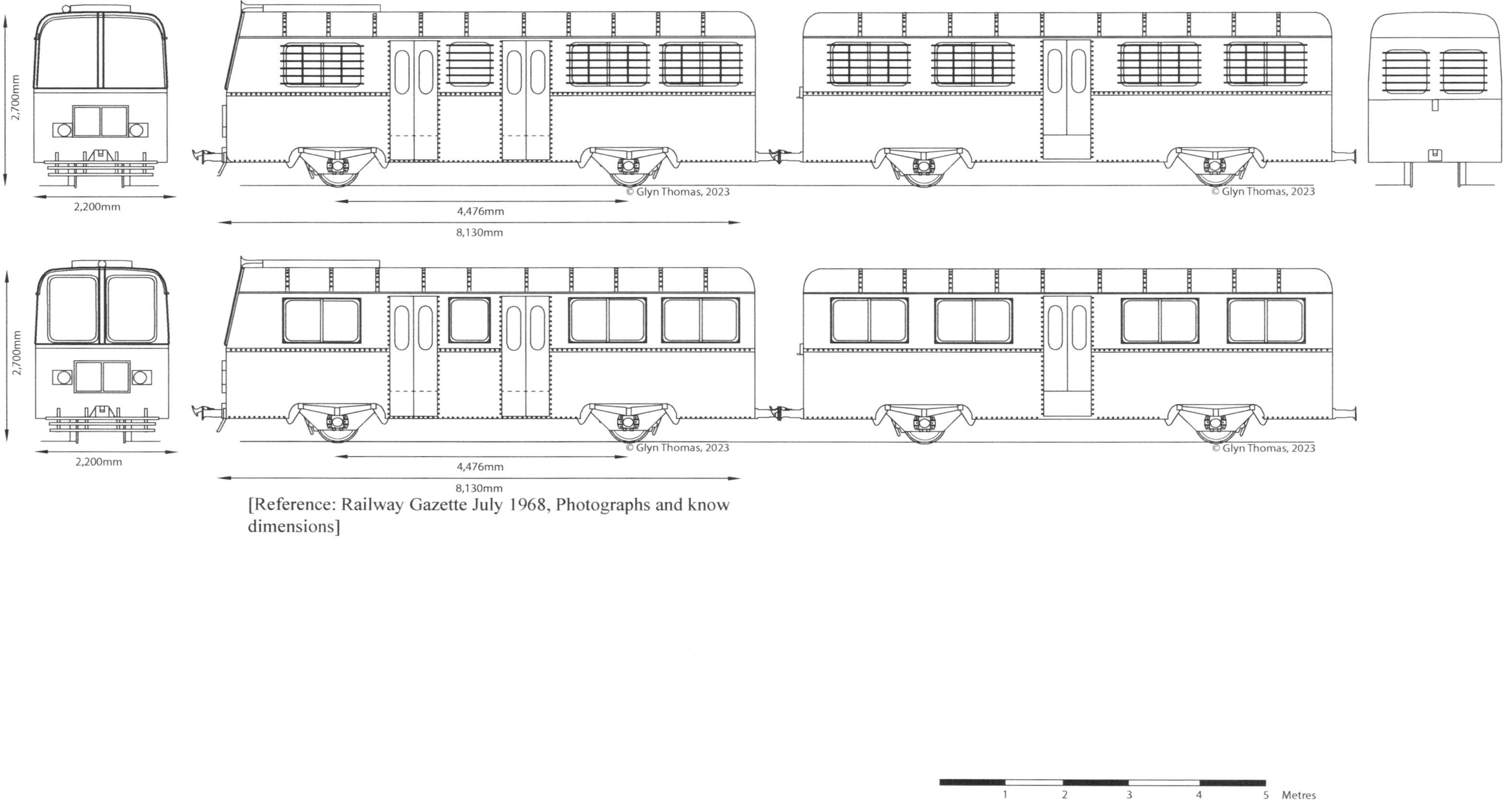

[Reference: Railway Gazette July 1968, Photographs and know dimensions]

Electric Vehicles

GIPR EMU, 1925 (Broad Gauge)

GIPR EMU in monsoon conditions, 1936 [IRFCA]

The Great Indian Peninsula Railway (GIPR) was the first railway in India to adopt electric traction, in 1925. Mainline electric traction was required to improve operating conditions on the ghats (heavily graded sections on the escarpments between the coast and the Deccan Plateau). Electrification of suburban services around Bombay would increase capacity and frequency of trains to tackle overcrowding, which was becoming an issue even at this time. At the time, the GIPR was embarking on a major new construction project, the partially elevated "Harbour Branch", intended entirely for suburban traffic. 1,500V DC traction was 'state of the art' at the time, and overhead lines were used to mitigate the impact of flooding during the monsoon season. Trains were designed to operate in flood waters up to 2' above rail height[1].

EMUs from Cammell-Laird with traction motors by British Thomson-Houston of Rugby were used on the line from Victoria Terminus to Kurla (which would become the core of the CR suburban service). Unusually for the time, the sets were equipped with MCB (knuckle-style) couplings within the set and conventional screw links at the outer ends.

Based on David Churchill's analysis of Administrative Reports for Indian Railways, in appears that 53 4-car sets plus two spare motor cars were delivered between 1925 and 1931. This is largely consistent with the Report of the Suburban Train (Bombay, Calcutta and Madras) Overcrowding enquiry committee of 1956, which listed the "old" stock of the GIPR as:

- 10' wide wooden stock - 18 units
- 10' wide steel stock - 20 units
- 12' wide steel stock - 13 units

12' wide stock was not permitted to run on the Harbour Branch or beyond Kalyan, although there was work underway in 1956 to widen the loading gauge on the outer sections of the mainline.

In service, trains initially consisted of 4-cars. In 1927, this was increased to 8-car trains.

The early 1925 stock was withdrawn around 1966.

---

1 Reported in "Railway Wonders of the World"

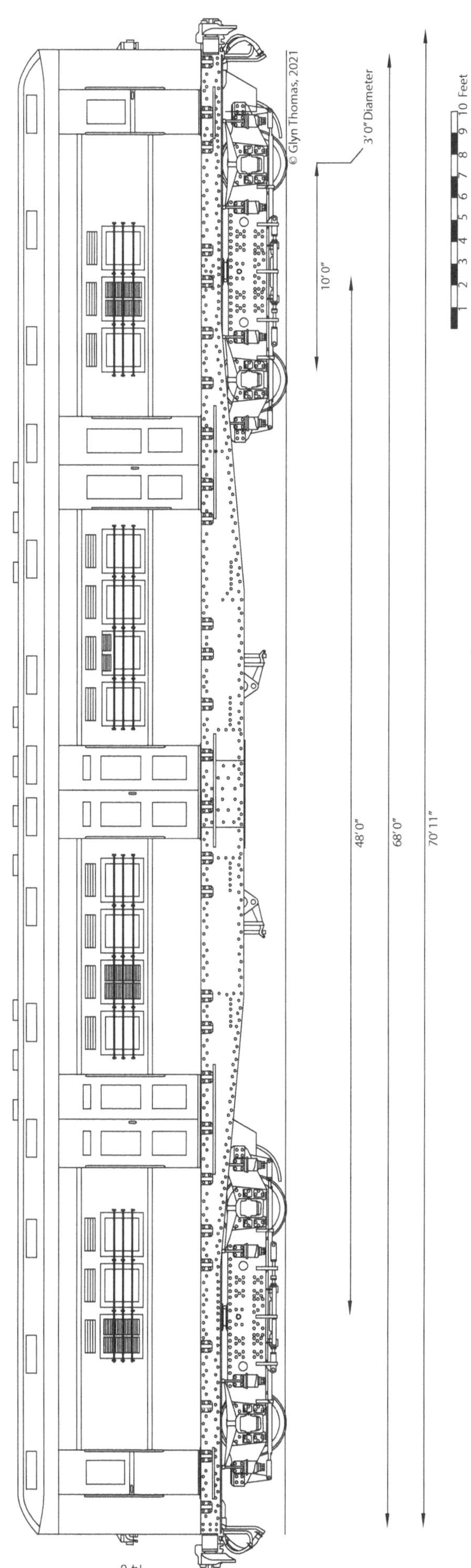

GIPR Electric Driving Trailer, 1925

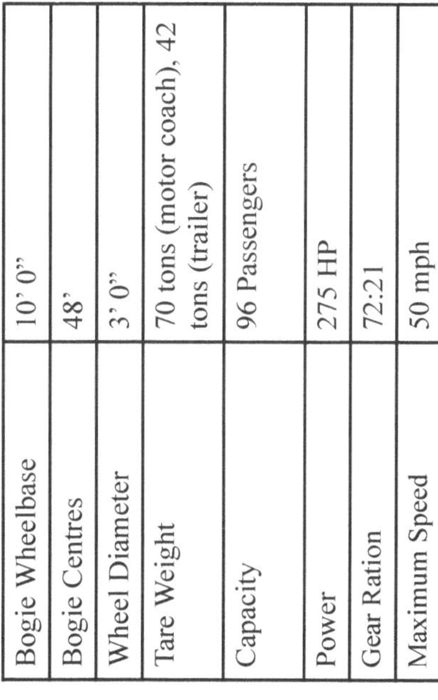

Bogie Wheelbase	10' 0"
Bogie Centres	48'
Wheel Diameter	3' 0"
Tare Weight	70 tons (motor coach), 42 tons (trailer)
Capacity	96 Passengers
Power	275 HP
Gear Ration	72:21
Maximum Speed	50 mph

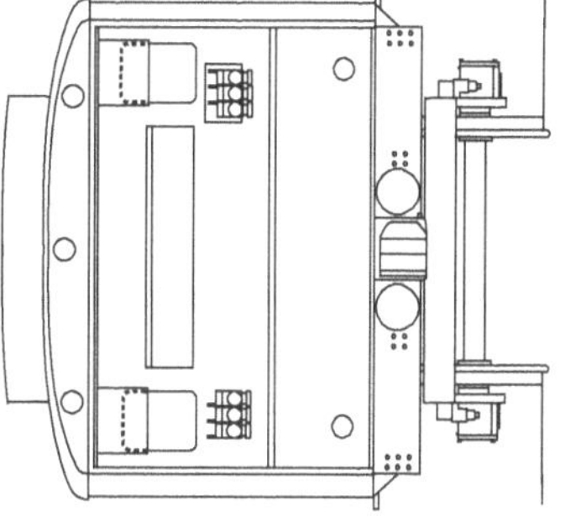

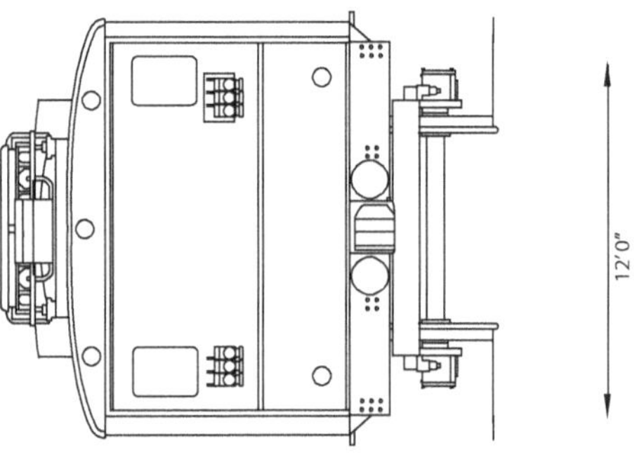

GIPR Electric Motor Car, 1925
© Glyn Thomas, 2021
3'0" Diameter
10'0"
48'0"
68'0"
70'11"
14'6"
12'0"
1 2 3 4 5 6 7 8 9 10 Feet

BBCIR EMU, 1928 (Broad Gauge)

BBCIR EMU on Andheri service [Kelland Collection, BRCT, 47021]

The Bombay, Baroda and Central India Railway (BBCIR) were quick to follow the GIPR in electrifying its suburban service from Colaba to Borivali in 1928. The system also used 1,500V DC power and overhead wires. 169 motor cars and trailers (40 four-car sets plus 9 spares) were ordered from Cammell Laird. British Thomson-Houston (BTH) of Rugby supplied the electrical equipment for the trains. The types were:

- 40 Composite I & II Class Carriages.

- 40 Composite II & III Class Carriages.

- 49 Luggage Van and II Class Carriages.

- 40 Motor coaches III Class Carriages (9 spare cars provided from the outset)[1]

These were similar to the stock used by GIPR on their suburban lines, but all BBCIR stock was 12' wide because the loading gauge was more generous across the system. Initially, the rake composition was: A - driver, third and luggage; B - third motor; C - second-third composite; D - first-second composite. Due to the all-steel construction, the coaches were fabricated entirely in Nottingham, England and shipped ready-to-run. The bogies for trailer units were shipped separately, while the motor coaches were shipped with the bogies attached. The coaches were too wide to be transferred to Hull by rail, so they were transferred from Nottingham to Hull by barge. The stock was shipped from Hull to Bombay on the SS Belpareil and SS Beljeanne. The October 1927 (arriving November) shipment on the SS Beljeanne carrying 52 cars was covered by Pathé News in the UK at the time and this clip is available on the Internet.

The stock remained the same through the Second World War. In 1948, BBCIR was incorporated into the Western Railway. In 1953, it was reported that the stock was 162 cars. These cars were finally withdrawn in 1974.

One motor car is preserved at the National Railway Museum in Delhi.

BBCIR Electric Motor Car (End View)

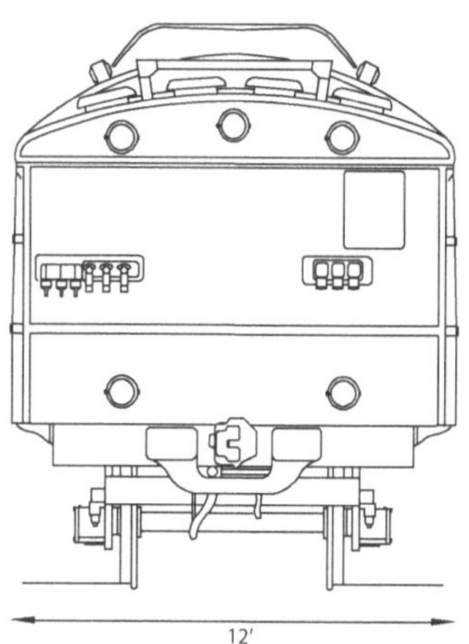

---

1 Dr. Ashok Kumar. The History of Bombay Suburban Railways

BBCIR Electric Motor Car

[Reference: Builder's publicity and known dimensions]

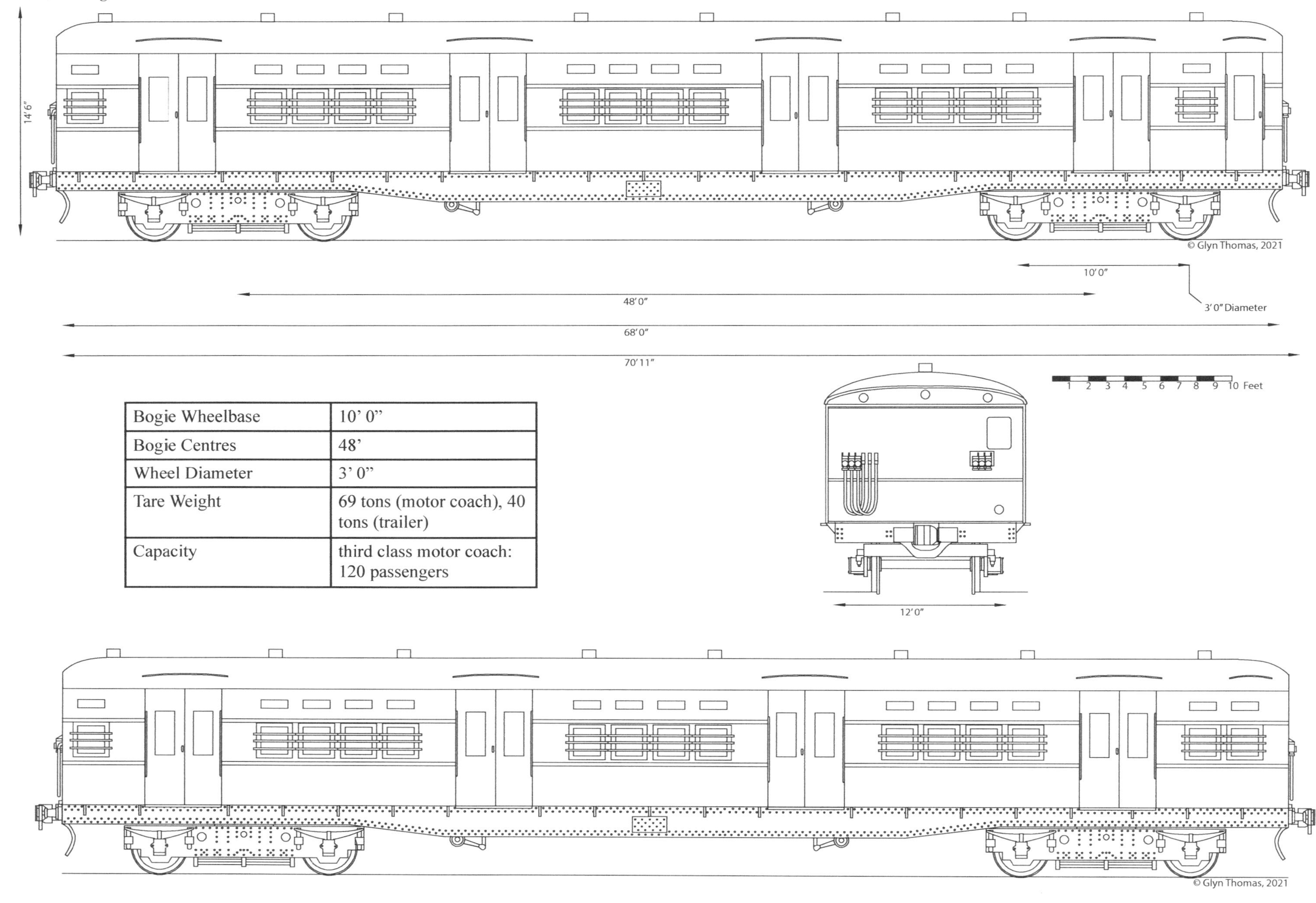

Bogie Wheelbase	10' 0"
Bogie Centres	48'
Wheel Diameter	3' 0"
Tare Weight	69 tons (motor coach), 40 tons (trailer)
Capacity	third class motor coach: 120 passengers

Metro-Cammell EMU, 1951 (Broad Gauge)

BRCW EMU in monsoon conditions, 1957 [Builder's Publicity Photo via IRFCA]

By the early 1950's no new equipment had been supplied to the Bombay suburban lines since they opened. The GIPR lines were now part of the Central Railway (CR), and the BBCIR lines were part of the Western Railway (WR). There had been relatively little expansion of the Bombay suburban network since the early 1930s, with the most notable addition being the electrification of Kurla to Mankhurd as an extension of CR's Harbour Branch. Shortage of stock and electrical power meant that shortly after the Mankhurd electrification program completed, services on the extension reverted to steam.

A combined order were placed with Metropolitan Cammell for stock to be used on both the CR and WR. The 1951 order would mitigate shortages on the Mankhurd section and also permit increasing the frequency of trains elsewhere in order to reduce overcrowding. According to the 1956 Suburban Train Overcrowding Enquiry Commission the CR received 16 units, and the WR received 12 units. The first GIPR units were received via the SS Empire Spartan on May 8th, 1951.

Variations of the Metro-Cammell Design

The Metro-Cammell EMU design became the standard for the Bombay suburban network for decades, and also influenced development of Howrah/Calcutta electrification. Subsequent orders from other manufacturers generally used the same dimensions and body profiles as the Metro-Cammell cars, although windows and interior layout varied, especially in the motor cars. Notable orders that followed the same general design include:

- 24 4-car sets from Ernesto Breda of Milan in 1956 (half with English Electric electrical gear, and half with electrical gear from Ansaldo San Giorgio of Genoa); by 1978, 25% of these units were out of service due to problems with getting replacement traction motors.

- 74 4-car sets from Nippon, Toshiba and Hitachi of Japan in 1958

The stock was built as a collaboration between Metropolitan Vickers, BTH, Metropolitan Cammell and Birmingham Railway Carriage and Wagon (BRCW). Unlike the earlier stock, which consisted of one motor coach and three trailers, the new stock had two motor cars and two trailers per unit. The stock was equipped with electro-pneumatic brakes. By this time all trains on both railways were operating with eight cars (two units). It is reported that these sets reverted to using one motor car after a while in order to reduce load on the electricity grid.

A further order for 18 trailer cars was placed with Metropolitan Cammell in 1955 for use on the CR.

In service, it was reported that this design suffered from bowing in the centres of the cars due to excessive weight from overcrowding. Indian Railways remediated this by strengthening the side sills in the 1960s. [IRFCA article]

The Metropolitan Cammell stock operated until the 1980's.

Due to the perennial problem of excessive overcrowding train lengths have steadily increased over time[1].

- Starting in 1963, additional trailers were added to Bombay suburban EMUs, making the standard train length 9-cars.

- In 1964, the Kalyan-Kasara/Karjat section increased EMU lengths from 4- to 6-cars.

- In 1986, mainline EMU services were increased to 12-cars. Karjat services followed in 1987, but it took until 2008 for Kasara services to start 12-car service.

---

1 Numbers from "Whistling Ahead - Story of Growth & Modernisation", Indian Railways Electrical Department, publicity booklet, c. 2016

3,000V DC Electrification at Howrah

When it came to electrifying suburban services in the Howrah/Calcutta area, the 1,500V DC system used in the Bombay and Madras areas was already considered obsolete. The more-efficient 3,000V DC system was selected and initial suburban orders used this technology:

- 16 3-car units from MAN with AEG electrical equipment in 1958-9

- 16 3-car units from Jessop in 1959

- 15 3-car units from SIG in 1958-9. These three-car sets had the same passenger capacity as an 8-car steam-hauled set[2].

The SIG units were notable as being the first totally new EMU design on Indian Railways since the BRCW design of 1951. They were built by a consortium of Swiss manufacturers led by SIG. SIG built all the motor cars, and Swiss Car and Elevator Manufacturing Corp Ltd of Schileiren ("Schilieren") built the trailers. The sets consisted of: A driving trailer - drivers compartment, 1st class 26 seat compartment and 3rd class 50 seat compartment; B motor coach - 2 x 3rd class 50 seat compartments, HT cabinet, and auxiliary drivers compartment; and C driving trailer - 3rd class compartment 62 seat, 3rd class compartment 26 seats, 4 tons luggage, driving compartment. Up to three 3-car sets could be combined to create a 9-car train. The sets were also able to work in multiple with the Jessop and MAN units. They used a welded integral stressed skin car construction similar to the design of ICF coaches. Majex automatic centre couplers were provided on the ends of units for MU working and they had Westinghouse electro-pneumatic brakes. Four 260hp traction motors fitted in the motor coach. Leading dimensions are provided in the table below[3].

Body height	12' 6"
Length over buffers (3-car set)	211"
Distance between bogie centres	48"
Bogie wheelbase	9' 6"
Wheel diameter	3' 1½"
Tare	51 tons motor coach 62 tons trailers (2) 113 tons total
Capacity	264 seats and 290 standing (crush load 580 people) plus 4 tons luggage
Gear ratio	21:65
Maximum Tractive Effort	20,500 lbs
Maximum speed	65 mph

The 47 initial sets were the only 3,000V DC EMUs ever built for India. Even as these units were being introduced, Indian Railways was taking advice from French railway engineers to convert the electrified network to 25kV AC. 25kV AC power systems incur lower transmission losses (higher efficiency) than lower voltage DC systems, because the current required to deliver the same amount of power is lower. 1950s-60s development of high-power rectifiers that were small and reliable enough to be used in power cars and locomotives facilitated conversion from DC to AC. By this time, many railways around the world were using this technology and it would also permit Indian Railways to tap into worldwide technology developments. The services from Sealdah were electrified on this system from the outset.

28 of the 3,000V DC sets were converted to dual-voltage to avoid the need for passengers to change trains at Baudel while voltage conversion progressed - 12 of the SIG/Brown Boveri/Oerlikon/Secheron units and 16 of the Jessops/AEI units were converted at Kanchrapara works[4]. The SIG units had a 15.5 ton axle load (vs. 18.8 ton permitted), so an additional 11.7 tons of electrical equipment in the power car could be accommodated and the existing pantographs could be used for both power systems. The Jessops cars already had a 18.3 ton axle load, so additional power equipment was placed on one of the power trailers, with a separate single pantograph for 25kV AC. The first converted units were delivered in June 1965 and the final units in April 1966. The costs of conversion was 2.12 lakhs per Jessop unit and 2.10 lakhs per SIG units[5] . 25kV AC conversion of the lines from Howrah was completed in 1968.

Following completion of 25kV AC conversion, six 9-car 3,000V DC units were sent from Calcutta to Bombay for conversion to 1,500V DC. Five had been put in service by April 1969[6]. Conversion cost was 65 lakh[7] Rupees, of which 16 lakh was foreign exchange[8].

---

2 Railway Gazette, Dec 1966

3 Indian Railway Gazette, Jan 1959

4 Indian Railway Gazette, April 1965

5 Indian Railway Gazette, July 1966

6 Indian Railway Gazette, April 1969

7 A lakh is 100,000

8 Indian Railway Gazette, April 1968

Jessops EMUs

The Jessops EMU was essentially an Indian-built version of the Metro-Cammell EMU and contained a large proportion of British-built components in the early years.

The first Jessops 3,000V DC rake was delivered for use on Howrah-Burdwan service in 1959, joining 31 imported units. The 3-car set had seating for 290 people - 52 women, 26 1st class, 212 3rd class and 4 tons of luggage. It cost 15 lakh Rupees. At the time, 34 3-car units were on order to be shared between Calcutta and Bombay. The second set was due to be delivered in August, then 2 sets to be delivered each month. 16 coaches and 2 spare motor cars were 3,000VDC units to be used in Calcutta, with the remainder were 1,500V DC units for Bombay. Metro-Cammell designed the motor coach and provided underframes and bodies. Metropolitan Vickers designed the electrical equipment[9]. Initially, electrical equipment was manufactured by Associated Electrical Industries Manufacturing Co. Ltd..

In 1964, Jessops started to receive traction equipment from Heavy Electricals (India) Ltd. (HEIL), although the amount of imported content was still high initially. By 1969, 112 sets of electrical traction equipment for 1,500V DC had been ordered, 65 sets had been delivered and installed in 38 3-car trains plus 3 spare motor cars. Domestic content increased from 50% to 80% between 1964 and 1969[10].

In the late 1960's India suffered supply chain issues due to lack of foreign exchange. No Jessops units were delivered in 1968. In mid-1969, Western Railway received three 9-car sets from Jessops[11].

Jessops EMU at Bombay Bandra Jct, 12/11/1977 [John Tolson, Transport Treasury, JMT2615]

Bogie Wheelbase	10'
Bogie Centres	48'
Wheel Diameter	36"
Tare Weight	175 tons (4-car train)
Power	4 x 175 HP motors
Gear Ration	61:19
Maximum Speed	70 mph

[Reference: Metro-Cammell diagrams via Historical Model Railway Society]

---

9 Indian Railway Gazette, July 1959

10 Indian Railway Gazette, June 1969

11 Indian Railway Gazette, April 1969

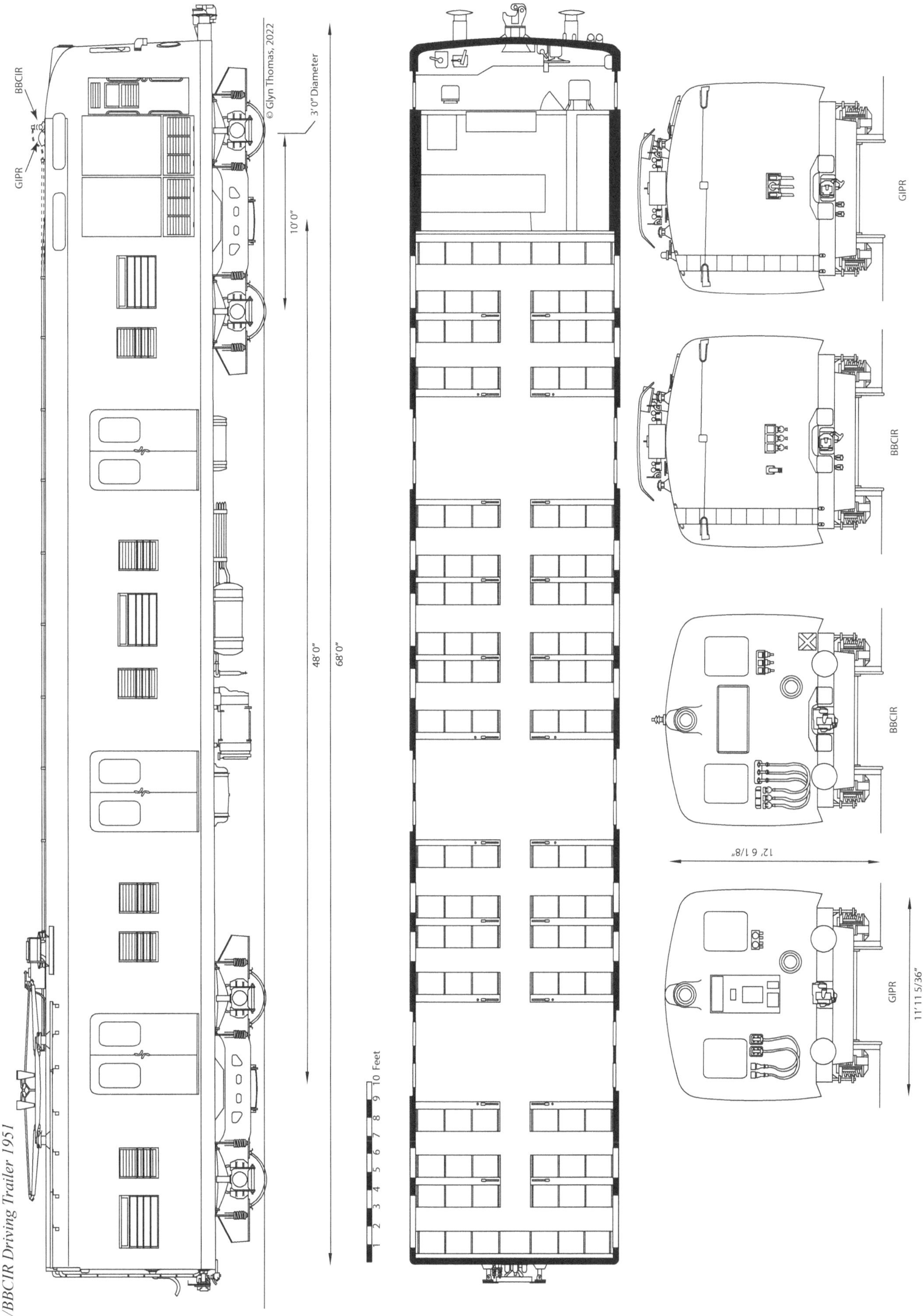

GIPR/BBCIR Driving Trailer 1951
GIPR
BBCIR
© Glyn Thomas, 2022
10' 0"
3' 0" Diameter
48' 0"
68' 0"
1 2 3 4 5 6 7 8 9 10 Feet
12' 6 1/8"
GIPR
BBCIR
BBCIR
GIPR
11' 11 5/36"
103

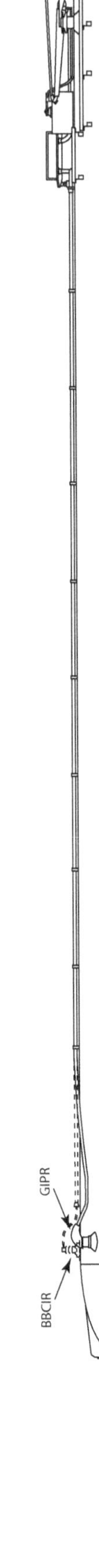
GIPR/BBCIR Driving Trailer 1951
GIPR
BBCIR
© Glyn Thomas, 2022
3' 0" Diameter
10' 0"
48' 0"
68' 0"
12' 6 1/8"
11' 11 5/36"
1 2 3 4 5 6 7 8 9 10 Feet

ICF EMU, 1962 (Broad Gauge)

ICF EMU in Mumbai, 8/1/2011 [Author]

Independent India's long-term objective was to become self-sufficient in the construction of railway rolling stock. As described in "Indian Rolling Stock in HO Scale", the Integral Coach Factory (ICF) was established in 1955 at Perambur, Madras.

For the domestic production of EMUs, it was initially decided to place 1,500V DC and 3,000V DC orders with Jessops, and 25kV AC orders with ICF. Jessop's DC EMUs generally followed the Metro-Cammell EMU pattern, while the ICF design had a different body profile and window design. The long-term plan was to provide domestic electrical equipment from Heavy Electricals (India) Ltd. (HEI, later to become Hindustan Engineering and Industrial) of Bhopal. HEI's large scale capacity only came online in around 1968, and in the meantime domestic EMU production used either British or Japanese electrical equipment. BG EMUs used air brakes for faster braking.

The initial Calcutta 25kV AC order, placed with ICF in 1961, was for 64 coaches in 4-car sets[1]. Four prototype sets were ordered - two with British electrical equipment from AEI/ English Electric and two with Japanese electrical equipment from Hitachi. The first prototype was delivered in 1962. All had been delivered by 1964. By that time, there were 70 sets of electrical equipment on order from the HEI for delivery from April 1965[2].

As an interim measure 26 push-pull sets with ICF EMU driving-trailers and regular trailers (8-car trains with a locomotive in the middle) were put in service on the northern section of the ER Sealdah division by 1966.

An order for additional electrical equipment was offered on global tender[3]. 32 sets of BG 25kV AC equipment was ordered from a Japanese group led by Hitachi, and the resulting units put into service by 1966.

The EMU shell was adapted from the standard ICF coach shell, with an integrated body designed to be load-bearing and dispense with a heavyweight underframe, In addition to existing ICF coaches, the design made reference to the shells of the SIG 3,000V DC EMUs provided for Howrah electrification. The EMU stock was 12' wide as opposed to the 10' 8" of mainline coaches, and were 68' over headstocks. Motor cars needed additional work to determine weight distribution for the 20 tons of electrical equipment[4]. The motor bogies had a box-frame design that was stronger than the I-frame trailer bogies. Each set was coupled with Schafenberg semi-permanent couplings and through air connections, The motor coach has most of the electrical equipment on the cross frames of the underframe, Motor coaches had two small electrical compartments, and a small driver's compartment at one end for use in shunting. An AEI lightweight pantograph was mounted on the roof (no inset) above the No. 1 end (driver's compartment).

The standard 4-car ICF train consisted of: A - driving trailer (102 seats); B - motor coach (100 seats); C - trailer (114 seats); D - driving trailer (75 seats + 4 tons luggage). In service, these trains were often paired to provide 8 coaches, and could also have an additional trailer between the units to take capacity to 9-cars. The maximum speed was 65 mph (105 kph).

Following completion of 25kV AC electrification in the Calcutta area and Madras, ICF switched to building 1,500V DC EMUs with HEIL electrical equipment. The first sets appeared in Bombay in 1969. Production peaked in the mid-1970s (see table in the ICF EMU section). It appears that construction of further Jessops 1,500 V DC units finished around the same time.

See the following table for statistics on ICF EMU production in the 20th Century.

---

1 Railway Gazette, July 1961

2 Indian Railway Gazette, October 1966

3 Railway Gazette, May 1964

4 Indian Railway Gazette, October 1966

ICF EMU Production - 1962-2000

Type	1962-3	1963-4	1964-5	1965-6	1966-7	1967-8	1968-9	1969-70	1970-1	1971-2	1972-3	1973-4	1974-5	1975-6	1976-7	1977-8	1978-9	1979-80	1980-1	1981-2	1982-3	1983-4	1984-5	1985-6	1986-7
EMU 25kV Motor B		4	21	19	37	28	29	13	24	14	19	9				22	31	23	30	33	33	18	6	10	20
EMU 25kV Motor B (disc brake)																									
EMU 25kV Trailer A & D	11	80	58	65	9	75	62	12	2							40	26	52	68	48	48				
EMU 25kV Trailer C	10	79	49	40		23													31	24					
Cumulative BG 25kV AC	21	184	291	417	445	580	670	711	726	750	764	783	792	792	792	854	911	986	1,115	1,220	1,301	1,319	1,325	1,335	1,355
EMU 1,500V Motor B								2	7	10	17	30	31	18	16								6	20	8
EMU 1,500V Trailer D								7	6	6	17	31	31	19	5	22	10	30						26	
EMU 1,500V Trailer C								7	8	8	17	32	28	18	8									26	
EMU 1,500V Trailer D (Disc Brake)																									
EMU 1,500V Trailer C (Disc Brake)																									
Cumulative 1,500V DC	0	0	0	0	0	0	0	16	37	61	112	205	295	350	379	401	411	441	441	441	441	441	447	519	527
MG EMU 25kV Motor			3	25	17																				
MG EMU 25kV Coach				38									24			12					22		12	7	
MG EMU 25kV Driving Trailer				19									24			6									
Cumulative MG 25kV AC	0	0	0	60	85	102	102	102	102	102	102	102	150	150	150	168	168	168	168	168	190	190	202	209	209

Type	1987-8	1988-9	1989-90	1990-1	1991-2	1992-3	1993-4	1994-5	1995-6	1996-7	1997-8	1998-9	1999-2000
EMU 25kV Motor B		33	40		24	50	21	32	30	59	52	55	45
EMU 25kV Motor B (disc brake)									9				
EMU 25kV Trailer A & D		12	48	40	45	35	43		42	84	25	25	20
EMU 25kV Trailer C		2	58	32	45	40	43	53	69	50	87	85	60
Cumulative BG 25kV AC	1,355	1,402	1,548	1,620	1,734	1,859	1,966	2,051	2,201	2,394	2,558	2,723	2,848
EMU 1,500V Motor B	2	8					30	16	33				4
EMU 1,500V Trailer D	12	6					30	18	31				4
EMU 1,500V Trailer C	12	6					30	18	31				23
EMU 1,500V Trailer D (Disc Brake)							10						
EMU 1,500V Trailer C (Disc Brake)							10						
Cumulative 1,500V DC	553	573	573	573	573	573	683	735	830	830	830	830	861
MG EMU 25kV Motor		6			15	4							
MG EMU 25kV Coach													
MG EMU 25kV Driving Trailer													
Cumulative MG 25kV AC	209	215	215	215	230	234	234	234	234	234	234	234	234

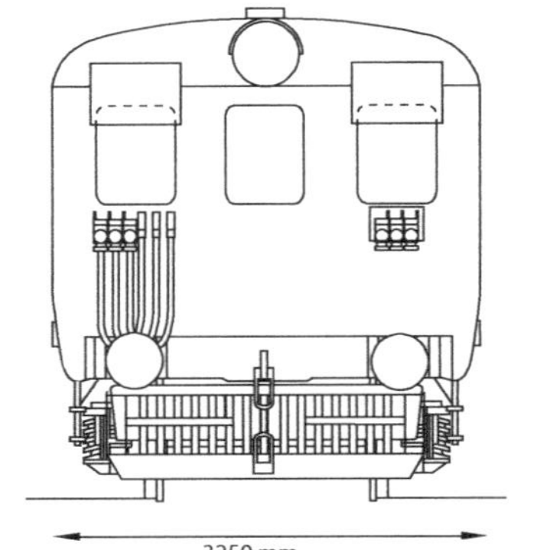

Overall Length	20,726 mm
Width	3,658 mm
Height	3,810 mm
Height to panto in lock-down	4,398 mm
Capacity	391 passengers and 4 tons of luggage (4 car set)
Maximum Speed	106 km/h

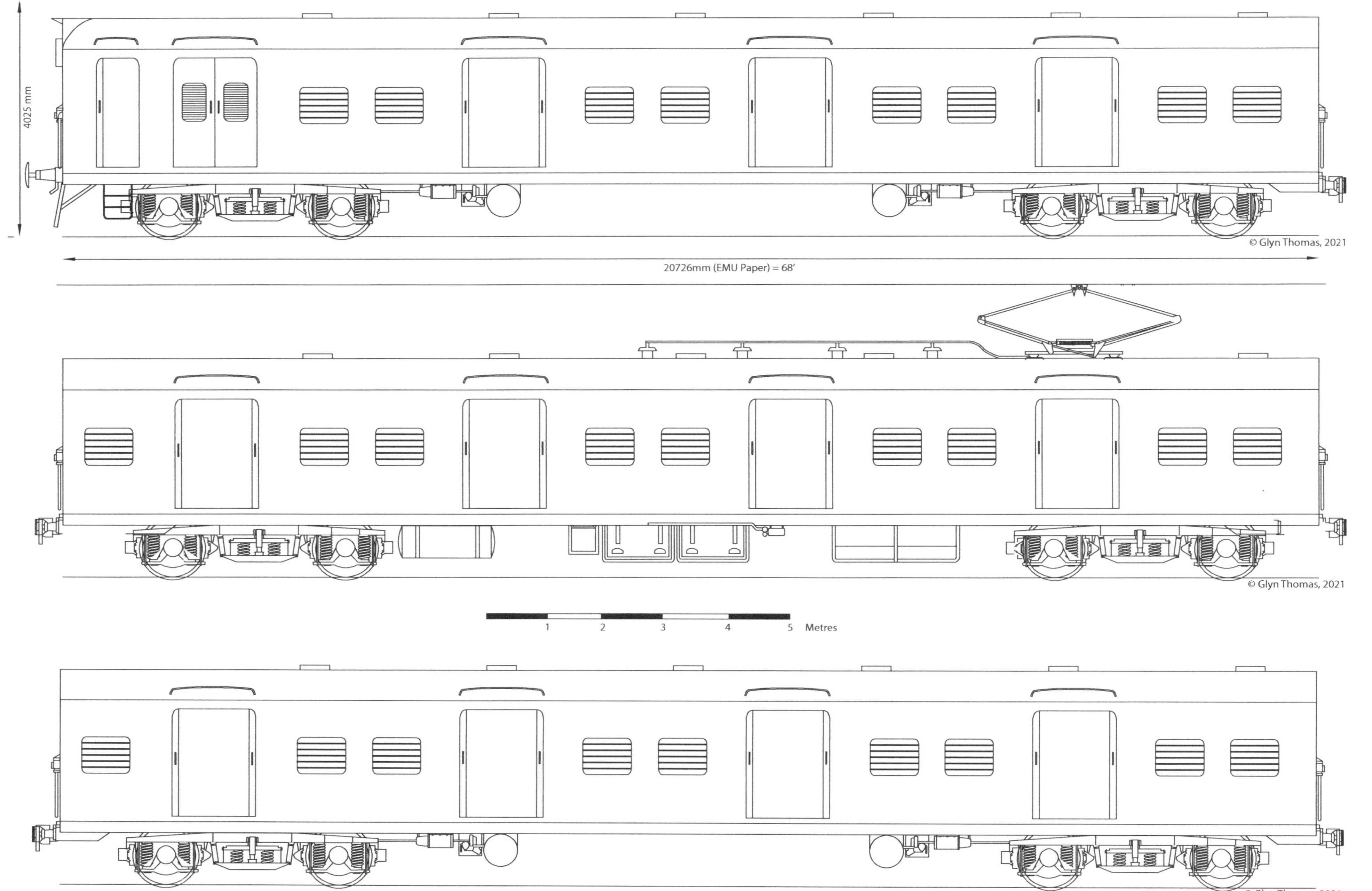

[Reference: Known Dimensions and Photographs (Internet Diagram)]

Madras EMU, 1930 (Metre Gauge)

Madras 1930 EMU [Kelland Collection, BRCT, 49213]

As discussed in the introduction, Madras electrified its major metre gauge suburban line between Madras Beach to Tambaram in 1930 on the 1,500V DC system with overhead wires.

English Electric Co Ltd supplied 17 3-coach articulated trains (motor and 2 trailers) to operate the suburban service. The stock was built and tested in Preston, England before being shipped to Madras for final assembly. The sets were equipped for multiple-unit working and were usually run in 6-car trains during rush hour; 9-car trains were also possible. It was also possible to add a YT third-class coach to sets in order to increase capacity.

While outside the scope of this book, 7 Bo-Bo electric locomotives, class EM/1 (later YCG-1) were also provided for freight service on the line. Battery tenders, class ET, were provided to permit these locomotives to reach sections beyond the overhead wires[1].

A further 7 3-car sets were acquired from English Electric and put into service in 1934.

Following introduction, services on the line appear to have remained largely unchanged until the 1950's. The Suburban Train Overcrowding Enquiry Commission of 1956 noted severe peak-hour overcrowding by this time. Around that time, additional units of a more modern design were bought from Breda to supplement services (see later).

In the 1960's it was decided to extend electrification south to Viluppurum. With the English Electric stock reaching the end of their useful life, it was decided to convert the entire line to 25kV AC and withdraw the older stock. It was originally planned to switch voltage in 1965, but foreign exchange issues delayed production of replacement stock. Eventually, complete voltage conversion occurred on January 15th, 1967. Supply chain issues resulted in ICF concentrating on construction of 25kV AC motor cars, and the English Electric sets had their traction equipment stripped out and were used as trailer sets until sufficient ICF trailers were produced (possibly in phases between 1974 and 1978, see "ICF EMU Production - 1962-2000" on page 106). 24 or 26 of the older English Electric sets were treated this way[2].

Unfortunately, none of these units were preserved. A YCG-1 locomotive is preserved at the National Railway Museum, Delhi.

Madras EMU Train. Note the extra coach coupled between the two 3-car EMU units [IRFCA]

---

1 See Daboo, "Diesel and Electric Locomotives of India" for more details.

2 Indian Railway Gazette, July 1966, Indian Railway Gazette, October 1966

Madras EMU. 1930

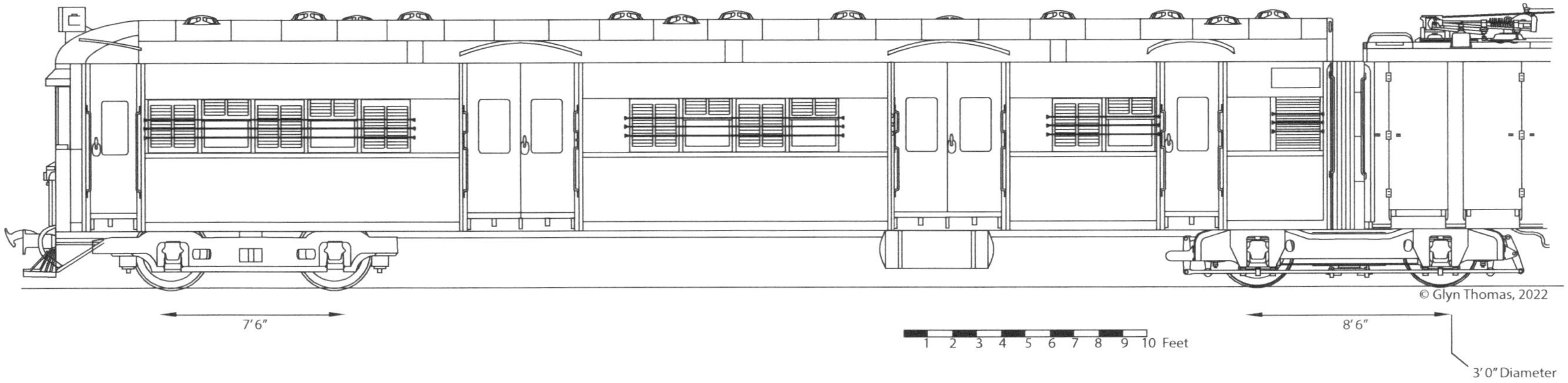

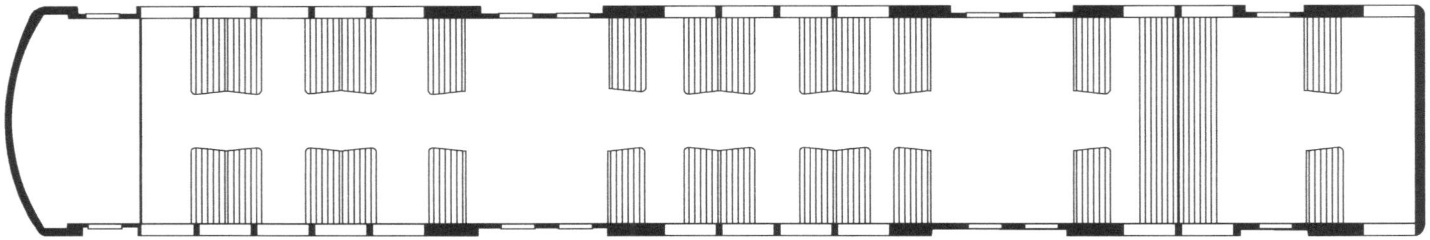

© Glyn Thomas, 2022

3' 0" Diameter

8' 6"

7' 6"

1 2 3 4 5 6 7 8 9 10 Feet

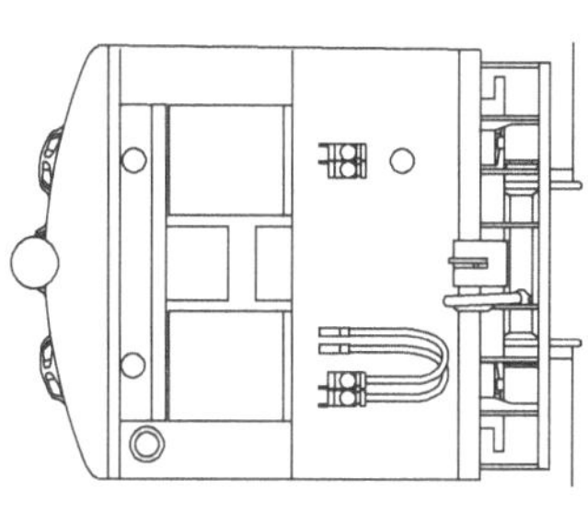

Bogie Wheelbase	7' 6" outer, 8' 6" inner
Wheel Diameter	36"
Tare Weight	79 tons
Power	4 x 122 HP
Gear Ratio	65:15
Maximum Speed	55 MPH

[Reference: GA diagram republished in Rail Enthusiast's magazine]

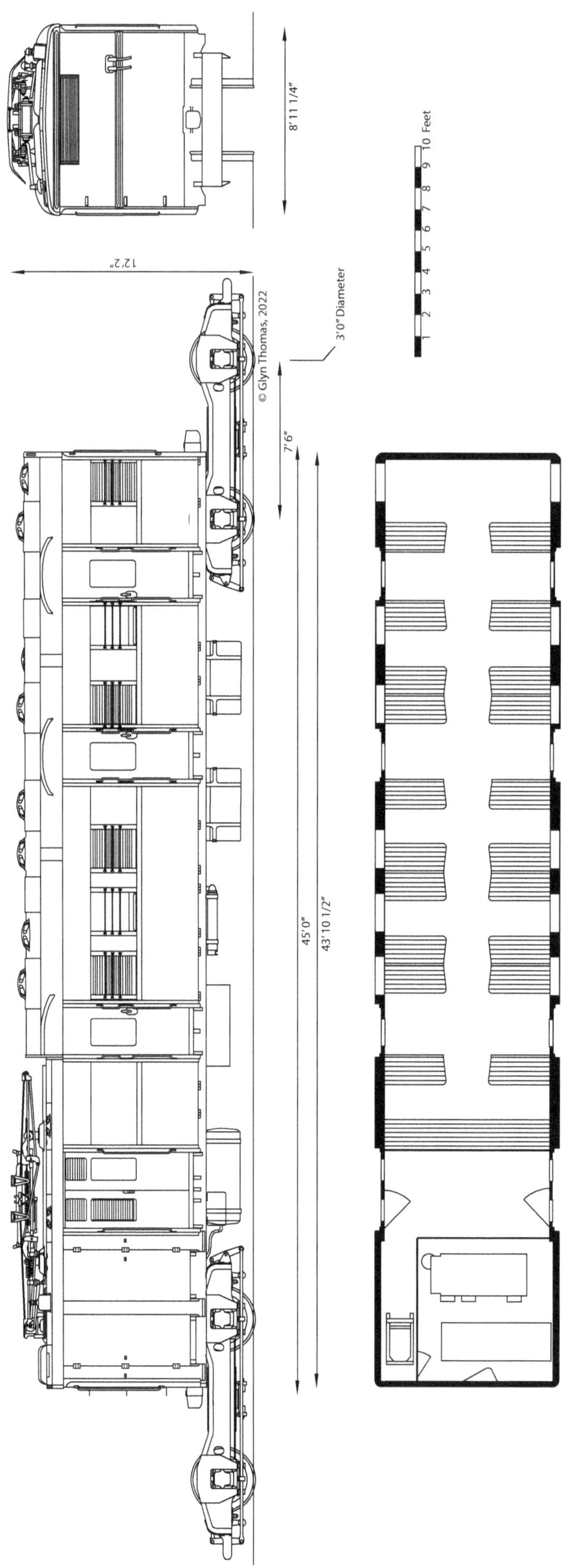

[Reference: English Electric Diagram via Historical Model Railway Society]

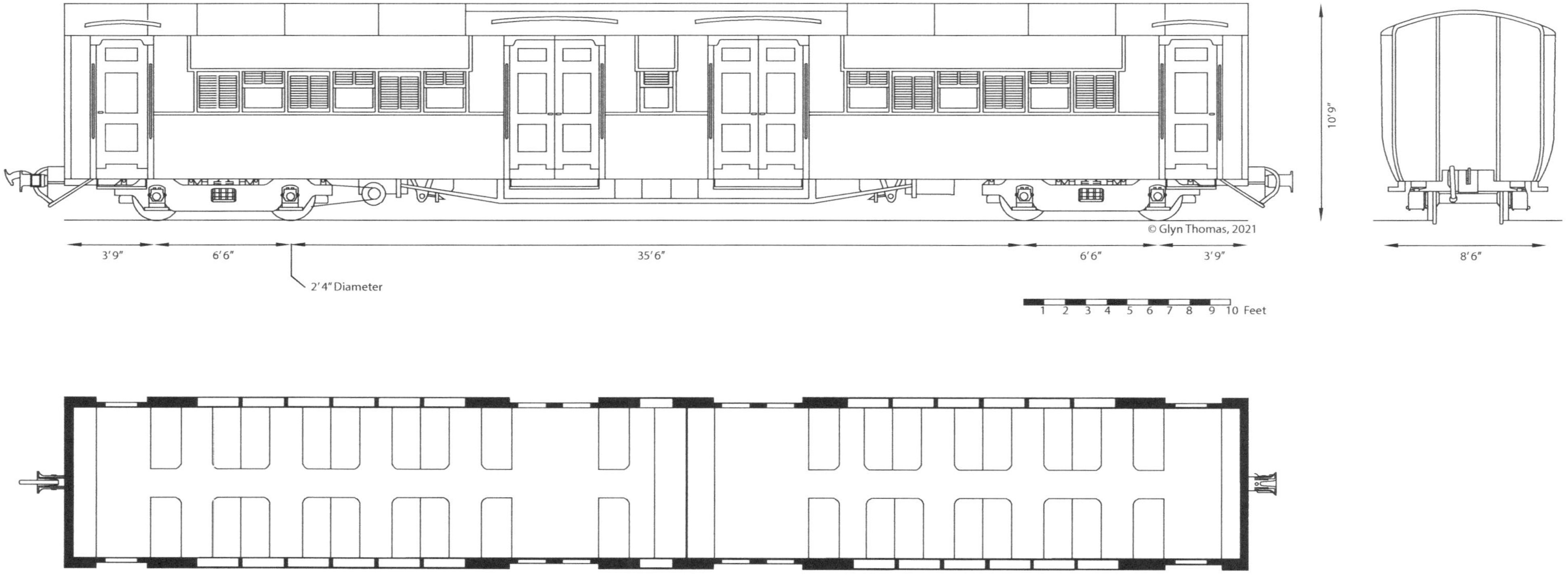

SIR Suburban Coach

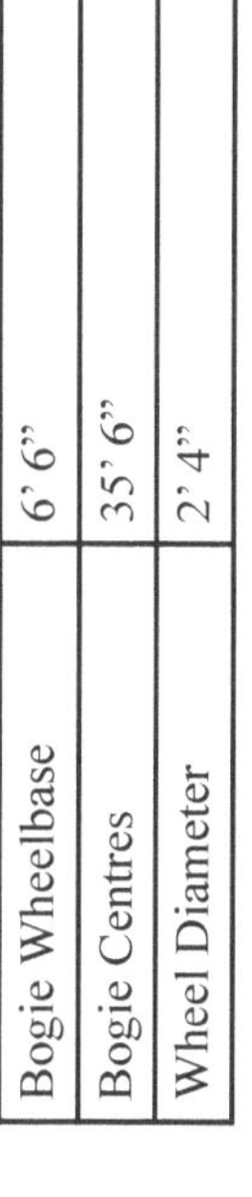

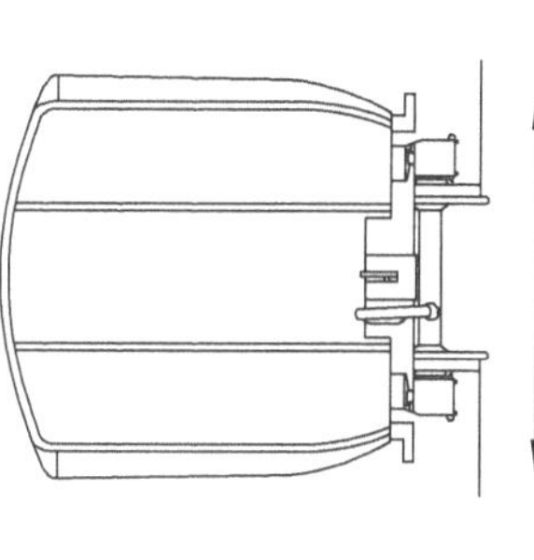

Bogie Wheelbase	6' 6"
Bogie Centres	35' 6"
Wheel Diameter	2' 4"

[Reference: Diagram from Ernie Webber Collection, Otago University]

Madras Breda EMU, 1956 (Metre Gauge)

Newly Delivered Breda EMU, 1956 [Overseas Railways]

Post-Independence, the Southern Railway ordered six 4-car EMUs from Ernesto Breda to supplement Madras suburban services and these entered service on April 13th. 1956. These were of a more modern appearance than the English Electric cars. The 1956 Suburban Train Overcrowding Enquiry Commission report documents 24 EMUs in service, which probably includes the Breda sets, plus possibly an extra built from spares?

In line with developments elsewhere on Indian Railways, when the English Electric units reached end of life, the decision was made to convert the entire Madras suburban line to 25kV AC. In 1964, tenders were sought to convert the Breda 1,500V DC sets to 25kV AC. This order was won by Nichimen of Japan, and was paired with a wider order to supply traction equipment for ICF-built EMUs (see later)[1].

The conversion of the Madras-Tambaram section to 25kV AC was completed in 1967.

The final withdrawal dates of the Breda units is not known, but it possibly coincided with ICF producing six additional power cars in 1988.

Overall Length (4 cars)	237' 1½"
Width	8' 11"
Height (pantograph locked)	12'
Tare Weight	86.9 tons (4-car train)
Capacity	Lower class 280 Upper class 26
Power	4 x 160 HP motors

---

1 See Indian Railway Gazette, April 1964

Breda EMU for Madras. 1956

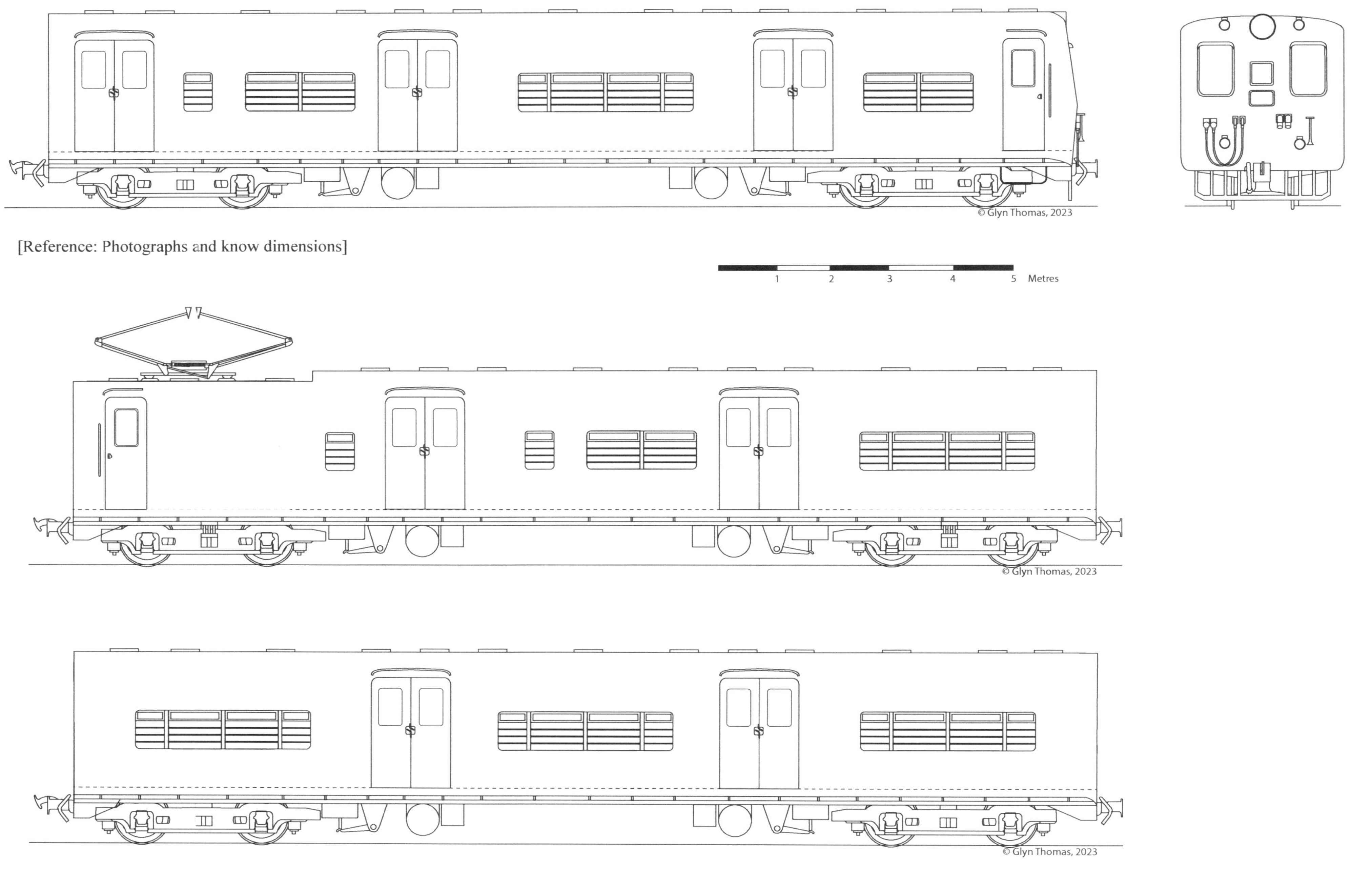

[Reference: Photographs and know dimensions]

Madras ICF EMU, 1965-1993 (Metre Gauge)

25kV AC EMU at Madras Egmore, 21/11/1977 [John Tolson, Transport Treasury JMT2929]

In 1964, following the decision to convert the entire Madras suburban line to 25kV AC, a worldwide tender was issued for 39 sets of electrical equipment for use in new AC sets (the cars themselves to be built by ICF). This tender was won by a group of Japanese companies led by Nichimen and combined with equipment to convert the Breda EMUs (see earlier)[1].

Initially, conversion of Madras-Tambaram section to 25kV AC was due to be complete by December 1965, with ICF stock to be delivered by then[2]. In fact, only 10 motor cars had been completed by October 1966, including the Breda conversions. 25kV AC conversion was completed on January 15th, 1967 using 22 four-car units built by ICF. These sets had a 300 seat capacity compared to 198 seats in the 1,500V DC stock. The plan was to eventually expand the fleet to 49 units in order to increase frequency and also allow longer trains (three sets coupled together). Already, traffic had increased from 33M rides in 1956-7 to 63M in 1966[3].

The ICF sets were classified YAU1. Due to restricted space between the roof and the overhead wire, the pantograph needed to be set on a lower roof section. This resulted in reduced headroom inside the coach, and the space was reserved for vendors bringing produce to market (or later, the ladies section). The motor cars had only 45 seats. Maximum speed for these units was 85kph.

During the transition period, 25kV AC power cars were coupled to the older 1,500V DC trailers to operate AC sections. To facilitate this, early ICF motor cars were fitted with the older style couplings, and vacuum brakes instead of air brakes.

Most of these ICF EMUs survived until the conversion of the Chennai metre gauge suburban lines to broad gauge in the early 2000s. ICF produced a few more cars in the 1980s and 1990s (see the table on page 106).

A power car and trailer from the 1965 ICF stock has been preserved at the Chennai Railway Museum.

Madras ICF EMU near Madras Beach, 27/12/1979 [Fuzz Jordan, DHRS Collection]

---

1 Railway Gazette, May 1964; Indian Railway Gazette, October 1966

2 Indian Railway Gazette, April 1964

3 Indian Railway Gazette, April 1967

ICF EMU for Madras 25kV AC. 1965

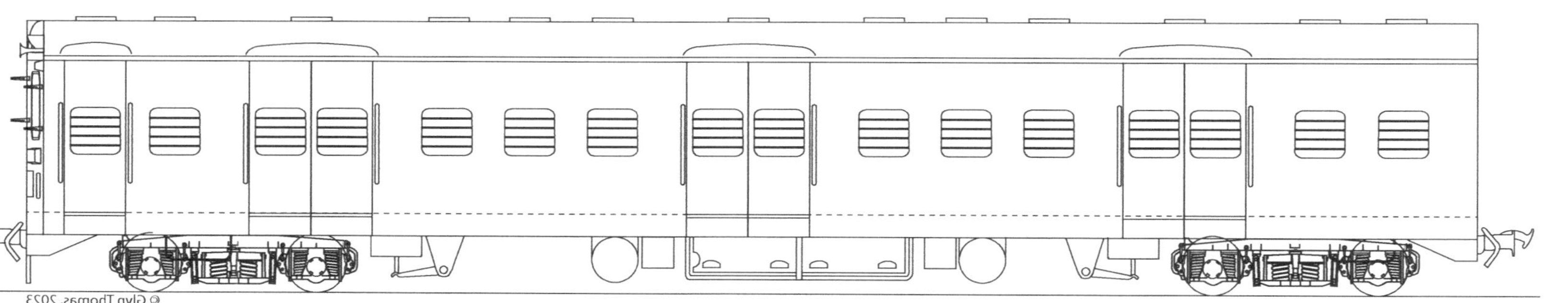

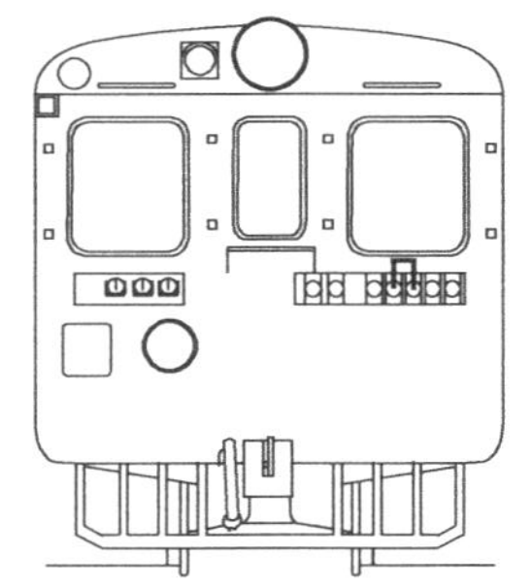

[Reference: Photographs and know dimensions]

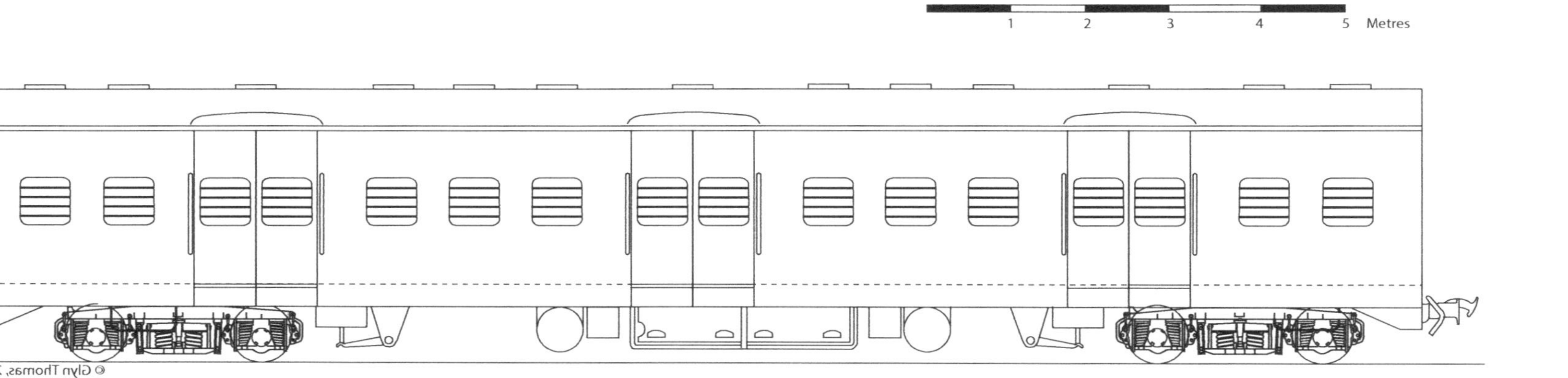

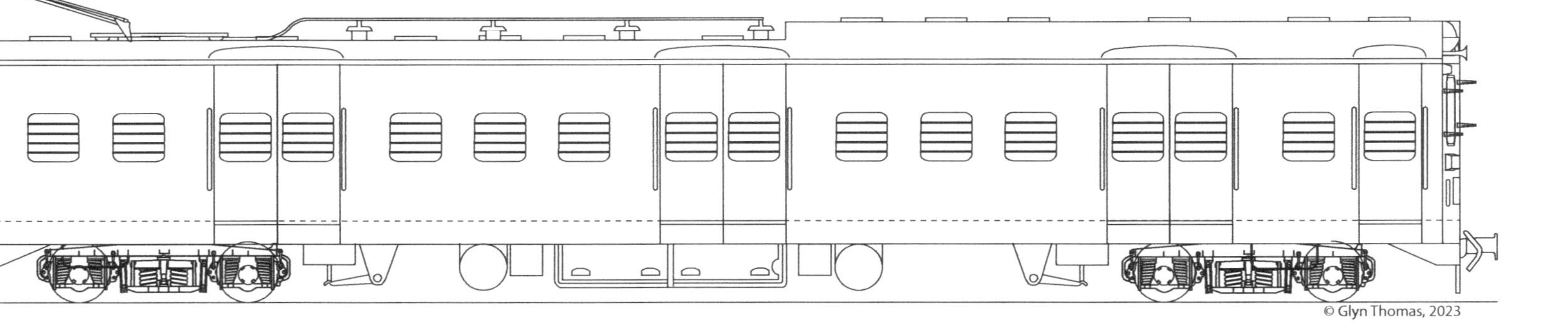

Pakistan

LHB Railcars and Trailers, 1958 (Broad Gauge)

LHB diesel railcar and trailer for Pakistan, 1958 [Manufacturer's catalogue, via Historical Railway Images]

Following partition, the North Western Railway in West Pakistan became the Pakistan Western Railway (PWR) As discussed earlier, the NWR had started to experiment Ganz railcar services in 1939. Following their rebuilds, the Ganz railcars were performing well and continued in service around Lahore until at least 1962.

In 1958, PWR placed an order with Linke-Hofmann-Busch (LHB) for 24 matching pairs of railcars and trailers. The railcars were powered by two Daimler-Benz 228HP diesel engines with hydraulic transmission. Air brakes were used on these units. They were used on the Lahore to Qasur line, and possibly elsewhere.

Railway Gazette of March 1968 reported that a further 36 railcars and trailers had been ordered from Germany. The details of this order have not been confirmed, but they may have been further examples of this type. These were intended for Rawalpindi-Rohri services.

	Railcar	Trailer
Bogie Wheelbase	2440mm	2440mm
Pivot Centres	14780mm	14780mm
Wheel Diameter	864mm	864mm
Tare Weight	44 t	30 t
Engines	2 x Daimler-Benz	
Power	2 x 228 HP	
Capacity	90 seats	102 seats
Maximum Speed	90 kph	

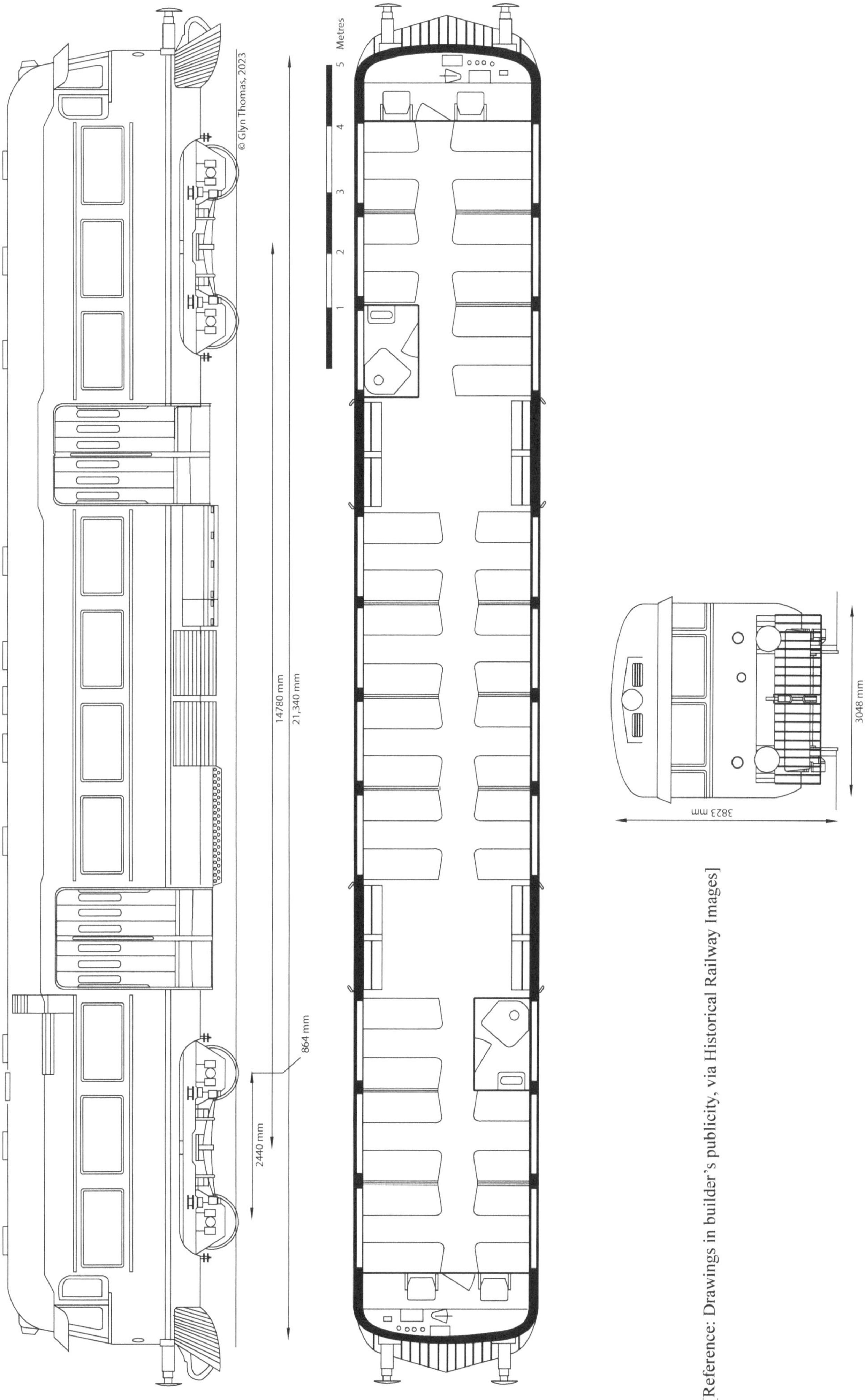

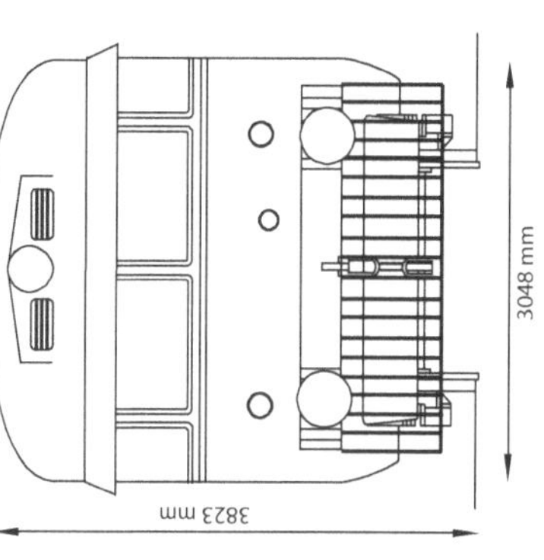

[Reference: Drawings in builder's publicity, via Historical Railway Images]

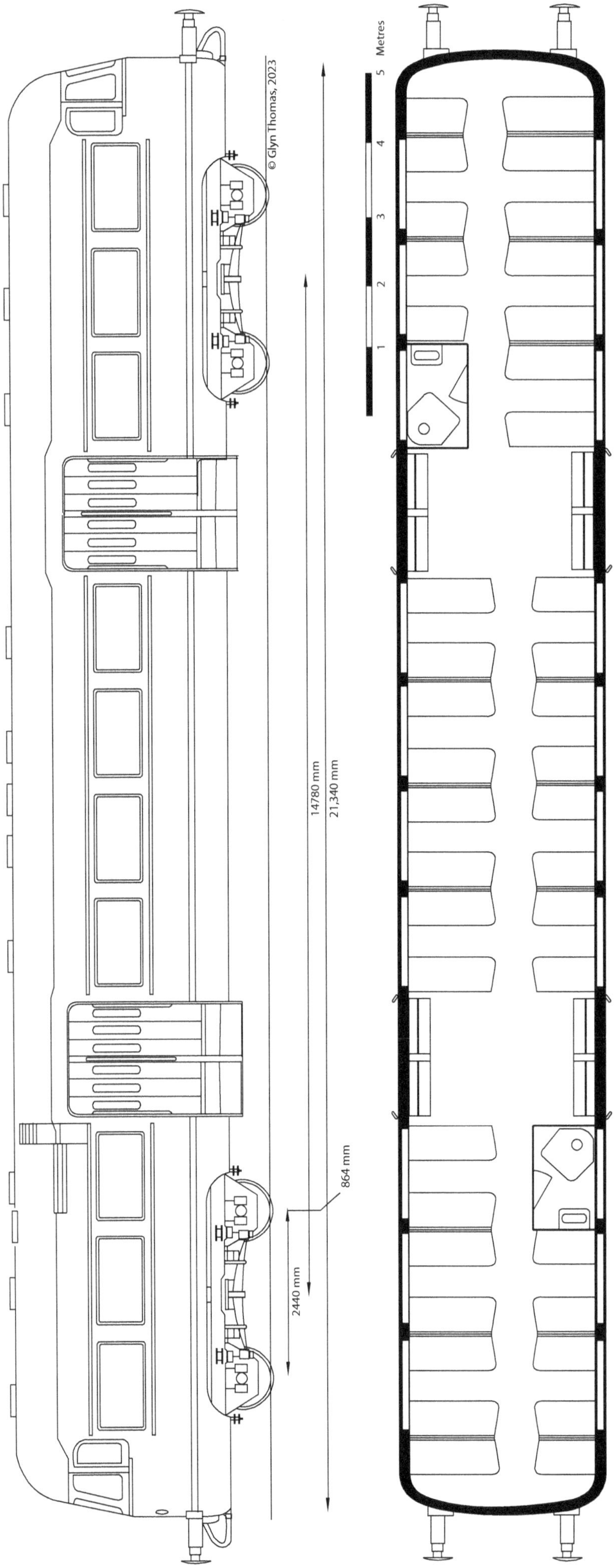

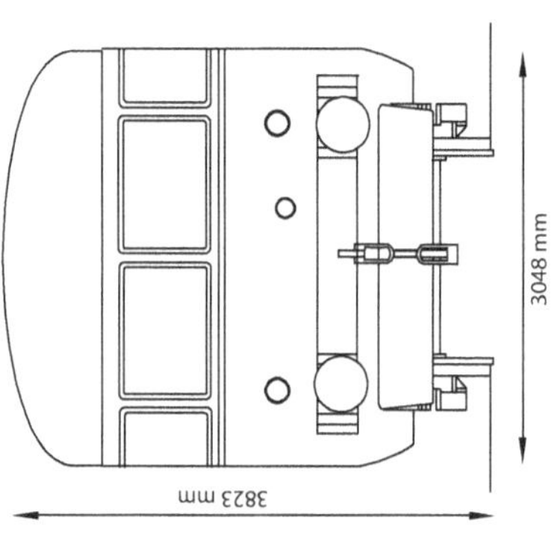

[Reference: Drawings in builder's publicity, via Historical Railway Images]

Hitachi Railcars and Trailers, 1968 (Broad Gauge)

Hitachi diesel railcars (4182 in front) at Rawalpindi 11/03/1978 [George Woods, Flickr]

Following the relative success of the LHB railcar sets in service, in 1964, PWR built at least one domestic railcar, in collaboration with a Japanese manufacturer. This railcar remained in service until the 1980's.

It's possible that the experiment with domestic railcar manufacture proved that it was impractical to build railcars in volume inside Pakistan. In 1965 Pakistan Railways put out a tender for a much larger order of railcars. Hitachi Group, representing a group of Japanese manufacturers including Hitachi Group, Kisha Sezo Kaisha Ltd, and Fuji Heavy Industries won the order against competition from MAN, LHB, FERROSTAL, Metro-Cammell and Italian and Hungarian companies. The order consisted of 126 cars - 34 railcars (each fitted with two above floor engines) and 89 trailers plus 3 AC trailers. The total order value was 2,600,000,000 Japanese Yen[1].

One railcar and 2 trailers were to be delivered within 15 months and the remainder to follow after trials by June 1968.

In service, these railcars were used on several major routes, including Rawalpindi to Lahore, Rawalpindi to Peshawar, Rawalpindi to Kundian, Lahore to Multan. When initially put in service, they operated as a railcar plus trailer set, but subsequently 2 or 3 trailers became common. This may have been necessary because the passenger accommodation in the motor car was limited due to the two above-floor engines.

In service, these appear to have been classified ZZT. Observed numbers include 4171 (possibly the prototype), 4177, 4182, and 4183.

These railcars were popular with passengers due to their enhanced level of comfort compared to steam-hauled coaches. George Woods photographed a long line of the units apparently out of service at Rawalpindi in 1978, but some remained in operation into the 1990s so these may have just been waiting for repairs. 4177 was photographed on a Malakwal Jn. to Bhera train in 1988. An unidentified unit was filmed in service as late as 1994.

4171 remained in the derelict line at Rawalpindi until recent years and still appeared to be in reasonably good external condition.

Bogie Wheelbase	2440mm
Pivot Centres	14776mm
Wheel Diameter	864mm
Engines	2 x General Motors GM12V-71M
Maximum Speed	68 MPH

---

1 Indian Railway Gazette, April 1965

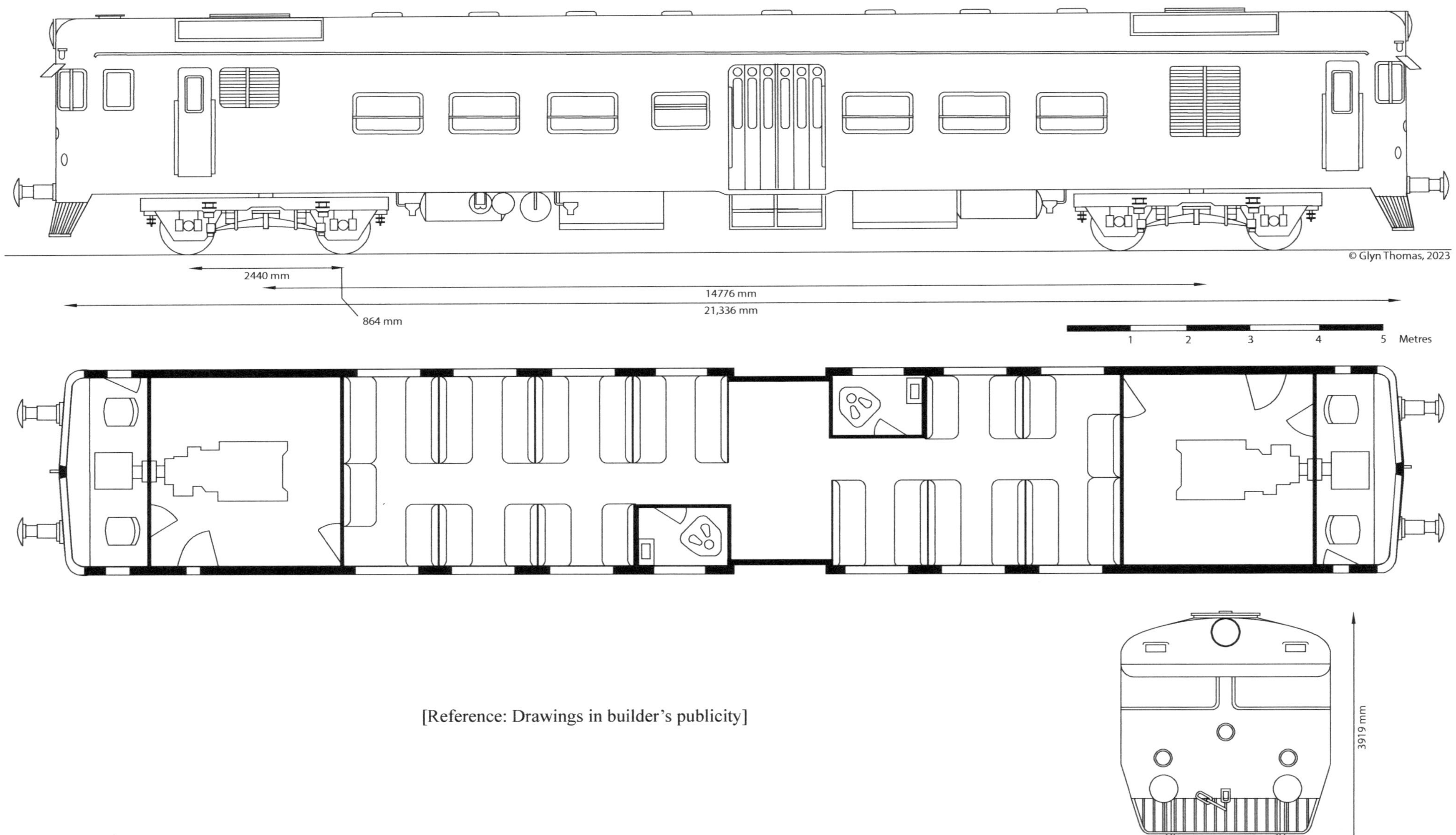

© Glyn Thomas, 2023
2440 mm
14776 mm
21,336 mm
864 mm
1   2   3   4   5   Metres
3919 mm
3251 mm
[Reference: Drawings in builder's publicity]

Additional Photographs

One of two BRCW metre-gauge railcars for the Junagad State Railway, 1934, see table in "Petrol and Diesel"
on page 6 [David Churchill Collection]

Maharajah's metre-gauge railcar for Jamnagar & Dwarka State Railway, see table in
"Petrol and Diesel" on page 6 [David Churchill Collection]

This 140 bhp (brake horsepower) diesel-electric railcar (AW DT41/1934) was introduced on the Pulgaon-Arvi line in 1935. It was fitted with a Armstrong-Saurer 6-cylinder engine. The lightweight body with Seating for 58 third-class passengers was built at the GIPR Matunga Workshops. . In 1967 it was working the weekly market day passenger service: journey time was one hour and twenty-five minutes as compared with the mixed-train timing of two hours and thirty minutes. See table in "Petrol and Diesel" on page 6 [The late Peter Bawcutt courtesy of Peter Tiller]

GIPR railcar fitted with a Ford engine. See "Appendix: The Ones That Got Away" on page 151 [Administrative Report for Indian Railways, 1936]

Eleven 250 bhp diesel-mechanical railcars, manufactured by Ganz, Budapest, were introduced in 1939. One of these railcars NWR 95 was noted at Mian Mur south of Lahore in 1958. See "NWR Ganz Railcar, 1939 (Broad Gauge)" on page 67 [The late Peter Bawcutt courtesy of Peter Tiller]

Walford Bogie Locomotive on Martins' Baraset-Basirhat Light Railway. See "Martin and Co. Railcars, 1935-1952 (2'6" Gauge)" on page 62 [David Churchill Collection]

Walford Bogie Locomotive on Martins' Baraset-Basirhat Light Railway. See "Martin and Co. Railcars, 1935-1952 (2'6" Gauge)" on page 62 [David Churchill Collection]

This photo is tentatively identified as one of the railbuses built locally for the Morvi Tramway. It appears to be based on a 1940 Dodge truck chassis. See table in "Petrol and Diesel" on page 6 [Photo courtesy of Roger West]

Small Western Railway narrow-gauge railbus No. 51s was powered by a 30hp Chevrolet engine. See "Western Railway and its Predecessor's Railcars" on page 54 [The late Peter Bawcutt courtesy of Peter Tiller]

HALR RC1 at Howrah Maidan, 1965. See "Martin and Co. Railcars, 1935-1952 (2' 6" Gauge)" on page 62 [The late Peter Bawcutt courtesy of Peter Tiller]

CR 798 Wickham railcar built in 1934 and seating twelve persons outside its shed at Gwalior in 1966 This was fitted with a 30hp ford engine. This photo shows an early livery - white with blue stripes? See "Matheran Railcars, 1909-1930s (2' Gauge)" on page 37 [The late Peter Bawcutt courtesy of Peter Tiller]

Twelve Japanese-built diesel railcars with 180hp Nippon engines classed YRD/2 were acquired by the Southern Railway in 1954 and based at Tiruchchirappalli. 209 Karaikkudi-Tiruchchirappalli Passenger crossing the main road near Padukkottai under the watchful eye of the crossing keeper in 1969. The railcar is YRD/2 10. See "Appendix: The Ones That Got Away" on page 151 [The late Peter Bawcutt courtesy of Peter Tiller]

Twelve diesel railcars (later classified as YRD1) came from Fiat of Italy in 1955. They were fitted with Fiat 210hp 700A engines; six had hydro-mechanical transmission and six had hydraulic transmission. NR 1004 was seen at Delhi Cantonment in 1958 en route from Rewari to Delhi Sarai Rohilla. See "YRD-1 DMU, 1955 (Metre Gauge)" on page 71 [The late Peter Bawcutt courtesy of Peter Tiller]

Commonwealth Engineering DMU, with unit 1012 leading, on the Southern Railway during commissioning, 1958. See "Commonwealth Engineering Railcars, 1958 (Broad Gauge)" on page 73 [BUT photo, David Churchill Collection]

Commonwealth Engineering DMU, with unit 1011 leading, on the Southern Railway during commissioning, 1958. See "Commonwealth Engineering Railcars, 1958 (Broad Gauge)" on page 73 [BUT photo, David Churchill Collection]

Railbus at Katwa, 7/2/1991. See "Standard Railbus, 1966 (2' 6" Gauge)" on page 78 [Laurie Marshall, DHRS Collection]

Railbus 7000 at Katwa, 9/11/1975. See "Standard Railbus, 1966 (2'6" Gauge)" on page 78 [Laurie Marshall, DHRS Collection]

Bardhaman (Burdwan) 2ft 6in gauge ZRD railbus and trailer set (31-12-1985). See "Updated Standard Railbus, 1980s (2'6" Gauge)" on page 81 [Tim Edmonds]

Yelahanka 2ft 6in gauge ZRD railbus (28-11-1981). See "Updated Standard Railbus, 1980s (2' 6" Gauge)" on page 81 [Tim Edmonds]

Railbus 7041 at Nabadwip Ghat on the Shantipur line, 2010. These railbuses needed to be turned at each end of the line.
See "Updated Standard Railbus, 1980s (2' 6" Gauge)" on page 81 [Fuzz Jordan, DHRS Collection]

Railbus 7041 on the Shantipur line, 2010. The line closed for gauge conversion shortly afterwards. See "Updated Standard Railbus, 1980s (2'6" Gauge)" on page 81 [Fuzz Jordan, DHRS Collection]

ZRB Railcar 10607 at Ahmadpur Jn. on the Katwa line, 2004. See "ZRB Railbus, c. 1999 (2'6" Gauge)" on page 92 [Samit Roychoudhury]

ZRB Railcars meet on the Katwa line, 2004. See "ZRB Railbus, c. 1999 (2'6" Gauge)" on page 92 [Samit Roychoudhury]

Trailer 10612 on the Katwa line, 2009-10. The later railcars were built in 3-car sets, but obviously could be supplemented with older trailers. See "ZRB Railbus, c. 1999 (2'6" Gauge)" on page 92 [Fuzz Jordan, DHRS Collection]

Railbus 10607 at Katwa, 2009-10. See "ZRB Railbus, c. 1999 (2'6" Gauge)" on page 92 [Fuzz Jordan, DHRS Collection]

Small narrow gauge railcar at Rawalpindi, Pakistan on 11/3/78. It was probably there for repairs because there were no narrow gauge lines at that location. The coaches in the background are trailers for the broad gauge diesel railcars [George Woods]

The following section is illustrated with photographs from an album titled "Electrification B.B.&C.I.Rly - Colaba-Borivli" in the BORHT collection. This was presumably provided to one of the engineers working on the project, possibly as a leaving gift. Additional subjects from the album are included due to their historical interest.

BBCIR Electrification, 1928. See "Bombay/ Mumbai" on page 13 [BORHT Collection]

BBCIR Electrification, 1928. See "Bombay/ Mumbai" on page 13 [BORHT Collection]

BBCIR Electrification, approach to Churchgate station, 1928. See "Bombay/ Mumbai" on page 13 [BORHT Collection]

BBCIR Electrification near Churchgate, 1928. See "Bombay/ Mumbai" on page 13 [BORHT Collection]

BBCIR Electrification, 1928. Facilities for the new Bombay Central station. See "Bombay/ Mumbai" on page 13 [BORHT Collection]

BBCIR Electrification, 1928. This is probably the light machine shop at Bombay Central EMU shed. See "Bombay/ Mumbai" on page 13 [BORHT Collection]

BBCIR Electrification, 1928. Construction of Bombay Central EMU shed. See "Bombay/ Mumbai" on page 13
[BORHT Collection]

Tata power station for BBCIR electrification, 1928. In the early years, power was provided by three hydroelectric plants at the foot of the ghats; one of these was at Khopoli. From here power was transmitted at 110kV 3-phase AC to a receiving station at Dharavi (near Matunga). Dharavi fed three sub-stations via 22kV 3-phase AC lines[1] See "Bombay/ Mumbai" on page 13
[BORHT Collection]

1 See JE Daboo, "The First Major Railway Electrification in India", British Overseas Railway Journal no. 19 for more details

BBCIR Electrification, trailers arriving at Bombay Docks, 1928. See "BBCIR EMU, 1928 (Broad Gauge)" on page 97
[BORHT Collection]

BBCIR Electrification, trailers arriving at Bombay Docks, 1928. See "BBCIR EMU, 1928 (Broad Gauge)" on page 97
[BORHT Collection]

BBCIR Electrification, trailers arriving at Bombay Docks, 1928. See "BBCIR EMU, 1928 (Broad Gauge)" on page 97
[BORHT Collection]

BBCIR Electrification, trailers arriving at Bombay Docks, 1928. See "BBCIR EMU, 1928 (Broad Gauge)" on page 97
[BORHT Collection]

BBCIR Electrification, trailers arriving at Bombay Docks on SS Beljeanne, 1928. See "BBCIR EMU, 1928 (Broad Gauge)" on page 97 [BORHT Collection]

BBCIR Electrification, painting the trailers at Parel, 1928. See "BBCIR EMU, 1928 (Broad Gauge)" on page 97 [BORHT Collection]

BBCIR, 1928 trailer interior, 1st class. See "BBCIR EMU, 1928 (Broad Gauge)" on page 97 [BORHT Collection]

BBCIR, 1928 trailer interior, 3rd class. See "BBCIR EMU, 1928 (Broad Gauge)" on page 97 [BORHT Collection]

BBCIR electrification at Andheri South, 1928. See "BBCIR EMU, 1928 (Broad Gauge)" on page 97 [BORHT Collection]

BBCIR, 1928 train. See "BBCIR EMU, 1928 (Broad Gauge)" on page 97 [BORHT Collection]

BBCIR, 1928 train near Churchgate. This section from Colaba to Churchgate was closed for redevelopment in 1933. See "BBCIR EMU, 1928 (Broad Gauge)" on page 97 [BORHT Collection]

BBCIR, 1928 train of two 4-car sets. See "BBCIR EMU, 1928 (Broad Gauge)" on page 97 [BORHT Collection]

BBCIR, 1928 train, motor car with 3rd class accommodation. See "BBCIR EMU, 1928 (Broad Gauge)" on page 97
[BORHT Collection]

BBCIR, 1928 trailer car, Cammell Laird. See "BBCIR EMU, 1928 (Broad Gauge)" on page 97 [BORHT Collection]

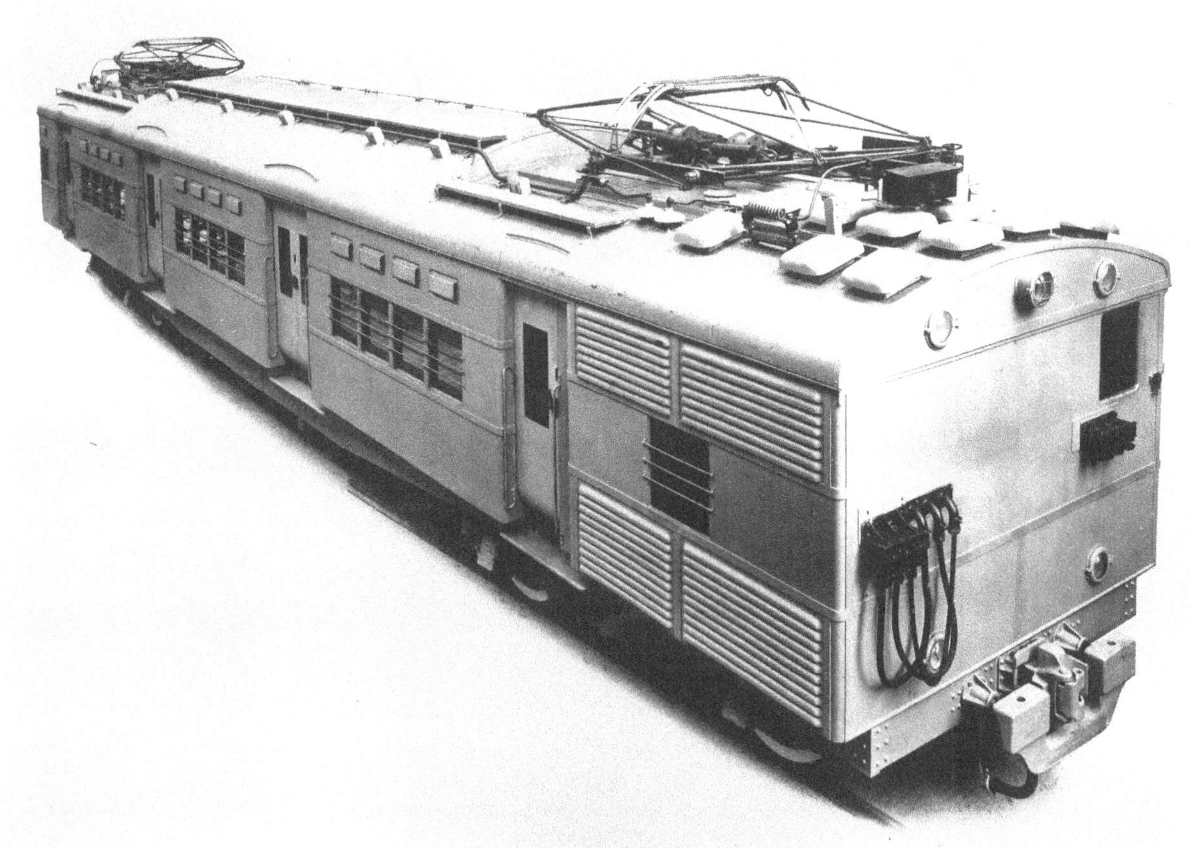

BBCIR, 1928 motor car, Cammell Laird with BTH electrical equipment. See "BBCIR EMU, 1928 (Broad Gauge)" on page 97 [BORHT Collection]

BBCIR, 1928 motor car, Cammell Laird with BTH electrical equipment. See "BBCIR EMU, 1928 (Broad Gauge)" on page 97 [BORHT Collection]

Cammell Laird power car 35B for 1928 BBCIR EMU, as restored at the National Railway Museum in Delhi, 12/2/78. See "BBCIR EMU, 1928 (Broad Gauge)" on page 97 [George Woods]

ICF EMU near Howrah, 19/11/1974. See "ICF EMU, 1962 (Broad Gauge)" on page 105 [Fuzz Jordan, DHRS Collection]

Appendix: Builders

Colonial Era Builders

Armstrong Whitworth (AW)

William George Armstrong founded an engineering works in 1847 with headquarters in Newcastle Upon Tyne. In 1882, it merged with Charles Mitchell's shipbuilding company to become Armstrong Mitchell and Co.. In 1897, it merged with Joseph Whitworth's company to become Sir WG Armstrong Whitworth and Co. Ltd. (AW). Shipbuilding was the company's primary business, but it developed markets in armaments, aviation and railways. In 1927, AW merged with Vickers Ltd. to become Vickers-Armstrong.

Railway locomotive production started at AW's Scotswood Works in 1919 and continued through to 1937, when they transitioned back to armament manufacture. AW were notable early proponents of diesel-electric traction for locomotives and railcars, and was a licensee of the Sulzer diesel engine.

AW supplied a large number of steam locomotives to Indian railways. They also provided experimental diesel locomotives and diesel railcars.

Brookville

Brookville was founded at Brookville, Pennsylvania as a subsidiary of Pennbro Corp. in 1917 to build locomotives and railcars based on road truck and tractor designs. Early models were based on Ford truck or Fordson tractor engines and transmissions. These were considered to be a rugged, successful design, and many survived in industrial use for many years.

Starting around 1928, Brookville progressed to more advanced designs with purpose-built chassis driven by Ford engines.

In 1942, Brookville was acquired by Joseph Horky of Pittsburgh and built many locomotives during World War 2. It was re-acquired by Pennbro Corp. in 1974 and continues to build industrial locomotives.

Hughes reports 10 Brookville vehicles supplied to India, which included at least 2 small railcars (2'-gauge for Matheran, and 2' 6"-gauge for the Railway Board in Calcutta).

Clayton Wagons (Clayton)

Clayton and Shuttleworth was an engineering company established in Lincoln in 1842. In 1920, they setup Clayton Wagons Ltd. to concentrate on road and railway vehicles. Their road steam motor wagon was popular in the 1920's, and they built rolling stock, including many wagons for India. A steam railcar design, based on the road motor wagon engine and boiler, was introduced in 1922 and improved in following years - several were provided to British mainline railways and for export to the Commonwealth.

Clayton Wagons Ltd. went out of business in 1930. Chief Draughtsman, Stanley Reid Devlin, went on to setup in the Clayton Equipment Company in 1931. Clayton Equipment initially provided spares for Clayton Wagons products. They later added new designs. Clayton Equipment continues to build railway products today.

Only one steam railcar from Clayton Wagons is known to have operated in India, on the Eastern Bengal State Railway.

D. Wickham and Co. Ltd. (Wkm)

Denis Wickham founded a general engineering company in 1886 as Motor Car and General Engineers. The company operated as D. Wickham and Co. Ltd., and was known as 'Wickham of Ware', although they also had a plant in Stevenage. In the early years, they mainly built brewing equipment.

Wickham started building railway equipment in 1922. They are best known for a very successful range of small petrol-engined railcars intended for industrial and maintenance of permanent way use.

Wickham was a major supplier of powered and unpowered railway equipment to India through the colonial era and early Independence era. Their railcars were mainly used for maintenance of permanent way and only a few instances of passenger carrying vehicles occurred. A well-known example was the 2'-gauge Gwalior railcar, built in 1934 and a similar car was produced for use by the Maharajah's entourage in 1947.

Wickham was acquired by BM Group in 1987. The rail side of the business was sold to Bruff and merged with Bruff Rail Ltd. in 1990 as Wickham Rail Ltd. but they were unable to maintain production. The rights to the products were sold to Wickham Rail Cars of Goodyear, Arizona, which ceased business in 1999. Most of the company records were lost during these acquisitions.

Drewry Car Co. Ltd. (DrC) and Related Companies

Drewry Car Co. Ltd. (DrC) was registered in London in 1906 to build small railway motor cars. They established a works at Teddington, but were unable to build cars economically. In 1908, they subcontracted manufacturing to Birmingham Small Arms Co. Ltd (BSA). The Manager of BSA's Motor Division was Ernest E. Baguley, who subsequently setup his own company, Baguley Cars Ltd. of Burton. Baguley Cars Ltd. won the contract for DrC car manufacture from 1912 onwards. In 1930, DrC cancelled their contract with Baguley (Engineers) Ltd. (successor to Baguley Cars Ltd.), and transferred production to English Electric. In 1945, production was again transferred, this time to Vulcan Foundry. Vulcan Foundry was acquired by English Electric in 1954. Production of new railcars and locomotives ceased in 1963.

There was still a significant market in spare parts for DrC equipment. Baguley acquired DrC in 1966 and the company became Baguley-Drewry Ltd. The company was bought by Hunslet (Holdings) Ltd. in 1969-70.

An interesting addendum to this story is that in 1912 Baguley acquired the interests of McEwan, Pratt and Co. Ltd.. McEwan, Pratt and Co. were founded by Robert Henry McEwan, Arthur Wellesley Pratt, and Robert Davison in Wickford, Essex. They were an early innovator of petrol driven locomotives and railcars, and provided what was probably the first petrol-driven railcar in India for the Matheran Steam Light Tramway in 1909[1].

DrC provided a number of interesting vehicles to Indian railways. The most famous of these were a successful series of petrol-mechanical railcars for the Kalka-Simla Railway. The final batch of these were modified with diesel engines by the railway and continue to be used today.

English Electric (EE)

The English Electric Company Ltd. (EE) was formed in 1919 by the merger of three major electrical engineering companies as they transitioned from war-time to peace-time demands. The <u>constituents were:</u> Coventry Ordnance Works, Phoenix Dynamo

1 See "The Railway Products of Baguley-Drewry Ltd and its Predecessors"

Manufacturing Co., and Dick Kerr and Co.. Dick Kerr's subsidiaries, United Electric Car Co. and Willans and Robinson were included in the merger. Soon after its formation, the company also acquired Siemens Brothers Dynamo Works in Stafford. The resulting electrical engineering company had significant capabilities across a wide range of markets.

In the early years, the company was managed from London. In 1930 the centre of operations was moved to Stafford.

In the railways market, EE provided traction equipment for the rapidly expanding electric railway sector. By the 1930's capability had expanded to the production of entire diesel and electric locomotives and trains. Following World War 2, EE acquired steam locomotive manufacturers: Robert Stephenson and Hawthorns in 1955, and Vulcan Foundry in 1957. The company became a leading supplier of railway equipment to Britain and the world, especially the Commonwealth.

In 1968, EE merged with the General Electric Company (GEC). GEC merged with Alstom in 1989 to form GEC Alstom. GEC Alstom was floated on the Paris Stock Exchange in 1998 and re-branded as Alstom the same year. Alstom remains a major global manufacturer of railway equipment.

In India, EE supplied EMUs for the Madras suburban scheme. They also provided electrical equipment for EMUs on the Bombay and Calcutta suburban networks, and locomotives for mainline services from Bombay.

Ganz

Ganz was founded as Ganz and Partner Iron Mill and Machine Factory in Budapest, Hungary in 1845. It later became Ganz Művek (Ganz Works). They became known for tramcar and railway manufacturing, but also had shipbuilding and other heavy engineering interests. They were particularly notable as advocates of Kálmán Kandó's three-phase AC railway electrification scheme.

Ganz's railway business was acquired by Telfos Holdings of Britain in 1989 and became Ganz-Hunslet Co. Ltd. In 1991, this business was sold to Jenbacher Transport Systeme of Austria. In 2001, the railcar division was sold to Connex of Germany, and this is now part of Trasndev, which is a regional rail operator that doesn't build rolling stock any more.

In India, Ganz provide a class of diesel-mechanical railcars to the North Western Railway.

Koppel Industrial Car and Equipment Co. (Koppel)

Orenstein and Koppel of Berlin, Germany (O&K) established a US subsidiary, Arthur Koppel, at the purpose-built town of Koppel, Pennsylvania in 1906. The works there built a range of railway equipment, including wagons, track, and possibly locomotives. These were mostly based on their parent's German designs, but including boxcar-derived standard-gauge wagons for the American market. In 1912, the works reverted to the O&K organization.

During the first world war, the US government commandeered the works and converted it to war production. After the war, the works were sold to the Pressed Steel Car Company of Pittsburgh, Pennsylvania as Koppel Industrial Car and Equipment Co. From this time onwards there was no connection with O&K.

The Depression wasn't kind to Koppel, and it ceased production from 1929-c.1932. When it restarted production it built railcars derived from standard Dodge Brothers road truck engines and transmissions. It is believed that this company was the source of the chassis used for two successful railcars supplied to the

Matheran Light Railway in 1932 and 1934.

The Koppel works was consolidated into Pressed Steel's McKees Rocks plant in 1938 and the US brand disappeared.

Motor Rail and Tram Car Co. (MR)

The Motor Rail and Tram Car Co. was founded in London in 1911. It's founder, JD Abbott, was the Resident Executive Engineer of the East India Tramway Co. , which operated tramways in Karachi. JD Abbott developed and patented the Dixon-Abbott gearbox, which was successfully used in an early series of petrol-mechanical tramcars. In the early years, production was sub-contracted to local engineering companies in the Lewes area of England.

MR developed the Karachi tramcar design into a number of derivatives for tram and railway use, and was influential in demonstrating the practicality of petrol engines for railway use. In India, a railcar was supplied to Bhavnagar State Railways in 1915, and three bogie railcars were ordered by the South Indian Railway in 1914-15 (one of which was diverted to Aden). A further SIR car of similar design was dispatched in 1925.

The First World War changed the destiny of MR. Its 20 HP 'Simplex' rail tractor found favour with the War Department and was built in large numbers for light railways that served the front line. MR started in-house manufacturing at a plant in Bedford in 1916. Although a few railcars were built in the post-war years, most subsequent production was concentrated on small locomotives for light railway and industrial use. A notable 1920 addition was a railcar for the Darjeeling Himalayan Railway.

It has been suggested that a 'gentleman's agreement' was made with the similar D. Wickham and Co. Ltd. (see above), whereby MR would concentrate on locomotives, while Wickham concentrated on railcars. This may explain the dearth of railcars in MR's later production.

MR was renamed as Motor Rail Ltd. in 1931. It continued to build locomotives until 1987 when it was sold to Alan Keef Ltd.

Sentinel

Sentinel Wagon Works Ltd traces its origins to Alley and MacLellan Ltd. (AML), a general engineering company founded in Glasgow in 1875. In 1906, AML introduced its 'Sentinel' steam motor wagon for road use. This vehicle was sufficiently successful to justify setup of a separate manufacturing plant at Battlefield, near Shrewsbury in 1914. In 1918, the plant was divested from AML and became the "Sentinel" Works Ltd..

The company started offering a steam rail coach from 1922 in partnership with Cammell-Laird (discussed in the rolling stock book). Sentinel also offered chain-driven steam locomotives.

Sentinel's steam rail coach business was successful through the 1920's and 1930's until the design was overtaken by more modern diesel-driven railcars. The chain-driven steam locomotives and a few railcars continued to be built until 1957.

Sentinel was acquired by Metal Industries Ltd in 1941, and was renamed as Sentinel (Shrewsbury) Ltd in 1945. In 1956, Rolls-Royce took a controlling interest in the company and used it to develop a diesel-hydraulic locomotive for industrial use. These locomotives were built from 1959 to 1971. Remaining business was transferred to Thomas Hill in 1970. The works closed in 1993.

India received several of the Sentinel-Cammell steam motor coaches, as well as a number of the Sentinel chain-driven steam locomotives.

Independence Era Foreign Builders

Breda

Società Italiana Ernesto Breda was founded by Ernesto Breda in 1882. It initially concentrated on railway equipment, but subsequently also built armaments and aircraft. The company was nationalized in 1962 as part of Ente Partecipazioni e Finanziamento Industria Manifatturiera (EFIM). When EFIM was liquidated in 1992, the railway division was spun off as AnsaldoBreda S.p.A.. AnsaldoBreda was acquired by Hitachi Rail in 2015.

Breda provided electric multiple units (EMUs) to Bombay and Madras in the 1950s.

Commonwealth Engineering

Commonwealth Engineering was founded as Smith and Waddington of Camperdown (near Sydney, Australia) in 1921. It initially provided coachwork for motor cars. Following bankruptcy during the Depression, it was reformed as Waddingtons Body Works and moved to a larger plant in Granville. The larger plant permitted diversification, including into railway rolling stock.

The company provided major engineering contributions during World War 2 and was nationalized in 1946, and the name changed to Commonwealth Engineering (later shortened to Comeng). During the post-War period several new plants were opened across Australia. In 1955, Commonwealth Engineering received a license from the Budd Company of Philadelphia, USA, to build stainless steel coaches and railcars.

Comeng was privatized in 1982 by a sale to Australian National Industries. In 1990, its railway assets were sold to ABB Transportation. In 1995, ABB Transportation was merged with the rail operations of Daimler-Benz AG to form Adtranz. In 2001, Adtranz was acquired by Bombardier Transportation, and in 2020, Bombardier was acquired by Alstom.

In India, Commonwealth Engineering provide a class of diesel multiple units (DMUs) in the 1950s.

Fiat Ferroviaria

Fiat Ferroviaria S.p.A. was the rail division of automobile manufacturer Fiat. It was founded in 1880 as Società Nazionale Officine di Savigliano. Fiat Ferroviaria began building locomotives in the 1930s. It became part of Fiat in 1970. Fiat Ferroviaria acquired the rail business of SIG of Switzerland in 1995, forming the subsidiary Fiat-SIG[2].

Fiat Ferroviaria S.p.A. and its subsidiaries were acquired by Alstrom in 2000, to become Alstom Ferroviaria S.p.A., the Italian division of Alstom.

In India, Fiat provided a class of metre gauge DMUs in the 1950s. While stylish, these DMUs were unreliable in service.

Hitachi

Hitachi as formed by Namihei Odaira in Japan in 1910 to exploit an electric motor developed for the Kuhara Mining Company, based in Hitachi. In 1918, the headquarters was moved to Tokyo. In 1921, they established Hitachi Works and started building electric locomotives for Japanese railways (first locomotives introduced in 1924).

Hitachi suffered significant damage during World War 2, but eventually recovered and became a major multinational across many industries. In 1964, they built the first Shinkansen (bullet train) for Japanese railways.

Hitachi acquired AnsaldoBreda (see above) and rebranded the combined rail operations as Hitachi Rail in 2015. They remain a major builder of railway equipment.

Hitachi delivered some complete EMU trains to Indian Railways, but was more influential in providing electrical equipment for use in Indian EMUs developed by domestic manufacturers.

MAN

Sander'sche Maschinenfabrik was founded at Augsburg in 1840 by Ludwin Sander. By 1898, the company had been renamed Maschinenfabrik Augsburg AG, when it merged with Maschinenbau-AG Nürnberg (founded 1841). The combined company was called Vereinigte Maschinenfabrik Augsburg und Maschinenbaugesellschaft Nürnberg A.G., Augsburg ("United Machine Works Augsburg and Nuremberg Ltd."). In 1908, the company was renamed Maschinenfabrik Augsburg Nürnberg AG, (MAN)[3].

The combined MAN company was a major vertically integrated conglomerate with mining, iron and steel, and manufacturing capabilities. Among many other interests, they built locomotives, rolling stock, and railway infrastructure such as bridges.

Following World War 2, the company was restructured to remove the vertical integration of mining and iron and steel production, but it continued to be a major manufacturer.

In 2011, Volkswagen AG took a controlling interest in the company. The MAN brand is still active at the time of writing, and is most closely associated with commercial road vehicles.

In 1958, MAN provided 3,000V DC electric multiple units for Calcutta/Howrah electrification. The body style was based on the 1950's Metro-Cammell design for Bombay modernisation. These units were subsequently transferred to Bombay when the Calcutta electrification switched to 25kV AC.

SIG

The Schweizerische Waggonfabrik was founded in Neuhausen am Rheinfall, Switzerland in 1852 to supply railway rolling stock. In 1859, they diversified into firearm manufacturing and changed the name to Schweizerische Industrie Gesellschaft (SIG). The rail business of SIG was acquired by Fiat Ferroviaria in 1995 to become Fiat-SIG. Fiat-SIG was acquired by Alstom in 2000.

In 1957, SIG provided 3-car EMUs for the 3,000V DC electrification of the Howrah suburban network. When the network was converted to 25kV AC, most of these units were converted to dual voltage. Subsequently, they were converted again, to 1,500V DC, for use in Bombay.

---

2 See Wikipedia

3 See Wikipedia

Independence Era Domestic Builders

BEML

The Rail Coach Factory in Bangalore (Bengaluru) was established in 1948 to build an all-steel coach designed by MAN of Germany. It was initially managed by M/s. Hindustan Aircraft Ltd. In 1964, Bharat Earth Movers Limited (BEML) was founded as a government-owned entity to build earth-moving equipment, and also took over control of the Rail Coach Factory.

BEML started building EMUs for Indian Railways in 1994, with 63 units provided to the Mumbai network on 1,500V DC. More than 500 25kV AC units have been provided to suburban networks in New Delhi, Chennai and Kolkata (most of which were provided after the period covered by this book). BEML also now builds mainline DEMUs and EMUs.

In the late 1990's, BEML built 20 broad gauge diesel railcars for local service on Indian Railways. They may have also built the similar metre gauge examples. They have also provided many maintenance of way vehicles.

HEIL

India planned to become self-sufficient in the manufacture of railway electrical equipment. In 1956, Heavy Electricals (India) Ltd. (HEIL) established a plant in Bhopal to build transformers and traction motors for locomotives and multiple units under a technology transfer agreement with Associated Electrical Industries Ltd. (AEI) of Sheffield, England. The original planned capacity was 200 traction motors per year. In response to increasing electrification of the railways, target capacity was increased to 800 units per year in the early 1960's and was planned to increase again to 2,000 units a year by 1970. However, initial ramp-up was slow due to foreign exchange and supply chain issues and by 1964, only approximately 100 DC traction motors had been built in India.

More recently, HEIL has renamed itself to Hindustan Engineering and Industries Limited and continues to be a major manufacturer of railway equipment.

ICF

Integral Coach Factory (ICF) of Madras (later Chennai) was founded by the Indian government in 1955 as part of a strategy to become self-sufficient in construction of railway equipment. It initially concentrated on the construction of modern lightweight steel coaches to a design by the Swiss Car and Elevator Manufacturing Company (Schlieren).

ICF started building electric multiple units (EMUs) in the early 1960s, initially supplying 25kV AC stock for the Calcutta suburban network, and using electrical equipment imported from AEI of Britain and Hitachi of Japan.

By 1968, ICF was able to start using domestically-built traction equipment, supplied by Hindustan Engineering & Industries Ltd. (HEIL).

ICF remains the predominant supplier of EMUs for Indian Railways. In the modern era (post the period covered by this book), they have also introduced DMU and Mainline EMU (MEMU) designs.

Jessop

For the history of Jessop, see the rolling stock book. Management of Jessop was taken over by the Indian government in 1958. Jessop received its first orders for 3,000V DC EMUs for Calcutta (Kolkata) and 1,500V DC EMUs for Bombay (Mumbai) in 1958, and delivered the first vehicles in 1959.

Despite the auspicious beginnings in EMU manufacture, Jessop never achieved the scale of ICF in terms of units delivered. They continue to construct EMUs and other railway rolling stock today.

ICF metre-gauge EMU at Madras Beach, 27/12/1979. See "Madras ICF EMU, 1965-1993 (Metre Gauge)" on page 114 [Fuzz Jordan]

Appendix: The Ones That Got Away

The American "World Survey of Foreign Railways" was an annual booklet of railway statistics and the data below from the 1939 edition provides an insight into the Indian railcar and EMU scene at the time. Some railcars listed have not been identified elsewhere, but could have been inspection vehicles instead of passenger vehicles. The figures given in the American survey generally agree with those in the Railway Board Annual Reports (RBARs) for the previous 2 or 3 years, although there are exceptions as noted below.

The local construction of railcars based on commercial road truck chassis in the 1930s and 1940s is not well documented and it is likely that variations on the basic concept existed and went out of service before frequent visits by enthusiasts. Hopefully this record will be filled out with reference to original documents in future

Railway	Number of Railcars listed in World Survey of Foreign Railways	Notes (RBAR indicates references in the statistics tables of the Railway Board Annual Reports in the late 1930s)
BNR	5 railcars, including 2 steam.	Should be 5 steam (2 BG and 3NG) all Sentinels
BBCIR	3 steam railcars, 40 EMUs.	MG Sentinels
EBSR	3 steam railcars.	One of these was probably the MG Clayton. Another possibly counts a Sentinel locomotive which ran with special lightweight coaches , otherwise unknown.
GIPR	53 EMUs, 4 railcars.	One NG railcar was for Pulgaon-Arvi. RBAR also lists 1 BG I/C coach 1937-39. Others unknown
NSR	2 steam railcars.	MG Sentinels
NWR	18 railcars includes 6 steam and 1 electric.	Steam probably the BG railcars; I/C are mainly the KSR railcars; electric may refer to the KSR diesel-electric railcar. The figures do not agree with RBAR which records 10 steam (7BG and 3 NG Sentinels) and 7 I/C (1BG and 6 NG)
SIR	48 electric trailers, 27 railcars (includes 24 electric motor coaches).	The 3 non electric railcars are MR petrol.cars
Barsi Light Railway 2' 6"	6 steam railcars.	Includes the 2 Sentinels; others unknown (did they count the Sentinel locomotives as railcars?). However RBAR lists 1 railmotor 2 steam
Bhavnagar State Railway (MG)	1 railcar.	MR car of 1915, which remained on the books until 1951
DHR 2'	2 railcars.	Includes the 1920 MR; other unknown
GBSR 2' 6"	3 railcars (includes 1 steam).	Should include the 4 AW railcars; steam railcar is unknown. RBAR give 7 railcars (6 I/C,1 steam) in late 1930s
Jamnagar and Dwar-ka Railway (MG)	3 railcars.	Probably railcars based on road vehicle parts.
Junagad State Rail-way (MG)	2 railcars.	BRCW railcars
Morvi Railway (MG)	3 railcars.	This is before the Maharaja's railcar - These were MG (RBAR)
Shahdara-Sahararapur Light Railway 2' 6"	1 railcar.	Wkm petrol railcar from 1935 per Hughes.
Cutch State Railway	7 railcars.	May still include the shooting car, others unknown. Only 1 listed in RBAR
Dehri-Rohtas Light Railway 2' 6"	3 railcars (1 electric).	Unknown. RBAR records 3 rail motors and 1 steam – latter probably a converted steam lorry.
Jessore-Jhenidah Railway 2' 6"	1 railcar.	Unknown; Line was closed on 1 May1936.
Jorhat Provincial Railway 2'	1 railcar.	Unknown. Listed in RBAR.
Kulasekharapatnam Light Railway 2'	3 diesel railcars, 3 petrol railcars.	Hughes reports 4 petrol cars. Diesel cars unknown. RBAR report 6 railmotors in late 1930s. Line closed 1 Feb 1940
Matheran Light Rail-way 2'	4 railcars.	Based on road vehicle parts. Widely use in the 1930s.
Trivellare Light Railway 2'	3 railcars.	Railcars unknown. Closed 1939/40.
Bengal Iron Co.Ltd. (Nano-harpur Light Railway) 2'	5 railcars.	One of these may be open body inspection car, 2w-2PMR Bg/DrC C type 1112/19201 Others unknown.

(Table includes corrections by David Churchill)

Broad Gauge

It hasn't been possible to fully reconcile the numbers of Electric Multiple Units (EMUs) delivered to the Bombay suburban network. The author is reasonably confident that the gap was filled by Jessop deliveries in the 1970's (these numbers aren't readily available) and are not the result of missing an entire class.

No information has been found on the BBCIR articulated railcar illustrated below. It appears to be a simple adaptation of two road trucks coupled back to back. It is interesting in being possibly the only railway vehicle to have run with rubber tyres in India.

BBCIR Articulated Railcar [MeMumbai Blog]

Metre Gauge

David Churchill analysed Railway Board reports and identified several additional MG railcars that aren't included in the tables above. Differences are listed below, including David's notes from Bradshaw timetables:

- Bhavnagar State Railway had 2 railcars in 1937 4 in 1938-1940, 5 in 1941, and 4 in 1942-1946.

- Jaipur State Railway had 2 railmotors in 1940, 4 in 1941, and 6 from 1942-1946. Bradshaw for Jan 1944 has one train in each direction [24/25] indicated as RMC on the Sikar–Fatehour Shekhawati line, 30 miles in about 2 hours.

- Jamnagar and Dwarka Railway had 5 railcars in 1939, 6 in 1940, 7 in 1941, 6 in 1942, 8 in 1943 to 1946. Bradshaw for Jan 1944 has one train (22 up) indicated as RMC on the Jamnagar–Rozi line, 9 miles in 30 minutes; 21 down was probably also RMC.

- Junagad State Railway reported 3 railcars in 1946 (only 2 identified above). Bradshaw for Jan 1944 has one train in each direction (23/24) indicated as RMC on the Talala–Dalvadai line, about 3 hours. Bradshaw Oct 1946 ha one train in each direction (23/24) Indicated as RM on Junadagh Jn–Visavadar line, about 1½ hours.

- Mysore State Railway had 1 railcar from 1933-1935, 5 in 1936, 1 railmotor and 6 i/c coaches from 1937-1938.

Isao Tsujimuraand quotes JARI statistics from 1977, showing that the Southern Railway received 12 DMUs from Japan in 1953. Peter Bawcutt photographed a couple of these units in 1969 (see Additional Photographs), The Japanese company Niigata advertised quite heavily in Indian Railway Gazette in the 1950s with illustrations of KiHa 44,600 and 45,000 class bogie railcars with hydraulic transmissions, so the Southern Railway cars may have been based on that design. These railcars were designed for 3' 6" gauge Japanese minor railways, so they would have been an easy adaptation to Indian metre gauge.

The provenance and quantity of railcars and DMUs built at Indian railway workshops in the 1990s hasn't been fully determined.

Narrow Gauge

A number of areas would benefit from further research:

- Further details of how many standard post-war railcars (EZZx and ZRD) were built and manufacturing workshops.

- Dimensions of the LP railcars 1-3 for KSR, built 1911-13.

- More details on the rebuilding of the KSR Drewry railcars 8-11, later renumbered 1-4.

East Pakistan/ Bangladesh

In 1963-4, East Pakistan received four railcars and 8 trailers to run as 3-car trains on the metre gauge. The author hasn't been able to obtain further details on these units.

References

Sources and Acknowledgements

I am particularly indebted to my editor, Julian Rainbow, for his usual diligent and thoughtful review of this text.

David Churchill of the Darjeeling Himalayan Railway Society (DHRS) provided copious comments and additions, as well as several critical photographs to supplement the text. Membership of DHRS is strongly recommended for anyone with an interest in Indian Railways.

Tim Edmonds, Fuzz Jordan, Laurie Marshall via David Churchill, Samit Roychoudhury, Wilson Lythgoe, Mike Tisdale, Aravind Gundumane, George Woods, the late Peter Bawcutt via Peter Tiller, Protik Maitra, Jay Balakrishna, 'Indian Rail Road', and Brian Manktelow via Rob Dickinson all provided additional photographs.

One of my longest friends, Derek Turner, provided a good "layman's view" of the content in order to prevent me using too much railway jargon.

My wife, Annie, and sons, Gavin and Duncan, have provided unwavering support through this and my previous book - thanks.

Many sources have provided material for this book, including:

- The Great Eastern Railway Society (gersociety.org.uk) has made the complete set of "Locomotive, Carriage, and Wagon Review" available for download at a modest cost - this is a great source of diagrams and general information

- A number of engineering journals up to about 1920 are now available on-line via Google Play and were a good source for high-quality plans - these include some issues of "Locomotive, Carriage, and Wagon Review" (sometimes called "The Locomotive"), "Railway Engineer", and "Engineer"

- Grace's Guide on-line has the complete set of "Engineer" available to download including the period after 1920, but it is necessary to pay for downloads

- The Mike Satow collection at the British Library is useful for locomotive and railcar diagrams

A number of photographic sources are also used:

- IRFCA

- The Kelland Collection, available via the Bournemouth Railway Club Trust (www.brc-trust.com)

- British Overseas Railways Historical Trust (www.borht.org.uk) and Julian Rainbow Collection

- Transport Treasury

- Adobe Stock

- Alon Siton's Historical Railway Images collection on Flickr

Thanks are due to the following people for assistance:

- The staff of the Asian Collection at the British Library

- The staff of the Stephen A. Schwarzman Building, New York Public Library.

Additions to Bibliography

A comprehensive bibliography of Indian railway books was provided in "Indian Seam Locomotives in HO Scale" and won't be reproduced here.

- The Wickham Works List, Keith Gunner and Mike Kennard, Dennis Duck Publications 2004

- Armstrong Whitworth A Pioneer of World Diesel Traction, Brian Webb, Lightmoor Press and RCTS, 2010, ISBN: 9731899889 45 7

- Wickham of Ware: a history of D. Wickham & Co. Ltd. Railcar Manufacturers, Loxley G. Ford, Rockingham Press, 2003 ISBN: 1 873468 40 7

- The Railway Products of Baguley-Drewry Ltd and its Predecessors, Allen Civil and Roy Etherington, IRS, 2008, ISBN 978 901556 44 1

- The Early Years of the Motor Rail & Tram Car Company 1911-1931, W.J.K. Davies, Plateway Press, 2008, ISBN: 1 871980 58 5

- Sentinel Locomotives and Sentinel-Cammell Railcars Their Design and Development, John M. Hutchings, IRS, 2020 ISBN: 978 1 912995 02-8

- The History of Bombay Suburban Railways (1853-1985), Dr. A.K. Arora, originally published 1985, ebook: www.bronato.com.

- Report of the Suburban Train (Bombay, Calcutta and Madras) Overcrowding Enquiry Committee, 1956 , Government of India Press, Nasik, available online at indianculture.gov.in

- Proceedings of the Institution of Mechanical Engineers, 1944_151_019_02 - Diesel Traction on the NWR (India), available via rhe Institution's website (www.imeche.org)

- See the "Reference Sources for Indian Railways" web page on the BORHT website (http://borht.org.uk/india.htm) for an extended bibliography that is updated periodically.

Diagrams from Other Sources

The following table lists plans that are available from publications that are readily available at the time of writing.

Gauge	Subject	Railway	Source	Author
5' 6"	Bogie Railcar 1934	MSMR	Armstrong Whitworth, a Pioneer of World Diesel Traction	Brian Webb
4'	1909-1944 Tramcars (5 plans)*	Karachi Tramways	The Early Years of the Motor Rail and Tram Car Company, 1911-1931	W.J.K. Davies
Metre	Railcar, 1911	South Indian Railway	The Early Years of the Motor Rail and Tram Car Company, 1911-1931	W.J.K. Davies
Metre	Railcar, 1915	Bhavnagar State Railway	The Early Years of the Motor Rail and Tram Car Company, 1911-1931	W.J.K. Davies
2' 6"	Sentinel Steam Railcar	BNR	Indian Railway Study Group newslettter, January 1992	
2' 6"	2-A Railcar 1932	GBSR	Indian Railway Study Group newslettter, July 1991	
2' 6"	2-A Railcar 1932	GBSR	Armstrong Whitworth, a Pioneer of World Diesel Traction	Brian Webb
2' 6"	Bogie Railcar 14 1934	KSR	Armstrong Whitworth, a Pioneer of World Diesel Traction	Brian Webb
2' 6"	Bogie Railcar 14 1934	KSR	Narrow Gauge and Shortline Gazette, March-April 2006	Jeff Scherb
2' 6"	Bogie Railcar 1934	CPR	Armstrong Whitworth, a Pioneer of World Diesel Traction	Brian Webb
2'	Steam Railcar	GLR	Narrow Gauge and Industrial Review 118	
2'	Petrol Railcars 898-899	Matheran	Indian Railway Study Group newslettter, July 1992	
2'	Petrol Railcars 898-899	Matheran	Narrow Gauge and Shortline Gazette, May-June 2005	Jeff Scherb
2'	Railcar, 1920	DHR	The Early Years of the Motor Rail and Tram Car Company, 1911-1931	W.J.K. Davies
2'	Railcar, 1940	DHR	The Iron Sherpa Volume 2	Terry Martin

* Note: Karachi Tramways are outside the scope of this book, but these plans are additional reasons to buy W.J.K. Davies' excellent book.

Abbreviations

The following table defines abbreviations used in this book.

AC	Alternating Current (electricity)		IR	Indian Railways
AEG	Allgemeine Elektricitäts-Gesellschaft AG, Berlin, Germany		IRCA	Indian Railways Conference Association
ASLR	Arrah–Sasaram Light Railway		IRFCA	Indian Railways Fan Club
AW	Sir WG Armstrong Whitworth and Co. Ltd., Newcastle, UK		IRS	Industrial Railway Society
			ISR	Indian State Railways
BBCIR	Bombay, Baroda and Central India Railway		K	Kitson and Co., Leeds, UK
BBLR	Baraset-Basirhat Light Railway		kph	Kilometres per Hour
BuBLR	Bukhtiarpur-Bihar Light Railway		KS	Kerr Stuart, Stoke-on-Trent, UK
BkSR	Bikaner State Railway		KSR	Kalka-Simla Railway
Bg	Baguley Cars Ltd., Burton, UK		LM	Locomotive Magazine (or Locomotive, Carriage and Wagon Review)
BG	Broad Gauge (5' 6")			
BLR	Barsi Light Railway		LHB	Linke-Hoffmann-Busch, Salzgitter, West Germany
BNR	Bengal Northern Railway			
BRCW	Birmingham Railway Carriage and Wagon, Birmingham, UK		MAN	Maschinenfabrik Augsburg-Nürnberg AG, Nürnberg Germany
Breda	Ernesto Breda, Milan, Italy		Mdws	Henry Meadows Ltd, Wolverhampton, UK
BSR	Bhavnagar State Railway		MEMU	Mainline Electric Multiple Unit
BTH	British Thomson-Houston, Rugby, UK		MetroVic	Metropolitan-Vickers
C	Hundredweight		MG	Metre Gauge
Clayton	Clayton Wagons Ltd., Lincoln, UK		MP	McEwan, Pratt and Co. Ltd., Wickford, UK
CR	Central Railway		mph	Miles per Hour
DrC	Drewry Car Co. Ltd., London, UK		MR	Motor Rail (manufacturer), London, UK
DC	Direct Current (electricity)		MSMR	Madras and Southern Maharatta Railway
DHR	Darjeeling Himalayan Railway		NER	North Eastern Railway
DMU	Diesel Multiple Unit		NFR	Northeast Frontier Railway
DEMU	Diesel-electric Multiple Unit		NSR	Nizam's State Railway
EE	English Electric Company Ltd., London (Stafford after 1930), UK		NW	Nasmyth, Wilson and Co., Manchester, UK
			NWR	North Western Railway
EMU	Electric Multiple Unit		O&K	Orenstein and Koppel of Berlin, Germany
EPB	Electro-pneumatic Brakes		PMR	Petrol-mechanical Railcar
ER	Eastern Railway		psi	Pounds per Square Inch (pressure)
EBSR	East Bengal State Railway		PWR	Pakistan Western Railway
EIR	East India Railway		RBAR	Railway Board Annual Report
F	Ford Motor Company, Dearborn, MI, USA		RDSO	Railway Design Standards Office
Ganz	Ganz Művek, Budapest, Hungary		RPM	Revolutions per Minute
GBSR	Gaekwar's Baroda State Railway		SCR	South Central Railway
GEC	General Electric Company, Schenectady, NY, USA		Sentinel	Sentinel Wagon Works Ltd, Battlefield, UK
			SER	South Eastern Railway
GIPR	Great Indian Peninsula Railway		SIG	Schweizerische Industrie Gesellschaft, Neuhausen am Rheinfall, Switzerland
GLR	Gwalior Light Railway			
HALR	Howrah-Amta Light Railway		SIR	South Indian Railway
HEI	Hindustan Engineering & Industries Ltd., Bhopal (originally Heavy Electrical (India) Ltd.)		SR	Southern Railway (India)
			SSLR	Shahdara-Saharanpur Light Railway
			T	Ton
HP	Horsepower		UK	United Kingdom
I/C	Internal Combustion		USA	United States of America
ICF	Integral Coach Factory. Chennai (Madras)		VF	Vulcan Foundry, Newton-le-Willows, UK

Abbreviations (Continued)

Walford	Walford Engineering, Calcutta
Wkm	D. Wickham and Co., Ware, UK
W&P	White and Poppe, Coventry, UK
WR	Western Railway

BBCIR, 1928 car construction. See "BBCIR EMU, 1928 (Broad Gauge)" on page 97[BORHT Collection]